Privacy Lost

How Technology Is Endangering Your Privacy

David H. Holtzman

Foreword by Senator Evan Bayh

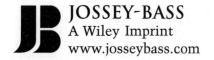

JOSSEY-BASS
A Wiley Imprint
www.josseybass.com

Published by Jossey-Bass
A Wiley Imprint
989 Market Street, San Francisco, CA 94103-1741   www.josseybass.com

Jossey-Bass books and products are available through most bookstores. To contact Jossey-Bass directly call our Customer Care Department within the U.S. at 800-956-7739, outside the U.S. at 317-572-3986, or fax 317-572-4002.

Jossey-Bass also publishes its books in a variety of electronic formats. Some content that appears in print may not be available in electronic books.

Library of Congress Cataloging-in-Publication Data

Holtzman, David H., date.
　　Privacy lost: how technology is endangering your privacy / David H. Holtzman.
　　　　p. cm.
　　Includes bibliographical references and index.
　　ISBN-13: 978-0-7879-8511-0 (cloth)
　　ISBN-10: 0-7879-8511-2 (cloth)
1. Privacy, Right of. 2. Information technology—Social aspects. I. Title.
　　JC596.H64　　2006
　　323.44'8—dc22

　　　　　　　　　　　　　　　　　　　　　　　　　　　　2006022977

Printed in the United States of America
FIRST EDITION
HB Printing　10 9 8 7 6 5 4 3 2 1

Contents

The Technology

The Watchers

What Can Be Done?

Foreword

Privacy is something that most Americans care deeply about, even if they can't always agree on what it means. For some, it means freedom from interruption, like not having their dinner hour invaded by telemarketers. For many Americans, privacy issues hit where it hurts most—the pocketbook; identity theft is the most publicized instance of privacy violation and affects tens of millions of Americans every year. For others, privacy is a principle that they believe to be constantly under assault from corporations, technology, and the government.

This book addresses these issues and more. Although I may not agree with all of David's conclusions, he is doing a public service by launching a discussion on this important issue. Ultimately, public debate is the most basic freedom that we have, and it is critical that we exercise this right loudly and often, especially on important and evolving issues such as privacy. David gets that debate started in a thoughtful way.

Since September 11th, we have taken important steps as a nation to protect the American people from another terrorist attack on our soil. We live in a dangerous world with suicidal terrorists, and we must use information technology to protect our country against those who want to hurt us. However, we must also remain ever vigilant to avoid unnecessary erosion of the basic rights that we are fighting to protect. This book does an excellent job of examining the tension between protecting the United States and protecting our civil rights.

Privacy Lost explores in great detail the force that's driving the privacy debate—technology. Technology can help and harm, depending on how it is used and who is using it. The same computer capabilities that the Transportation Security Administration uses to spot terrorists and stop them before they board airplanes can cause problems for innocent citizens whose profiles happen to match descriptions or names on a security watch list. Senator Edward Kennedy had trouble flying because his name was on a watch list. The solution is not to reject this technology and its ability to protect us from terrorists but to refine it, improve it, and enhance our security by targeting terrorists faster, while at the same time reducing the impact on the innocent.

In addition to the balance of security and privacy that must be managed by the government, there is a growing threat to consumers from data-management companies. *Privacy Lost* explains how advances in technology have enabled these businesses to maintain unprecedented amounts of information on each of us. This profiling makes many people uneasy, because of concerns about privacy in general as well as fear of being incorrectly labeled. An obvious example is credit scoring. These computer systems automatically decide whether we are worthy of credit or too big a risk, without the possibility of appeal or reconsideration, even if the facts are completely wrong. Traditional credit-reporting bureaus come under the Fair Credit Reporting Act, but the credit-scoring companies, whose reports are used to grant most consumer credit, are not regulated at all.

The biggest privacy problem for citizens comes from a disturbing and growing trend—data breaches. There have been numerous cases of inadvertent disclosures of consumers' personal information. Some of these involved literally millions of personal financial records that included Social Security numbers, credit-card numbers, and bank information. This threat to our privacy is also a threat to our security. In the Digital Age, we are only as safe as our computers. Bad commercial computer practices are potentially just as dangerous as mismanaged government databases.

The importance of a book like this is the light it shines on a growing challenge for our society. David points out that technology moves much faster than most of us can keep up with, but that doesn't mean that we shouldn't try.

I recommend this book to anyone who wants to try to keep up. David explains the implications of privacy in a way that is easily understandable. It's a good read for anyone, not just technologists or lawyers. Privacy is not just a legal concern; it is not just a technical phenomenon; it is an issue for all Americans.

Indianapolis, Indiana   Senator Evan Bayh
July 2006

To my children: Lauren, Sam, Ben, Alex, and Becca—
you are my greatest accomplishment

Preface: The Monkey House

*I've never looked through a keyhole without finding
someone was looking back.*

Judy Garland[1]

Technology advances society, but information technology
empowers the individual. It certainly did me. Before the Net,
I was a bookworm. Books helped me crawl into other people's heads
and peer out through their eyes. I was an information junkie and an
intellectual voyeur.

Later on, as a young cryptographic analyst in the Navy, I discovered the necessity of using computers when handling huge
amounts of information. No human being could sort through the
masses of signal intelligence collected during the Cold War, yet
those thirty-year-old thinking machines could hear a whisper in a
whirlwind, given enough processing time.

Ten years later I discovered the Internet. I was fortunate enough
to be at the center of the swirling information industry, the precursor
of today's commercial Internet. As waves of computers became
"wired," I discovered that I could use networking to reach out to other
peoples' computers and see what they saw, know what they knew, sift
through their online storehouses. The early information applications
like finger, telnet, Archie, and wais could access authoritative sources
like the Library of Congress as well as the mundane, like a Coke

machine in a computer lab in Boston (to see how many were cold). These hobbyist tools converged into a universal access protocol, http, setting the stage for the World Wide Web. On the web everything that anyone wanted to make public was.

For a junkie like me it was wonderful. The whole world became my zoo, each web site a new and entertaining exhibit. There was a voyeuristic quality about the experience; though information on the nascent web was freely displayed, flashes of the author's private thoughts still showed through, just as in books.

It took ten more years before I realized that I was also on display; I began to see my own bars. I gradually became aware of what was becoming available about me online as I sought information about others. I was divorced, and the documents became public. I was an officer of a public company (Network Solutions), and all kinds of personal information became accessible through Securities and Exchange Commission filings, including my Social Security number. Details of my house purchase popped up. Even my political contributions were searchable. Most of this information was public and had always been available in paper, but two things had changed by the end of the 1990s. The first was the digitization of everything. The second was networking. Material stored on a stand-alone computer required the questioner to be physically present to use the machine. Each separate repository of information had to be interrogated, a task that required expensive and time-consuming travel. Once computers were networked, however, the protective barriers of distance and cost melted away.

I became worried. Not about me, so much. . . . My life was an open book for several reasons. But I became concerned about society in general. The harm from unmanaged access to all this content had the potential to outweigh the benefits. I came to the profound realization that data never disappear. When information is digitized and stored on a networked computer, for all practical purposes it is eternal, even if thought deleted. Historically, privacy has been based on controlling one's own information. However, once someone's life has been sucked into the emerging mesh of interlocked computers, that definition of privacy is impossible.

The rush to digitization was quick and thorough. The analog world disappeared overnight, replaced by an ever-cheapening silicon matrix. Fifteen years of my adult life were completely contained on email. I had entire relationships splayed out on my monitor if I so chose. All my pictures were now digital, my music was MP3, my movies were on DVD, and I can't remember the last time that I wrote a letter. Yet others were collecting information on me too. Between the government and marketing companies, most of my life was being collected—far more than just credit reports and official paperwork. The trend toward centralized, managed health care wrested control of my medical information out of my doctor's hands, for example. My private life was only as secure as my computer. Computer viruses controlled by hackers and spybots managed by businesses swarmed onto every unprotected computer; the creators of these programs no longer caused havoc for kicks but stole personal information for profit.

Clearly the courts and Congress haven't "gotten it" yet. The courts have been scrupulously avoiding anything that might slow down Internet growth, and since 9/11, Congress has not shown any inclination to get involved in information protection if it constrained commercial database companies or counterintelligence efforts by the government. There has been media discussion of the legal ramifications of privacy, but the primary agent of change, technology, has largely been ignored.

I am a technologist and a businessman, and it is from that perspective that I wrote this book. Privacy is too important to be left to lawyers. As a starting point, I did a little violating of my own privacy, including running background checks and having my DNA analyzed. In a few days, I was able to put together a comprehensive report on myself from easily accessible sources. I've included a highly abridged version here. The full version was almost embarrassingly complete, with detailed financial and personal information.

Vital statistics

Age:	49
Address:	Herndon, Virginia
Birthplace:	Pittsburgh, Pennsylvania
DOB:	9/30/56
Height:	67"
Weight:	198 lbs
Hair:	Brown
Eyes:	Brown
Travels:	Canada, Italy, Spain, Netherlands, UK, BVI, Japan, Tahiti, France
Education:	BA Philosophy U of Pittsburgh, BS Computer Science U of Maryland
Veteran:	8 years as Cryptographic Interpretive Technician (Russian)
Special:	Qualified in Submarines (SS)
Family:	5 children, divorced
Source:	*Passports and driver's license,* Who's Who *entry, resume*

Medical

Blood type:	A+
Genetic variations:	Possible heart complications
Dental work:	Two bridges, three crowns
Marks:	Circumcised, no tattoos, small birthmark left collarbone
Surgery:	Tonsillitis
Physical:	Exercises regularly, doesn't smoke, social drinker
Other:	Type II diabetes
Source:	*DNA test from a cheek swab, medical records from HMO*

Legal and financial

Felonies:	None
Traffic:	Two speeding tickets since 2000
Credit cards:	Amex, Visa, MC
Debt:	$230,000 mortgage, minor credit-card debt
Voted:	2000 and 2004 general election
Political contribution	$2,000 Wes Clark in 2000
Source:	*Credit reports, opensecrets.org (political-donation tracking)*

Entertainment

Books:	Mysteries, science fiction, thrillers, varied nonfiction
Music:	Jazz, blues, modern rock
Television:	Comedy and news, likes *The Daily Show*
Movies:	Varied, documentaries, comedies, foreign
Source:	*TiVo, Amazon.com records*

Online behavior

News:	*Washington Post, NY Times,* C/Net
Blogs:	Slashdot, Daily Koz, Gizmodo, boing-boing, Wired, thecoolhunter
Personal site:	www.davidholtzman.com
Blog site:	www.globalpov.com
Book site:	www.privacylost.us
Email address:	david@globalpov.com
Daily email load:	250–350 pieces, 75 percent spam
Source:	*Wi-Fi monitoring, packet sniffing*

Personality

Intelligence:	High
Myers-Briggs:	ENTP
Political leanings:	Moderate-Liberal
Source:	*Passive psychological tests, analysis of online behavior*

Threat potential

Online gambling	None
Buys subversive books	Some
Browses counterculture sites	Some
Emails known terrorists	None
Visits known terrorist sites	Never
Travels to suspect countries	Never
Uses encrypted email	Occasionally
Threat risk	Low
Source:	*Overall analysis of behavior patterns, credit reports, emails, travel history*

Welcome to the monkey house. We're the monkeys and the tourists both—the exhibitionist and the voyeur. Each bar in our cage is smelted from the same metal—technology. If you want privacy, pay cash, send postal mail, use a television antenna, and don't travel by airplane or leave the country. That strategy might work right up until the inevitable national ID card is mandated. Of course, you'll give up many of the benefits of our society; renting cars requires a credit card, for example.

Technology is wonderful. It extends our life span, feeds the poor, and helps us thrive in harsh environments like tundra and deserts. Just as the railroads opened up the United States in the nineteenth century, networked smart devices are opening up new business areas in the twenty-first. But there are consequences. Building the railroads killed off the buffalo. What will building the Information Superhighway kill off?

Technology has changed our culture: how we communicate and how we don't. It has affected our ability to control our personal information: who sees it, what they see, what they do with it. Our privacy is already lost, whether we know it or not. Whether we can find it again is still unclear.

Herndon, Virginia   David H. Holtzman
July 2006

Acknowledgments

My extremely competent, vivacious, and super-smart assistant, Beth Watson, has helped me in innumerable ways, not least by keeping the home fires burning when I disappeared to write this book. Plus she keeps my cat, Helen, happy when I'm away.

My extraordinarily intelligent and articulate researcher, Moya Mason, kept me on the straight and narrow with timely and thorough material as well as encouraging words when I needed them the most, and in the process proved that not everything in Newfoundland is cold.

Dorothy Hearst and Jesse Wiley at Jossey-Bass championed this project, and Jesse spent many weekend hours working with me on the editing.

My agent, Grace Freedson, stuck with me and sold this book, even when prospects were less than rosy. She always cheerfully took a call, even for stupid questions.

Friends of many decades have always been supportive of my writing: Jim and Kathy Carr, Rich and Cindy Burkhart, and Cathy, who supported me early on.

Helpful readers and friends gave me feedback. Mike Sheridan and Rick Garvin offered helpful insight into both privacy and technology. Tim Skinner from SRA was great at reviewing the legal bits. My old friend Hatte Blejer read material, kibitzed, and made some good introductions. Jack Lewis often talked to me about the law and history at diners and helped more than he realized. My lawyerly daughter, Lauren, always made time for me that she didn't have. My lawyer, Max Miller, was always glad to share his opinions and to occasionally listen to mine. Travis Van was very generous with his time and public relations advice.

Tara gave me the great gift of believing in me.

The beautiful Canadian province of Prince Edward Island nurtured me while I wrote, entertained me when I was bored, and challenged me when I got too comfortable.

To curmudgeons everywhere, and you know who you are: keep fighting the good fight.

Introduction
How and Why Our Privacy Is at Risk

> *The Central Intelligence Agency is committed to
> protecting your privacy and will collect no personal
> information about you unless you choose to provide
> that information to us.*
>
> Central Intelligence Agency[1]

Privacy is a universally cherished prerogative that isn't much of a right at all. Few laws protect our seclusion, and they weaken every year. Our privacy is shrinking quicker than the polar ice cap; technology is eroding it faster than the legal system can protect it. This trend cannot be reversed in any obvious way. Privacy, as we know it today, is lost.

At its most basic level, privacy is about information control—who owns knowledge about us? The German term *informationelle Selbstbestimmung*, which means "informational self-determination," suggests that we control our own information. But today our information has slipped out of our control, and as a result we have lost our privacy. This loss has been caused by the most significant society-impacting science of our generation—computerized technology. My intention in writing this book is to explain the connection between technology and privacy and to speculate about where things might be headed.

This book is not written just for privacy advocates or for technologists, however. Rather, it's for all who are disturbed about the growing amount of data available on them, about who's doing the collecting, and about what the collectors are going to do with all that personal information. It's also for those who are concerned about the growing number of exceedingly well-publicized privacy violations and who are wondering how many other incidents haven't become public. It's hard not to notice the unending stream of news stories describing one egregious privacy violation after another: companies losing the financial information of millions of customers, a civil servant in the U.S. Department of Veteran's Affairs having a laptop stolen that contained personal information on nearly every American who's ever served in the military, a Boston newspaper wrapping papers in printouts of its customers' credit-card numbers. These stories are all documented and discussed in this book. They are, in themselves, a testament to the effect of technology on our privacy.

Privacy Lost is also for people who get nervous about privacy-hostile government actions like the Patriot Act. These counterterrorist programs give millions of government agents a get-out-of-jail-free card, permitting electronic probing of U.S. citizens on a scale that would have made even J. Edgar Hoover blush. None of these government activities would be possible without the availability of sophisticated information technology like data mining, which is used to sift through the rapidly growing data heaps of our newly digital civilization.

Our data include our emails, photographs, medical results, travels, and purchases. Eventually every transaction will be stored somewhere digitally and therefore will be accessible to a persistent searcher. As a rule of thumb, according to Moore's Law, digital storage devices get twice as powerful every eighteen months for the same price.[2] However, the cost of human labor stays the same. Therefore, it's cheaper to buy additional disks than to figure out what to delete. Digital data never disappear, and searching technology like Google is good enough that all information will be found. Like Poe's raven, our past may come back to haunt us when we least expect it. It's no coincidence that emails have been the key evidence at the center of most political and financial scandals since the mid-1990s. Data last forever. Privacy does not.

The digital universe parallels the one we live in, except it's littered with lost and forgotten information, data, and facts—a silicon twilight zone. Each of us has a twin in this universe, a digital Doppelgänger that reflects our lives and experiences and will be around when we're long gone. This electronic simulacrum shares our birth date and Social Security number and all our specifics: what we've bought, where we've traveled, the state of our health. Even though we may zealously guard our personal information, our double will tell anyone about us because that electronic twin is not under our control.

It's impossible to walk through this modern world without leaving behind indelible footprints in its silicon sand. Most financial activities, for example, leave a digital imprint somewhere because a record of every cashless transaction goes into someone's database. A whole industry has sprung up around selling and storing personal information about our behavior and activities. Each bit seems innocuous, but, in aggregate, this electronic montage provides a frighteningly detailed history of what we do, when and where we do it, and whom we do it with. As you'll read about later in the book, computer software is also beginning to make some good guesses as to what we think. Do we want new laws protecting our privacy from these intrusions, or are we willing to put up with them to have a better shopping experience?

We are also being tracked by our gadgets, such as cell phones (even when they're off) and Geographic Positioning Systems in our cars. A new technology called Radio Frequency Identification enables small chips to be hidden in packages, books, and even clothes. These little devices know essential information about us and can be surreptitiously interrogated from thirty feet away. Soon this technology will be prevalent in our lives. Are we willing to live without our gadgets if we know that they erode our privacy?

In addition, we're under constant observation by computerized sensors. In most modern cities our picture is snapped dozens of times a day by surveillance cameras. License-plate-reading and face-recognition programs are matching these pictures to names. So far, the worst result of this capability is the automatic issuing of speeding tickets, but additional uses will be developed. Will we ever get used to being watched twenty-four hours a day?

Even our bodies are being tagged, analyzed, and stored for future cross-reference. A simple cheek swab or drop of blood is enough to analyze our DNA, which indicates our tendency to inherit certain health problems. Health care providers and employers would naturally like to screen out those of us with genetic problems to keep down the overall cost of medical coverage. As a result, our genetic road map sometimes makes it difficult to get insurance or even a job. Several U.S. states and some nations are also building sweeping databases of citizens' DNA information for future use. Are we as a nation okay with a genetically biased health care system?

Some of these capabilities have been available for years, but weren't threatening because they were too expensive to be widely deployed on a large scale. Unfortunately digital technology is now cheap, very cheap—and it is getting more so every year. The best protection against wholesale privacy abuse has always been the cost. However, this fiscal barrier is effective only against physical, not virtual, items because the economics are different in the digital world. For example, the profitability point for spam (junk email), regardless of the volume, is insanely low compared with the break-even point for postal mail because the incremental cost per item of spam is close to zero. The cost of a postage stamp is a natural brake on the proliferation of junk mail. There's no equivalent friction for email. America Online (AOL) has instituted a program called Good Mail, which purports to cut back on spam by charging mass emailers who want to send to AOL recipients. The theory is that the payments will deter spammers. Are we willing to pay for all our email in the future, or is spam a nuisance that we're willing to put up with for free stuff?

Our lives are represented electronically in databases across the world. The decentralization of this information makes it difficult to regulate. These computerized storehouses are necessary for so many business and governmental purposes that most people do not view them as a threat. And the political climate is not favorable for changing the situation. These information tools are seen as important weapons in our nation's arsenal. We live in a turbulent time. All but the most snugly bundled liberties have been whipped by the wind of fear that has blown through the United States since the attacks on the World Trade Center and the Pentagon in 2001. The natural balance between national security and privacy has tipped precariously toward security. Are we as citizens in a democracy willing to grant our government indefinite powers to anonymously invade our privacy if it makes us safer? What if we only think it makes us safer? Should government be limited in what it can see and do with the information it collects on us?

But it's not just government tracking citizens. Every group that uses computers incrementally erodes the privacy of its constituents when it starts keeping lists. The newspapers are full of privacy-related stories, ranging from abuses of the Patriot Act to President George W. Bush's authorization of possibly illegal domestic surveillance. Every few weeks, we hear about massive data breaches caused by careless data handling by private companies, while others, like Google, are holding enormous amounts of personal information—so much so that the government is trying to forcibly get access to it. The privacy situation in the United States and Canada is at an Orange Alert level and will not be going back to Yellow again in my lifetime.

Information gathering is the new arms race. Superior knowledge gives the knower the ability to predict what's going to happen. And a lot of money can be made from predicting the future. Governments collect personal information to spot subversion. Merchandisers use it to target or persuade consumers. Financial institutions assess credit-worthiness. Politicians find donors. Terrorists hatch plots. This fungible information is easily transportable and can be converted into cash in any currency in the world. You often hear the old legend that our body is worth $4.50, stripped for parts. Our digital identity is worth far more than that. Information about us is worth $20–$50 to a business trying to sell us a product and is worth many thousands of dollars to an identity thief.

Our ethical sense is not yet fine-tuned to the changes brought about in the privacy arena by technology. Nor is our legal system. Western society views the universe through the lens of science. In this model, technological progress is ideologically pure and apolitical. Information is just data, just facts. We find it hard to accept the idea that knowledge can be dangerous. We don't have a cultural perspective that supports this idea, unlike people living under repressive regimes, who know that information, true or not, can get them jailed or even killed. This intellectual blind spot, refusing to believe that control of information should be regulated, is one of the major reasons why the United States has no comprehensive privacy laws today.

This book is different from other books about privacy because it's centered on technology, not the law. In this century, technology moves fast and sets the pace for social issues, leaving the law lagging behind. Legislation works best when fixing a problem that has clearly definable boundaries. However, information technology itself and the ways in which it's harvested and sold are developing at such a rapid rate that new laws are likely to address technology that industry has already abandoned. Congress has historically done a miserable job at providing protection against future problems, even the slow-moving ones. These kinds of problems cannot be resolved in Congress, just as they cannot be fixed solely in the courts. The law will always lag behind the technology.

Privacy legislation has also been difficult to enact because the damages from privacy loss are not clearly understood. To many people, privacy issues are linked to immediate annoyances, like telemarketing phone calls. Because the consequences are not directly apparent, the hardest situations to regulate in a democratic society are those, like smoking or environmental protection or control of information, that cause long-term damages.

Privacy Lost is divided into six parts. The first part is about the damages caused by the loss, including what I call the Seven Sins Against Privacy. The second part reviews some of the history behind our concept of privacy, how related technology has evolved, and how new technology leads to new invasions of privacy. The third part discusses the context of privacy; it includes a chapter on the legal basis in the United States, another on how privacy relates to identity, and a third on how the idea of privacy varies culturally. The fourth part deals with the mechanics of snooping, databases, surveillance, and networking technologies. The fifth part describes the snoopers themselves, the marketing companies and the government. The last part suggests some ways you can slow or staunch your loss of privacy. The Recommended Reading list at the end of the book provides suggestions for further reading on the topics covered.

Throughout the book you'll find numerous stories and examples, culled from newspapers, magazines, and the Internet, about how privacy invasions hurt people. Although privacy violations happen to celebrities more often they affect normal people, the ones who mistakenly think that the government or the law is protecting them. If you take one idea away from reading this book, it should be that you have the right to control information about yourself. Even if the law doesn't recognize this right, you should. Privacy is, in a legal and practical sense, based on our expectations. Even though Americans have no explicit constitutional right to privacy, most think that we do. People are constantly surprised that there is no mention of privacy in the Constitution. Government is, in fact, powerless to regulate the availability and flow of personal information; even more dangerously it believes that it can. This book discusses some steps individuals can take to protect themselves instead of relying on the government.

Polls indicate that people are willing to give up their privacy in exchange for safety. However, the damage caused by the loss of privacy could reach into other areas of our lives as well. For instance, the ability to keep our thoughts and opinions to ourselves gives us the freedom to exercise our other rights without fear of retribution. Privacy allows us to peacefully exercise other rights such as freedom of speech and religion and the right to bear arms. The answer to the question of who controls information about us touches many other areas such as intellectual property and genetic engineering. It may be the most important domestic policy question of this century.

A long-term danger to society resulting from a total loss of privacy protection is that our creative and freethinking culture could be replaced by one that rewards fear-driven mediocrity. It happened on a smaller scale in Hollywood after the Senator Joseph McCarthy hearings and was part of daily life in the Puritan colonies. Those who know that they're watched don't call attention to themselves, and thus they disappear. The economic might of Western innovation cannot be sustained by a nation of ghosts.

Part I

Privacy Invasions Hurt

Many, maybe most, people aren't worried about their privacy. Isn't it our right, already protected in the Constitution? The short answer is no. This part explains privacy by describing what happens when it gets violated: how privacy violations affect our culture, our government, and, most important, us. Chapter One breaks privacy violations into seven categories and provides accompanying "commandments" for improvement. Real examples of privacy problems are included to help explain each sin. Chapter Two describes how a lack of privacy can harm civilization in general and a country specifically.

1

The Seven Sins Against Privacy

*Privacy is not something that I'm merely entitled to;
it's an absolute prerequisite.*

Marlon Brando[1]

Privacy is a common word that is, like most overworked terms,
somewhat ambiguous. The *Oxford English Dictionary* defines it
as "a state in which one is not observed or disturbed by others."[2]
The *American Heritage Dictionary* says it's "the quality or condition
of being secluded from the presence or view of others."[3] *Merriam-
Webster's* alternatively defines it as "freedom from unauthorized intrusion."[4] But in its frequent press mentions these days, it has taken on
yet another connotation. There, it has come to mean the loss of control of personal information, generally because of technology.

A lack of consensus on the meaning of privacy creates equal
confusion about what constitutes a privacy violation. Generally violations are measured against a legal template—an act breaks a privacy law; therefore it's a violation. This approach doesn't work well
against technology-enabled privacy offenses because they're usually
too new to have generated restrictive laws.

Privacy invasion means something different to each of us; it's a
moving target. When you hear the term you may automatically think
of an invasion by a technology like wiretapping, while others may
think about having their identity stolen. To some it's an advertising

annoyance, like junk mail, while to others it's the exposure of private information, which can be demeaning and undermine their dignity. The understanding of privacy can also be cultural and generational, aspects that I discuss in Chapter Seven. Privacy means something different in urban and rural settings. Baby boomers feel that it's an entitlement; Gen Xers don't. Everyone seems to agree that privacy is or should be a right, although, as I will show, there is at best a tenuous basis for that belief. One thing is certain: the idea of privacy has changed and evolved throughout history, never more so than in this complex Information Age. Overall, I see three basic meanings for privacy:

- Seclusion—the right to be hidden from the perceptions of others

- Solitude—the right to be left alone

- Self-determination—the right to control information about oneself

Privacy is at the whip end of information technology. Even a small, incremental innovation can have profound effects on privacy. Take the camera phone, for example. The nationwide trend now is to ban all cell phones from gyms because of the phones' new ability to take surreptitious pictures. The enabling nature of technology constantly changes, transforming the context of privacy tangibly, shifting the underlying meaning itself.

To define privacy adequately requires understanding the extent of information technology. One reason the legal system is so poorly equipped to deal with privacy problems is that this scope is constantly expanding. In Chapter Five, I describe the U.S. legal definition. Many lawful activities that pertain to privacy are distasteful or undesirable to most people. Nevertheless, they are likely to remain legal.

Privacy, like pain, is personal and hard to describe even though the perception of its loss is universal. This lack of consensus about a definition makes discussing the topic difficult. Respecting privacy takes more than adherence to laws; it takes thoughtful ethical reasoning and consideration. When we agree about what is wrong, what is right becomes clearer. To that end, I've created a taxonomy of violations. The harms from lost privacy are considerable. Breaking them into categories, some obvious, some perhaps less so, helps us understand the concept of privacy and appreciate the scope of the potential harm as well as the actual harm. In my taxonomy, privacy violations can be viewed as seven sins: intrusion, latency, deception, profiling, identity theft, outing, and loss of dignity. Each sin is described here, and each description is followed by a "commandment," or ethical guiding principle.

Sin of Intrusion

The classical form of privacy abuse, intrusion, is the uninvited encroachment on a person's physical or virtual space. In the nineteenth century, intrusion often took the form of voyeurism or peeping. In the crowded Information Age, it's become a multidimensional offense, involving each of the five senses. Intrusion may mean being forced to sit next to someone on an airplane who's wearing a cloying amount of perfume. It may be simple voyeurism, as when you step out of the shower and see your neighbor staring across the alley at you. It may be auditory, as when you pull up to a stoplight and hear the booming bass of an amplified car stereo.

Technology has added complexity to the mix of potential intrusions. Miniature cameras and picture phones are inexpensive, popular, and powerful. Hidden listening devices can be smaller than a pinhead. Nicole Kidman found concealed cameras and listening devices planted in and around her home in Australia.[5] Fashion model Kate Moss lost lucrative endorsement and modeling contracts when she was captured snorting cocaine by a camera hidden in someone's clothes.[6]

Many were surprised when they found out that by attending the 2001 Super Bowl in Tampa, Florida, they were subjected to a biometric technology called facial recognition. All participants were scanned as they entered the stadium, and the images were then compared with a series of digital mug shots in hopes of capturing some known felons.[7]

Our picture is taken dozens of times a day as we pass by banks, convenience stores, or ATMs. It's taken hundreds of times if we live in a big city; for instance, the average person is caught on a surveillance camera three hundred times a day in London.[8]

Manalapan, Florida, is located near exclusive Palm Beach and is one of the wealthiest towns in the United States. It has decided to blanket the community with cameras and computers to check every vehicle and driver traveling through the area. Software will run the collected tag numbers through law-enforcement databases looking for matches.[9]

Voyeurism technology has gotten more and more sophisticated. web sites sell remote listening devices, digital optics, scanners for picking up cell-phone conversations, and even infrared scanners that spot body movements through the walls of a house or pick out the figure of a human being through clothing. Snooping software used to track online activities can have legitimate uses like monitoring children, but it can also be used by criminals to secretly collect personal information and harvest credit-card numbers.

The Radio Frequency Identification Device (RFID) is a new kind of technology that acts like a wireless bar code. Geographic Positioning System (GPS) receivers are satellite locating devices that are small enough to be put into cars and even cell phones. GPS trackers and RFID chips are being incorporated into all kinds of devices and services. The President's Commission on the Postal Service is recommending collaboration with the Department of Homeland Security to look into the possibility of developing sender-identification requirements using RFID technology that would use tracking codes to determine who sends and receives mail through the U.S. Postal Service.[10]

The commission cited the system as a way to improve the security of the postal network, but privacy critics warn that taking away the ability to send anonymous mail will infringe on civil and privacy rights. RFID technology is predicted to be one of the most invasive inventions of our time because it can be used on everyday objects: everything from passports and currency to running shoes and printers (see Chapter Nine).

Libraries are already in hot water with privacy advocates because of plans to institute RFID tracking tags for inventory control. San Francisco library officials approved a plan to implement the tags to replace bar codes and magnetic strips. Critics say the technology could be used to track residents and their reading habits via their possessions because RFID tags could be activated and used outside the library. Several large American libraries already use RFIDs for inventory purposes.[11]

GPS is also being used increasingly in consumer products. OnStar, the popular personal security system for General Motors cars, is also a location-tracking device equipped with GPS. Oregon wants to put GPS devices on all automobiles so it can track cars and levy travel taxes proportional to road usage."[12] The Pentagon is developing a system that will catalogue every car and driver in a city by using cameras and computers.[13] The Palm Beach County School District already uses the technology to monitor its bus drivers, including how fast they drive, where they stop, and whether they respect railway crossings.[14] Taxi drivers in Manhattan are fighting for their privacy amidst plans that would equip each car with a tracking system.[15]

Black boxes installed in more than forty million brand-new vehicles provide a feature not listed on the sticker—invisible surveillance. Without owners' permission or even their knowledge, data on seatbelt use, speed, and destinations are collected on American citizens. Only five states have laws requiring car dealerships to inform buyers of the technology.[16]

The Food and Drug Administration has approved the sale of an implantable human identification chip called the Verichip. Applied Digital Solutions of Palm Beach, Florida, is the maker of the RFID tag. The owner of the company argues that it is more secure to have a device planted under the skin than embedded in a bank card or key-chain dangler, which can be easily lost. The Verichip is being marketed as a security measure for providing access to buildings or as identification for financial transactions. The company says it will have a GPS version soon, enabling it to track people implanted with the device to within a few centimeters, no matter where in the world they are. The potential for abuse with this technology is obviously huge, especially because many people may have chips implanted against their will. The first people to be "chipped" will probably be registered sex offenders and paroled prisoners, but the program could be extended to many others, such as nannies, organ donors, or anyone with a security clearance. Without a cultural push-back on chipping human beings, it will almost certainly occur in the future. In May 2006, Wisconsin was the first state to pass a bill prohibiting forced chip implants in humans.[17]

Already in use in Europe and countries such as Malaysia, smart cards containing computer chips will further increase the amount of digitized personal information available on each of us.[18] Electronic health cards are also just around the corner in the United States, with Great Britain, Australia, and Canada leading the way.[19]

China is set to require new electronic identification cards for all its citizens.[20] By the end of 2006, all newly issued American passports will be equipped with RFID chips.[21] All these smart cards raise privacy concerns because they will store in-depth personal information, giving companies and the government access to an incredible amount of data on all of us.

Intrusion violations are amplified by the double threat of locational technologies such as implanted chips and enhanced sensing. It's no longer possible for you to control your privacy just by being aware of who's around. Not seeing anyone doesn't mean that no one's watching.

Devising an effective measure against intrusion will be difficult. The easy, if impractical, answer would be to bar, or at least license, intrusive technologies. Several states already restrict use of high-end surveillance technologies to accredited law enforcement. It would be difficult to mandate this restriction federally. The best solution would be to toughen the penalties for sinners who get caught and do a better job of writing the laws so as to cover both the newest technologies available today as well as those that will surely soon be commercially available.

Commandment: *Don't spy on me just because you can.*

Sin of Latency

Because most of the damage to privacy comes from stored information, the harm can be minimized if personal information isn't retained. Excessive hoarding of personal information is the sin of latency. It occurs when custodians of personal information keep information beyond an agreed-upon time. This is one of the most common sins; I've yet to find a company that has established and enforced a data-aging policy.

Latency is subtle; it reaches into the future to tweak your privacy, usually long after you've forgotten that you gave out personal information. Typical sinners are companies that you have a relationship with for a temporary period of time, such as utilities, credit-card companies, and Internet service providers (ISPs). Every time you open accounts with such companies, they create a database file. Throughout the lifetime of the relationship (and sometimes beyond), service companies attempt to fill their files with any information they can get—at a minimum, personal information from forms like names, addresses, and phone numbers. Many require additional data, like birthdays and spouses' names. Some try to get Social Security numbers (SSNs) or at least driver's license numbers, sometimes claiming that they use SSNs as account identification numbers.

The more information that businesses collect, the likelier it is that they'll be able to match those data to other information at some future date. Unique information that describes a single person is an absolute requirement for marketing databases. Without it, ambiguity may result—Which John Smith on First Street? Until the mid-1990s, a phone number was enough to guarantee uniqueness, but no longer. Most of us have more than one telephone number now and change it more frequently than in the past. The easiest information to match is an SSN because it's guaranteed to be unique.

You might assume that a company will delete your information from its records when you close your account, but most companies only mark your file as inactive. Your file won't be deleted now or at any conceivable time in the future (see Chapter Three). Service businesses like telephone, cellular, and credit-card companies have records on far more people than they have active accounts.

So what can a company do with your information after you are no longer a customer? They can sell it. A consumer record with up-to-date information is worth around $200 for cell phone information. Social Security information sells for $60 and a student's university class schedule goes for $80.[22] Ironically, many companies consider themselves freed from any self-imposed or contractual constraints once the relationship is terminated. Contractually, most can do anything they want with the data once you cancel your account.

An attractive part of e-commerce has always been the ability to monitor consumer behavior. Commercial interests, such as DoubleClick, the online marketing technology company, were initially responsible for institutionalizing online data collection. The company uses cookies, small text files containing unique identifiers that are stored on personal computers and used to monitor online activities and track the ads. Cookies help create an audit trail that defeats the expectation of anonymous web browsing. Most Internet users are unaware that they are tracked and monitored to that extent. In June 1999, DoubleClick purchased Abacus, a company that collects and sells data on offline catalogue customers and distributes print catalogues through the mail; it thus has the ability to merge online with real-world information.[23] Even though consumers never visit DoubleClick's web site, they pick up DoubleClick's cookies at participating third-party sites. The linking of invisible cookies to real-world marketing databases means that you can be identified: name, address, even credit rating, whether you buy something on the site or not.

The company eventually agreed to pay $1.8 million to settle lawsuits that claimed it violated privacy laws by gathering and selling consumer information. It also agreed to limit the life span of new cookies by routinely purging the information collected online and not linking online surfing habits with identifying personal information.[24]

The merger of online and real-world data means that whatever you do on the Internet—searching, purchasing, or just browsing—becomes transparent to hidden watchers who know who you are and where you live. Imagine looking up information on bankruptcy on the Internet and then getting a letter in the mail a couple of days later from a law firm stating that it heard you wanted information on Chapter 11.

Because of the lucrative value of consumer information, the highest scrutiny should be on companies that have the potential to "touch" millions of customers daily, even if they don't appear to be selling any product or service. Search engines such as Google should top the list. As Google has gained in popularity, its scrutiny by privacy advocates has increased. The company offers a suite of products that, by their very nature, collect a lot of personal information about the individuals who use them. In addition to being able to store every search for future analysis, Google has branched out into new areas, such as Google Maps, Google Earth, and even Google Shakespeare. Google Earth offers detailed satellite imagery of much of the world. In many areas the pictures are detailed enough to see the types of cars parked in driveways.

The large amount of personal data collected by Google, the potential for cross-connections, and the perpetual retention of the information make Google a serious future threat to privacy, regardless of its intentions. Web searching and blogging (using personal web logs) are impulsive, and although each instance may not be revealing, collectively searches and blog entries paint a detailed picture of a person's opinions and interests . . . and Google saves all searches forever.

The public teeth gnashing about Google is not based on any actions that the company has or hasn't yet taken; it's based on the potential for problems in the future. Because of Google's central position in the web (52 percent of all external referrals to most web sites come through Google),[25] most people use Google technology, directly or indirectly; this high level of use virtually guarantees that Google has information on almost every person in the Western world.

Because Google saves the results of consumer searches for a long time, perhaps forever, and because it has the search string and Internet address of many searchers, it can do real damage with database matching, which involves taking information from one context, like searching, and equating it to an unrelated venue, like product shopping on an e-commerce site or commenting on a blog. The only requirement is a shared piece of information, a key field that can be matched between databases. Its gmail product looks at the content of emails so that Google can serve up targeted banner ads. Google Desktop and related products index material stored on home and office computers. If Google were willing to exploit this information, it would become the biggest commercial threat to privacy in existence. The danger exists because of Google's indefinite retention of information coupled with its ability to cross-index many types of stored personal information. If the record of each transaction were purged after a short time, the menace would be greatly diminished.

In 2006, Google was involved in a legal battle with the U.S. government over its search history.[26] The Justice Department had subpoenaed a chunk of Google's log files to make the case that pornography constitutes a substantial part of Internet searching. Google had refused to comply with the order. A judge ruled in Google's favor, requiring it to turn over only a limited set of information with identifying notations stripped off. This case brings home the point that the company is in possession of huge amounts of information that could cause privacy problems if misused by the government, a hacker, or Google itself. Google provides no guarantee, contractual or legal, that such misuse will never occur. In the meantime, it keeps collecting information, apparently deleting none of it.

The more information that a company collects, the likelier it is that some of it can be matched to data saved elsewhere; and the more information that's matched, the deeper the insight gained. The lack of commercial data-retention policies and procedures turns this situation from an annoyance to a danger. Company privacy policies should address this issue, but they never do. Few companies state their long-term data-retention intentions in writing for a very simple reason . . . : they don't have to. This area absolutely requires government intervention: mandatory data-erasure policies enforced by fines for noncompliance. Companies should be legally required to purge consumer information after some minimally necessary time, which could be as little as 180 days from termination of the relationship. Firms that are found to keep data beyond the agreed-upon date could be sued. In such cases, data, including back-up tapes, network caches, and hard-copy printouts, must be purged completely and throughout the enterprise. Maintaining privacy in the era of digital information requires vigilant data destruction.

Commandment: *Thou shall erase my data.*

Sin of Deception

When too much electronic information is available in databases, the temptation for marketers to use it becomes great. Using personal information in a way that was not authorized by the person involved is the sin of deception.

If a company asks for personal information, it should state how long it's going to keep it, what it's going to do with it, and whom it's going to give those data to. When we give our information to a company, we are entering into a contract with them, just as we do when we lease a car or buy a house. Unfortunately, few companies see it that way. Most retain the right to sell your information or use it for other purposes under certain extremely broad conditions. You lose all control of your personal information if you don't know who has it and what they're going to do with it. The idea that you have the right to control information about yourself is a basic one. People in some cultures, most notably Tibetans, refuse to let anyone take their picture because they believe that the camera steals their souls. I wonder how they'd feel filling out a credit application.

If a phone company asks for your SSN so that it can run a credit check to turn on service, it shouldn't be able to use your SSN later to prequalify you for an unsolicited offer from a third party or to try to sell you another product. The company ought to purge the data after the initial qualification, but it does not. Some credit-card companies give these transaction data to businesses, providing comprehensive snapshots of cardholders and their spending behavior, including where and what they bought, at what time, the amounts of the purchases, the addresses of the stores, and even the demographic data either given to them by the customer or derived from the purchase history. Without notice and a chance to opt out, individuals have no say over the disposition of their personal information or awareness of how it is being used; they thus have no privacy.

Sometimes the courts can help. Wells Fargo was sued for selling its customer data to third parties, and a California Superior Court approved the settlement.[27] GeoCities, the web-community builder, was also sued for third-party selling of customer information. In this case, the company sold it to direct marketers without permission.[28] Several lawsuits have been filed against data broker ChoicePoint for the selling of personal information to identity thieves. In one case, ChoicePoint neglected to ask 140,000 individuals for permission and directly profited from the sale of SSNs and other private data.[29]

Not just commercial firms are guilty; the government is one of the worst offenders. Tax returns are used to gather information that has nothing to do with paying taxes, such as tracking "deadbeat dads" and student-loan scofflaws. With the No Child Left Behind Act the government also requires schools to hand over students' files to military recruiters upon request and without the permission or even the notification of the students or their parents. The phrase *no child left behind* takes on an ominous meaning when the country is at war and facing a severe shortage of military personnel.

Privacy policies sometimes address the deception issue, although they are so weasel-worded they are not an adequate consumer safeguard. One common statement appears to allow the handoff of your information to the company's "partners." As Roy Rogers would have said, *partner* is a pretty big word.

A related sin is the sharing of your information with a third party without your permission. Privacy policies sometimes address such sharing of data, but even if a company agrees to keep the information within its own organization, it can be a meaningless gesture. When you're dealing with AOL, you're dealing with Time Warner, a huge publishing conglomerate. With big or small companies, privacy policies protect the organization, not the consumer.

In 2001, Macy's announced it would sell the personal information it had collected from 1.5 million of its Internet customers, including their credit-card numbers, birth dates, and email addresses. The department store was asking $90 per thousand names, and, for an additional $15 per name, it included extra data such as household income and the ages of children. The company's position was that it had a right to sell the data unless a costumer opted out.[30]

Some cases involving unapproved third-party data sales have gone to court. But because no blanket federal laws prohibit data sales, these actions are usually successful only when a prohibitive contract between the institution and the consumer is in place. Generally speaking, banks and phone and credit-card companies can sell customer data unless they've limited themselves in their published policies.

U.S. Bank and its holding company, U.S. Bancorp, were sued for selling to a telemarketing company customer data that included credit scores, SSNs, credit-card numbers, and account balances. The price tag was $4 million plus a 22 percent commission on sales. The state of Minnesota claimed in the suit that the company was violating the federal Fair Credit Reporting Act. When the lawsuit was finally settled, the bank refused to acknowledge any wrongdoing but did agree to stop distributing personal information to other companies. It also agreed to give customers a way to opt out of data sharing with the bank's affiliates or partners.[31]

Companies should be forced to detail their information policies, specifying exactly what they will do with customer data, guaranteeing that this information will not be shared with other groups, even in the same organization. Terminology like "to notify our customers of special offers they might be interested in" is no restriction. The same goes for statements like "we will share information only with our strategic partners." It should be illegal for any organization to hand over information to third parties except for administrative functions like subcontracted data handling. Judging by the trend toward ambiguous and consumer-unfriendly privacy policies, the sin of deception badly needs legal policing to be kept in check.

The discussion of this sin has been focused on the knowing mishandling of data. But a huge problem also exists with inadvertent or sloppy custodianship of consumer information, often by the same companies mentioned in this section. The discussion of the sin of identity theft below provides additional information on this problem; more information on data breaches can be found in Chapters Three, Nine, and Ten.

The lack of laws punishing companies for fumbling our private information, either accidentally or on purpose, is appalling. By imposing escalating fines, legislation could easily force companies that want to be custodians of our personal data to improve their handling of those data.

Commandment: *Keep my information to thyself.*

Sin of Profiling

Not only original information needs to be protected. Data derived from raw information also can be mishandled. Misusing derived information is the sin of profiling.

Profiling is an important technique by which useful analytic information is derived from raw data like grocery-shopping histories; studying such transactions helps explain what customers did, but it does not explain what they will do. That's where profiling comes in. By using heuristics or artificial-intelligence technology, organizations can automatically categorize consumers based on rules created by database analysts, psychologists, or just good guessers. These rules enable companies to attempt to predict consumers' future behavior. Predictive intelligence can come only from profiling. Beginning with database merging and enrichment, profiling is built on a sophisticated form of information analysis known as data mining, using artificial-intelligence software to find patterns and connections of behavior.

Profiling is based on made-up rules. These can be as simple as "people who live in high-income zip codes are likely to buy a BMW" or as complex as "women who buy Haagen-Dazs ice cream twice in a week may be depressed and are likelier to impulse buy" or as stereotypical as "people who have a Hispanic surname make 20 percent less money than the average person in a given zip code." The harm from these guesses is that they may be wrong and, as a result, you may have a great deal of trouble changing your classification, or, even worse, you may not ever know that you've been labeled. Anyone who's ever been unfairly tagged as a credit risk can relate to this sin.

Often the result of profiling is *customer segmentation*, a marketing term for breaking people into groups (usually by demographics) that indicate their buying behavior. Segmentation is the ultimate goal of marketers because they can identify and catch people who are likely to bite at a given lure. Best Buy, the national electronics retail chain, is redesigning its stores around key market segments. They've named one group Jills—the so-called soccer moms who are the primary shoppers for their families but who are intimidated by electronics stores. The stores have trained special clerks to watch for the Jills, give them tailored assistance, and even escort them to private check-out lines festooned with pink and blue balloons with Jill-friendly music playing in the background.[32]

Profiling is a complicated sin. When it's right and inoffensive, it's helpful to the consumer because the softer side of profiling is personalization. When it's wrong, it can be insulting. When it reveals something that you'd rather keep hidden, it's a violation of privacy. The same technology that helpfully recommends a book that you might like could be making other guesses about you that you don't.

Experian is a provider of aggregated consumer information, much of it collected from the sale of magazines and from catalogue purchases. The company claims to have profiles on 98 percent of Americans. One of the databases they routinely sell contains the reading habits and activities of more than ninety million individuals; it covers 274 publications.[33]

Credit-card companies have used data-profiling technologies for decades. I worked with one card company that said it was able to pinpoint when its customers were having life crises such as mid-life depression by psychographically analyzing their buying patterns. Law enforcement uses similar techniques to predict the behavior of high-profile criminals like serial killers.

No laws protect people from profiling systems. Even though credit reporting is thinly regulated, credit-scoring systems (another word for profiling) are not. The most commonly used system, developed jointly by Equifax and the Fair Isaac Corporation in 1989, FICO is used to rate the risk in extending credit to a consumer.

Because of the credit-scoring company's dominant market position, the score is universally accepted as legitimate and factual. These scores are used by nearly all the large lending institutions to determine ability to pay off debt and as an indicator of creditworthiness. Besides providing financial services to companies in more than sixty countries, Fair Isaac supplies the ten largest banks in the world with credit scoring.[34] Equifax, Experian, and TransUnion— the big three consumer-reporting agencies in the United States and Canada—rely on FICO scores. Every year, billions of credit assessments are based on FICO numbers, including more than 75 percent of mortgage requests.[35] The higher the FICO score, a number between 300 and 850, the better. A lower score can result in higher interest rates for all forms of credit, but can also be used to deny employment or apartment rentals.

A July 2003 Consumer Federation of America survey found that only 2 percent of Americans knew their credit score.[36] In fact, during a conference, a Fair Isaac employee said that consumers derived no benefit from knowing their individual credit scores, that such information would be meaningless and confusing to them. The panelist went on to explain that the company doesn't want people trying to improve their scores because that would result in consumers' acting differently and thus skewing the company's model—a model that uses an unknown and unregulated mathematical formula to calculate the score.[37]

FICO's creditworthiness assessment is subjective. The analysis is based on facts contained in credit reports, but a study released by the U.S. Public Interest Research Group in June 2004 showed that as many as 79 percent of credit reports had errors, with more than 50 percent containing outdated information or data belonging to someone else, as well as 25 percent containing mistakes serious enough that credit could be denied.[38]

Scoring systems are the unseen accusers in the credit world. A bad score is essentially unchallengeable. You have no legal rights to see your score or understand how it was calculated; yet a bad score can hurt you for the rest of your life: it can keep you from buying a house, deny you credit, or even cost you a job. Setting the record straight in the case of an incorrect or unfair profile is like fixing a bad reputation spread by whispers. It's difficult when you can't confront your accuser directly.

The problems with credit-assessment businesses are thus threefold: the FICO scoring system is a mystery and is at best pseudoscientific; many credit reports that these businesses use for input contain substantive errors that affect the scores; and because there's no legal oversight, the scores are sold and shared everywhere without consumers' permission or knowledge.

Increasingly, insurance companies, Telcos, landlords, government agencies, retailers, health care organizations, and a slew of other organizations are getting access to credit scores and using them for many reasons having nothing to do with credit.

In September 2004, TXU Energy in Texas started charging clients with lower FICO scores higher rates for natural gas. TXU claims that the Experian data are an accurate predictor of payment performance.[39]

The government, especially the Internal Revenue Service (IRS) and the Department of Homeland Security, also uses profiling extensively. The IRS has a predictive profiling program called the Reveal System that is used to spot possible tax cheats.[40] Homeland Security has been experimenting with several systems designed to spot potential terrorists by categorizing them based on information like the books they buy, whom they talk to, and where they travel.[41] Catching a terrorist after an attack can be accomplished using conventional searching techniques, but identifying the act and the actor prior to commission takes intelligent software that can make educated guesses.

In an effort to fight terrorism, the Pentagon's Terrorist Information Awareness (TIA) program was designed to sift through data held in ultralarge databases looking for connections and relationships among people. Congress suspended funding for the TIA program in 2003, requiring the Defense Department to describe the project's privacy implications in detail. The program would give intelligence agencies access to every private database in the country. Communication, financial, travel, and medical records would be fed into centralized databases to create profiles and analyze patterns.[42] Although TIA is not operational yet, a scaled-down version will soon be running at local airports. Called the Computer Assisted Passenger Pre-screening System, the controversial program will run investigations of prospective passengers while they wait at check-in counters; it will search through a large number of databases to decide each flyer's risk level.[43] ChoicePoint, LexisNexis, and Acxiom are just a few of the many companies that will supply airports and law-enforcement authorities with personal data for the program. Presumably bad credit information could translate into a flying risk.

Industry and the government have been on parallel profiling tracks until now. However, their data-mining efforts have begun to become intertwined, with the results from one being fed as input into the analysis machinery of the other. Is a terrorist suspect inherently a bad credit risk? Is a credit threat a possible terrorist? The further that the resulting label strays from verifiable facts, the harder it will be for you to challenge the outcome. The problems that clearly innocent people (like Senator Edward Kennedy) have had in getting removed from the Transportation Security Administration's no-fly list illustrate this difficulty. Chapter Eleven discusses these cross-database issues in detail.

Profiling is just guessing. Developers often gussy up their results with jargon to obscure the essentially unverifiable nature of the process. The penalty for bad guessing is severe—the permanent nature of databases virtually guarantees that any labels attached to consumers by a profiling program can stigmatize them for life. Like actuarial tables, profiling is a statistical game, producing reasonable results in the aggregate but breaking down completely when applied to any particular individual. The potential victims of this kind of privacy violation include schoolchildren who are labeled learning disabled, customers termed bad credit risks because of job hopping, or citizens who are restricted from traveling because of a comment they made or a place they visited long ago or just because they happen to have the wrong name.

The basis of free societies is transparency in process. The ability to challenge an accuser is a fundamental principle of democracies. Profiling is insidious because of its stealthy, accusatory nature. Profiling systems are becoming too prevalent and important for us to blindly assume the good judgment of the companies that develop them. Full disclosure of the rules and score derivations is critical to our understanding and ungrudging acceptance of the process.

We should each have the right to see and challenge any entries made in any organizational database, especially those that label us, like credit scores and government threat profiles. Being categorized secretly with no ability to question and correct the label is not only at odds with the principles of a democracy but is the beginning of the slippery slope toward a closed and repressive society. True democracy abhors secrets.

Commandment: *Don't judge me by your data.*

Sin of Identity Theft

The previous sins are committed by institutions against individuals; identity theft is a one-to-one violation. Identity theft is exactly what it sounds like—a thief pretends to be you and steals your money. This is a modern crime, brought about by easily accessible personal information disseminated by computers. Remote-control robbery is one of the fastest growing crimes that the United States and Canada have ever seen, and it was the crime reported most frequently to the Federal Trade Commission (FTC) between 2000 and 2005.[44] In the electronic marketplace, vendors and customers don't meet face-to-face, so businesses identify a buyer by unique alphanumeric sequences—name, email address, and SSN. Sloppy handling of consumer data by both industry and government makes it all too easy for would-be identity snatchers to get the information that they need (see the descriptions of the sins of latency and deception).

A New York busboy was caught systematically stealing the identities of everyone on the annual Forbes 400 list. He used the Internet to do the research and had already been successful against Steven Spielberg, Oprah Winfrey, and Ted Turner.[45]

An identity-theft case in New York in which three men were caught stealing millions of dollars from thirty thousand people illustrates how easy and lucrative this kind of crime is and why people are motivated to commit it: one of the perpetrators was a poorly paid clerical worker at a credit-check agency.[46] At $30 per stolen credit file, the temptation for government workers to set up a side business selling databases is also going to be hard to resist. Such is the case of Jeffrey D. Fudge of Lancaster, Texas. A former FBI investigative analyst, he was charged with eight counts of unauthorized access to files on a government computer and with revealing private information to family and friends.[47]

Identity theft is a relatively recent crime. It's possible because of the vast amount of information available on each of us, some of which, like our SSN and mother's maiden name, is often sufficient identification to access our financial accounts. The easiest way to steal an identity is to use an SSN, yet many companies ask, even demand, SSNs for account information but fail to protect them adequately. Half of all universities still use the SSN as the student identification number. A half million identity-theft complaints were filed with the FTC from 2000 to 2005, with 214,000 in 2003—up 33 percent from 2002. Another 301,000 people reported consumer fraud in 2003, half of which was Internet related.[48] Other estimates put the numbers for identity theft much higher, anywhere from 750,000 to 12,000,000 victims each year. Two Gartner Research and Harris Interactive studies from July 2003 found that approximately seven million people had been victims of identity theft in the previous year—more than nineteen thousand per day. This crime increased by 80 percent between 2002 and 2003, with 49 percent of those polled saying they did not know how to protect their identities from theft.[49]

Business Week estimates that online identity-theft losses in the United States are running about $12 billion a year.[50] In 2003, the FTC conducted a telephone survey of 4,057 randomly selected respondents. Almost 5 percent said that they had been the victims of identity theft in the previous two years, and 13 percent claimed their identities had been stolen over the preceding five years. The FTC estimated that identity theft costs American businesses over $47 billion per year at an average cost of $4,800 per affected individual.[51]

A variety of techniques are used to steal identities. Phishing involves sending out mass emailings with a message purporting to come from a bank or a brokerage; customers are requested to go to a certain web page and validate their account information. The site is bogus, and the newly entered information is used by the crooks to clean out the mark's account. Phishers don't know which addresses are bank customers, but by targeting a huge mailing list, they're statistically bound to hit some. Phishing is a numbers game. If one person in a hundred thousand falls for the hoax, the crooks make a profit. Similar scams used to be run using postal mail, but such attempts had two drawbacks. First was the cost. A mailing to 100,000,000 people would cost at least $7 million for third-class bulk mail and so would hardly be profitable. Second, it is a federal crime to use postal mail to commit fraud. Phishing and spamming are not illegal in themselves. As a practical matter, few phishers are ever caught; many are located outside the United States and are probably not even prosecutable. (For additional information about phishing, see Chapter Six.)

Identity theft can be perpetrated by any strategy that leaves the thief in possession of enough information to empty out one or more of the target's accounts or, in rare cases, with title to a physical possession that can be sold. A couple who left town for an extended vacation had their identity snatched by thieves who wiped out their accounts, sold their possessions, and even disposed of their house. When the unlucky victims returned, they were penniless, carless, furniture-bereft, and staring at a big pit in the ground where their house used to be.[52]

Identity theft can start at a mailbox or a garbage can. Dumpster diving is a common method for getting a victim's financial information; so is prying open mailboxes. Some thieves are even unethical enough to use obituaries. Rondale Vonkeith Montgomery of

Houston fed the names of recently deceased people to his sister, an employee at a collection agency, so she could check credit histories. If a credit rating was good, the pair bought a sport utility vehicle in the dead person's name. In the end, Montgomery was given forty years in jail.[53] While a young woman from a small town in Utah was working as a Mormon missionary in Houston, a church member falsely acquired her personal information and used it to open sixteen credit-card accounts.[54] Olatunji Oluwatosin was arrested in Hollywood for identity theft. Oluwatosin had pretended to be a business and used ChoicePoint to get access to the personal data of more than 145,000 Americans.[55]

Paul Fairchild, a thirty-four-year-old web developer living in Edmond, Oklahoma, went through a crisis when his identity was stolen. After his credit card was turned down while he was renting a tuxedo for his sister's wedding, he learned that an identity thief had used his name and financial information to buy an apartment building in Brooklyn, run an escort service, acquire corporate credit cards for the business, rent cars, and buy luxury items such as furs, jewelry, and expensive shoes. Fairchild was $500,000 in debt before he knew what happened. It took him two years, working full time to clear his name and financial records.[56] Research shows that victims spend an average of six hundred hours recovering their identity after it is stolen.[57]

Identity theft can cost victims more than time. Michael Berry had his identity taken by a convicted killer, who then used it to spend thousands of dollars on credit cards. Michael still carries the letters that law-enforcement officials provided him with stating that he is not the convicted felon.[58] Ain Jones lost her identity to an imposter who stole her money. Warrants for Ms. Jones's arrest were issued, her insurance premiums skyrocketed, and fraud warnings were attached to every digital record connected to her.[59] An identity thief used John Harrison's SSN and good credit rating to go on a spending spree that lasted four months and cost over a quarter of a million dollars. The crook obtained credit cards, a motorcycle, two other vehicles, clothing, a vacation time-share, and home improvements. The criminal got three years in jail, while the victim still deals with the financial and emotional aftermath, including post-traumatic stress disorder and anxiety attacks.[60]

There are technical ways to snag a little piece of someone's identity without direct contact: cell-phone cloning, for instance. If an identity thief gets close enough to a person using a cell phone, the thief can copy information about the phone and "clone" a new phone that will bill to the target's account. Account information can literally be dragged out of the air now because of the widespread use of wireless technologies like 802.11 and Bluetooth. A technique known as "bluesnarfing" can tap into a person's Bluetooth gadget and access its information, some of which may be account information. This trick was used at the 2004 Oscars by a security company that conducted an experiment to raise privacy awareness. Standing near the red carpet with wireless laptops, the researchers detected over fifty smart phones whose contents were accessible.[61] In the summer of 2004, near Santa Monica, the same group was able to bluesnarf a cell phone from a mile away, accessing and transferring personal data from the target. A week later, they extended the range to 1.08 miles. During that incident they grabbed the address book and sent a message from the phone.[62]

A thief with access to a network can use a "packet-sniffer" and a pattern matcher trained to look for credit-card numbers to gain access to cell phones. If thieves know enough about their marks, they can figure out their passwords and get access to their cell-phone accounts. Contrary to media reports, password guessing, not bluesnarfing, was used to hack Paris Hilton's Sidekick. Her T-Mobile account was infiltrated because the password she used was something any of her fans would know: Tinkerbell, the name of her lap dog. In her case, the perpetrator posted everything on the Internet, including her entire celebrity address book, business memos, and private photos.[63]

Stories like these get a lot of press that publicizes how easy it is to get at data and steal identities. Yet companies continue greedily asking for more information than they need and store it in security-challenged computer systems. It's not practical to limit the technologies that make identity theft possible. The only real solution is to improve authentication strategies used by financial institutions. Combining techniques like biometrics and password control works well, although nothing will save the identity of someone stupid enough to give information to a complete stranger.

The first line of defense for deterring identity theft is consumer education. The second is instituting financial penalties for mishandling consumer data. As mentioned above, Congress should enact a graduated set of fines for data breaches. The only good way to force companies to beef up their security is to hit them in the bottom line. A simple system of, say, $2 per exposed record would probably be sufficient deterrence. As small as that amount is, several well-publicized cases in the early part of this decade would easily have generated tens of millions of dollars. The money could go into a national fund that could be used to help victims of identity theft. The potentially large cash penalties would hit database-centric companies like Acxiom, ChoicePoint, and Experian the hardest, rightly holding them to a much higher standard than companies in other industries.

Commandment: *Protect my data as if it were thine own.*

Sin of Outing

Identity theft is the consequence of sloppy data handling, which usually occurs because of a mistake at the data center. However, other privacy violations are deliberate, and when they are, they tend to cut to the core of a person's identity by revealing information that a person would rather remain hidden. This is the sin of outing.

This is a new violation, so new that most people haven't considered it yet. It comes from the slang term for the public revelation of a closet homosexual. It's taken on political significance because of the Bush Administration's apparent unveiling of an undercover

CIA agent. Outing is the unwanted connection of an alias to a real identity.

Outing has special significance in the Information Age because of the common use of alternate identities. Many people, especially young adults who grew up using the Internet, have spent considerable time establishing virtual identities for themselves online. Some are simple handles or aliases that provide a shield that allows them to safely express themselves on blogs and message boards. They prefer pseudonyms because false names give them protection against retribution in their "real" life. Privacy is about controlling all personal information, even that pertaining to alternate identities, because in the areas in which they are used and to the participants— they are real.

Most web sites that require identification and don't collect money just need to know the type of person someone is or says he or she is or would like to be. Usually an attribute is enough, like age, gender, sexual orientation, or profession. Providing personal information like name or address is unnecessary and needlessly exposes the customer to identity theft.

People don't want to use their real names for many reasons. Some don't want coworkers and bosses knowing their religious and political beliefs. Others use pseudonyms because real names indicate gender, which can potentially cause harassment in online communities. Sometimes they're professionals—doctors, lawyers, academics, executives, or politicians—who could face real-world retribution for online opinions. Doctors could be sued for malpractice, as could lawyers. Executives could be accused of stock manipulation, and politicians could be challenged for privately expressing opinions that are at odds with public statements. Fundamentally, pseudonyms provide online privacy protection.

Pseudonyms soon take on a life of their own. Unlike anonymity, they are persistent and the wearers of these "nyms" are as protective of them as ham radio operators used to be of their call signs. For many, these names not only provide identity protection but also are expressions of individuality. Hundreds of thousands of people around the world play online multiplayer games. Using pseudonyms is customary; they not only add to the role-playing atmosphere but protect the player from potential embarrassment in the real world. A corporate lawyer might feel silly if her partners found out that she was a level 10 Elf on weekends.

The Internet is quickly becoming the water cooler of the Western world. It's where people get their news, express their opinions, write and read entertainment reviews, and even research products before they buy them. People seem to talk more freely behind the informality and guise of an alias than they do when they don't have their identities protected. Identity outing can have a chilling effect on the freely flowing speech and casual conversations that are rapidly becoming the hallmark of the Internet.

Society benefits from open conversation. It's good for consumers to talk about their buying experiences; it's enlightening to read blog postings from people who are ideologically and demographically different; it's therapeutic to be able to blow off steam by bitching about politics. Even more important, institutional abuses are often uncovered by whistle-blowers, many of whom use the Internet.

However, some politicians and companies that have been the targets of anonymous Internet messages that they believe damaged their reputations have a different take on the anonymity of the Internet. There has been a flurry of court cases that try to force website managers to reveal the identity of people posting sensitive or purportedly libelous messages.

Les French, a former employee of Itex Corp, used his pseudonym, Whadayaknow, when he made postings that detailed Itex's earnings, which he said were misstated. The company sued him and he countersued. French was later awarded a $40,000 settlement and used it to establish a fund that others could access if sued under similar circumstances.[64]

Congress passed a cyber-stalking prohibition as part of the Violence Against Women and Justice Department Reauthorization Act. It makes posting annoying messages or sending annoying emails anonymously a crime. It's too early to tell whether this law will be used for prosecution by the Justice Department, but if applied to its fullest extent, it could have a disturbing effect on free speech on the Internet. It will almost certainly curtail whistle-blowing, making it more difficult than it now is for Americans to find out about institutional abuses and dangerous public-health situations. Speech on the Internet has become a new check on authorities, filling in the gap left by the growingly docile broadcast media.

Many people lose their jobs for discussing their workplace on the Internet. Mark Jen was fired for using his blog to discuss Google, his new employer.[65] Delta Airlines fired one of its flight attendants because she had posted photographs that the airline considered inappropriate on her personal blog.[66]

A growing number of students (in both high school and college and, in the case of Marquette University, dental school) have been punished for comments made on personal blogs. A twenty-two-year-old dental student was suspended because on his blog he bragged about his alcohol consumption, derided the intelligence of some of his fellow students, and called an instructor "a cockmaster of a teacher" (which is presumably bad).[67]

Blogs are gaining in popularity. The Pew Internet & American Life Project says that eight million Americans had blogs at the end of 2004.[68] Other estimates place the number around twelve million. Blogging is engaged in by all age groups but is most prevalent among those under twenty-five.[69]

Many social web sites, such as MySpace and Facebook, encourage the posting of personal information. Several, like myspace.com, are being looked at carefully by law enforcement as potential hunting grounds for would-be child molesters. Here is another excellent reason for not piercing the pseudonymous veil of bloggers—protection against child abuse and stalking. It's much safer for children to be able to use untraceable pseudonyms. Outing children and exposing them to real-world predators is inexcusable.

Other people have or would like to have alternative lifestyles that are not illegal but may be frowned on by their community or, in the case of the military, may subject the target to disciplinary action.

Timothy McVeigh, a highly decorated member of the U.S. Navy, was forced to resign from the military after he was outed by AOL. Someone from the Navy read an email from McVeigh, was disturbed by the screen name (handle), and called AOL to find out his identity. The sailor's dual lifestyle was referred to the Navy, who pressed charges against him, requesting his discharge in 1998 under President Bill Clinton's "Don't Ask, Don't Tell, Don't Pursue, Don't Harass" statute, which was enacted in 1993 by Congress to protect all lesbian, gay, bisexual, and transgender service members.[70]

After his discharge, McVeigh filed a lawsuit that requested his reinstatement in the U.S. Navy; he claimed that his discharge violated Homosexual Conduct Policy procedures because the Navy uncovered personal information about him without his consent and without legitimate authorization. A federal judge ruled that the U.S. Navy was barred from discharging McVeigh for allegedly talking about his homosexuality in an AOL chat room.[71] Reinstated, McVeigh faced a hostile work environment and was assigned to menial jobs like supervising trash removal and painting an office; this treatment caused him to retire from the military.

One of the freeing aspects of the Internet is the ability to communicate by presenting yourself as you wish to be perceived. This form of identity experimentation can be harmless, although some might argue that it protects criminals, who want to hide their identity for reasons other than free speech. The anonymous nature of the Internet does, in fact, make it difficult to catch wrongdoers who hide behind pseudonyms when committing crimes online. Many web-site owners' natural ethical inclination against outing their members serves to protect the felons and has encouraged some groups to take matters into their own hands and come up with creative ways to out online criminals. Volunteer organizations, such as Perverted Justice, scour the Internet, presenting themselves as underage children in order to entrap adults who prey on children into propositioning respondents who they think are kids. In 2003, a prominent New York rabbi was arrested on a number of charges, including attempted endangerment of a child and soliciting a minor on the Internet. Rabbi Israel Kestenbaum thought he was arranging a sexual liaison with a thirteen-year-old girl, but she was actually a he, an undercover police detective.[72]

Sting operations set up by law enforcement have led to similar arrests. In 1999, the founder of IBeam Broadcasting, William Michael Bowles, pleaded guilty to setting up a sexual rendezvous with a young boy who turned out to be a detective from the Sacramento sheriff's office.[73] Infoseek executive Patrick Naughton went across state lines in 2000 to meet a minor for sex. The thirteen-year-old girl was actually an FBI agent.[74] During the spring of 2005, nine sexual predators were picked up in just ten days as part of an online child-sex sting throughout the Washington, D.C., area. Thirteen undercover police officers from the Northern Virginia-D.C. Internet Crimes Against Children Task Force pretended to be children in online chat rooms, where they were quickly propositioned by sexual predators wanting to meet them face-to-face. The nine men arrested included an electrical engineer, a student, an auto painter, a Christian youth minister, and a volunteer firefighter.[75]

Many people use forums as extended support groups, like group therapy sessions. These forums have a common theme, often medical or psychological, and provide a safe venue for discussion of difficult topics by herpes sufferers, terminal cancer patients, abused spouses, and others. The damage that would be done to the participants by being outed is incalculable, ranging from personal embarrassment to professional ruin. It should be their choice to pick the venue and time for their disclosures, if any.

It should be a crime to out an identity, but practically speaking that will never happen. The pressure to protect children and other innocents by piercing the veil of would-be predators is too strong for that level of blanket protection to be legislated for everyone. Law enforcement will insist that they need to be able to uncover online identities to conduct arrests. Intelligence experts will say that terrorism will hide behind anonymity. It would be difficult to craft laws that didn't hamstring the legitimate needs of agents and investigators.

The solution may rest with the technologists, who will need to develop foolproof ways of cloaking an identity. Several open-source groups are developing ways of accomplishing bulletproof anonymity. A large missing piece of the Internet puzzle is a universal alias system that would protect personal information while allowing users to build reputations and transport them across all web sites.

The next several decades should see a furious battle between privacy technologists putting meat on virtual identities and government agencies stripping them back to the bone. Because identity-masking technology doesn't require huge capital investments, the contest is evenly matched; it's anyone's guess as to the outcome.

Commandment: *I am who I say I am.*

Sin of Lost Dignity

Outing is harmful because it affects a core value—someone's identity. A more common privacy harm inflicted by institutions on their constituencies attacks another core value—self-respect. This is the sin of lost dignity.

This last sin is the subtlest and the hardest to qualify; human dignity is the most difficult possession to protect. Comprehensive privacy legislation is impossible, but even if society tries to craft laws that will close the most egregious loopholes, in some areas uncomfortable, yet fully legal, activities could still happen. There will always be places where technology outruns the law, leaving gaps in its wake. There will also be cases where an offense is not bad enough to be deemed illegal but still humiliates the victim.

We can easily get worked up when falsified information that ruins a person's reputation is bandied about. But what about cases where information is revealed that is true but is personal, private, and nobody's business but the person's own? How would you feel if your medical records were public, with every silly question that you'd ever asked your doctor in plain view? How about a web site featuring your school essays containing opinions that might be better left in a dusty box in the attic? Information technology can easily dig up enough minute but embarrassing information on any of us to leave us exposed as if we were flapping around in a hospital gown.

Causing the loss of dignity has always been a favorite tactic for breaking down a group's spirit. Military boot camp is founded on this principle. From the first second that new recruits step off the bus, basic training is a deliberate attack on dignity, primarily through loss of privacy. The military takes the doors off bathroom stalls, sleeps everyone in open-bay-style rooms, and subjects recruits to constant verbal abuses while pushing them past the point of physical exhaustion.

The poor are historically subject to a similar kind of violation; lack of privacy is a tool of social control as is its resultant humiliation. A welfare recipient tolerating detailed and personal interview questions or a child forced to use a special brightly colored pass to get her subsidized school lunch is the subject of a public shredding of privacy that is often a blow to dignity, imposed almost as a punishment for being needy. The poor have no privacy. In some cases, the courts perpetuate the idea that poor people don't have the same rights as their wealthier neighbors. In the case of *Wyman v. James,* the Supreme Court used fraud prevention as the grounds for permitting welfare investigators to enter a recipient's home without a search warrant.[76]

Technology is also providing new ways for authorities to keep track of the poor and put them under surveillance. The government already makes use of SSNs to track individuals receiving welfare, and it wants to take the tracking to the next level by issuing benefit cards to track all purchases.[77] Plans are underway to create homeless management information systems, which will continuously track the homeless and keep extensive personal information in databases to be shared regionally.[78] The likely next step will be RFID monitoring of the indigent, like tagging bears or game fish.

Even those who can afford to sue for privacy violations often don't because they choose to avoid embarrassment and ridicule. Undertaking a public legal battle virtually guarantees that the details will be talked up throughout the community.

> The Rhode Island American Civil Liberties Union sued a police officer in 2002 on behalf of a woman who was arrested on suspicion of drunk driving and was then stripped, searched, and left in a camera-monitored jail cell with no clothes for five hours.[79]

Another type of humiliation and invasion of privacy often occurs when employees undergo urine testing for drugs. To prevent tampering with samples, employees are expected to urinate in front of attendants. Workplace monitoring, in general, significantly degrades dignity and compromises the privacy of employees.

Dignity comes from self-control. Those who maintain their dignity are said to hold their heads high and generally have an air of self-assurance about them. It's difficult to be self-assured when you can't govern what other people know about you and what they will do with the information, and today technology makes it all to easy to publish humiliating information, even pictures and video. Privacy and dignity are twinned, the yin and yang of the human spirit. It takes monumental perseverance to maintain dignity when privacy is stripped away.

Charity, government-assistance, and refugee relief workers should always take their clients' dignity into consideration. Television coverage of natural disasters, like Hurricane Katrina, shows the devastation panoramically but lingers on the contorted faces of the victims, stripped of their possessions, shorn of their pride. It was a tragedy when Princess Diana was surrounded by paparazzi as she lay dying on a Paris street. It was humiliating when a dying George Harrison was coerced into signing autographs for his doctor's children. His family sued because they also saw it as an invasion of his privacy and a slam against his dignity.

The best way to handle this sin against privacy is through cultural awareness and reform. Societies need to police themselves by treating egregious violations of the spirit as repugnant, legal or not. Truly democratic societies should zealously defend the right of their citizens, no matter how impoverished or needy, to wrap themselves in their dignity. Such measures will protect each and every citizen's privacy and will lead to the recognition that privacy is as much a human need as it is a community obligation.

Commandment: *Don't humiliate me with my private information.*

The Commandments

Another way to define privacy is by the negative, by what is left when information about us is not abused. When we are not secretly observed. When the information that we give merchants and government agencies is used only for the stated purpose, then erased. When we are the sum of our actions and are not punished before we've had the chance to make our own mistakes. When our intimate data are protected by custodians with as much care and caution as we ourselves would provide. When we are taken at face value and allowed to tell others who and what we are. When we are not embarrassed or humiliated and do not have our self-esteem taken away.

Information technology enables us as individuals and as a society. But to quote a great twentieth-century philosopher, "With great power comes great responsibility."[80] Just because technology allows us to do something doesn't mean that we should. It's too late to roll back the clock on the innovations that make possible spy cameras, data-mining software, RFID chips, and the complex social structure that is the Internet. Some new laws will have to be passed to protect us against these technological advances, but companies could stave off future privacy regulation by good-faith self-policing efforts. The ultimate answer is a new way of boardroom thinking—ethical reasoning and consideration of the rights of the individual balanced against organizational needs as part of the strategic business-planning process. Sometimes the law is not enough. Some actions that are legal are harmful, hurtful to each of us and, by extension, to society at large. They are sins for the new millennium, crimes so new that they're not even named, let alone outlawed.

Laws are necessary to stop individual cases of abuse. The moral prohibition against stealing is universally held, yet we still need laws and penalties to keep the peace by providing punishment for criminals. Institutional sinning is another story. Corporate abuse is the real danger. A single privacy-unfriendly policy of a large consumer company can violate more people than ten years of identity theft. If decision makers continue to disrespect our privacy, the prospects for us and them are not rosy. We will continue to lose our privacy until we've had enough. The privacy sinners will suffer under an onslaught of overreactive legislation, as angry constituents demand extreme action from their officials. The increasing mention of privacy-violation stories in the media is a good indicator of the growing public concern for privacy.

As a society, we should view willful privacy violators with the repugnance that we would show a serial drunk driver. Our artifice of allowing corporate privacy pillagers to hide behind an institutional shield must end, and the individuals, both managers and directors of companies that violate our privacy, should be exposed. Tolerating corporate or even governmental privacy intrusions is a slippery slope; allowing such abuses reduces our expectations of privacy and softens us up for future intrusions.

The commandments listed in this chapter are good precepts for the foundation of an ethical approach to privacy with far more depth than a sham privacy policy. The only way to adequately protect privacy, short of a tangled web of regulatory legislation, is to substitute a common sense and thoughtful methodology for privacy protection and to fall back on legal permissibility only as a last resort, not as policy. Just because you can do something, doesn't mean that you should.

Privacy violations are more than just a sin against individuals; they can have a pervasive and deleterious affect on society at large as described in the next chapter. A continued pattern of privacy erosion will hurt us as a culture and limit us as a society.

2

Collateral Damage
The Harm to Society

Good fences make good neighbors.

Robert Frost[1]

Chapter One described the Seven Sins Against Privacy and suggested some ethical commandments that organizations can use to create meaningful privacy policies. Reading the stories of violations contained in this book, watching television, or reading the newspapers should be enough to convince most people that technology is creating situations that are detrimental to privacy. Regardless of how one defines the right to privacy, most people would agree that we shouldn't have to contend with cameras hidden in our homes or have our phone calls monitored without very good reason, and we certainly should not be at risk of having our identity stolen. It's easy to believe that privacy violations hurt people, even if we don't understand how or agree on what to do about it. But a lack of privacy can hurt society too. When individuals lose control over their personal information, they act differently, more cautiously. The cumulative effect of this behavioral change can be hurtful to society in general. This chapter discusses why.

Imagine a culture where individual privacy is completely nonexistent. Think about the effects of technology, the metronome of the future. Most personal data will likely be in a database somewhere. Every moment in the real world will cause a ripple in the digital one. Our environment will be saturated with millions, maybe billions of silicon eyes and ears, bound together in a worldwide mesh; these watchers and listeners will fill institutional databases with copious amounts of minutiae on our doings, our whereabouts, and our conversations. The data will feed an army of profiling engines engaged in guessing our opinions, our tastes, perhaps someday our thoughts.

Why the Loss of Privacy Affects Society

Societies benefit from having untroubled citizens who can choose how much of themselves to share with others. They pick the content and the timing. This empowerment leads people to a well-founded sense of security, a feeling of self-control, self-respect, and self-esteem that is derived from believing that they're the masters of their own fate. Society benefits from a secure citizenry because people are more creative and productive when they're not looking over their shoulders.

When children feel insecure, they become sullen, focused inward, and withdrawn. Unsettled children are rarely at their creative best in school; they tend to do the minimum to get by and are happiest just fading into the crowd. In my experience, and I have raised five kids of my own, emotionally level children take chances; they experiment, both academically and personally, contributing to the micro society of a school and presumably later on to the world at large.

It's hard to feel secure when you have a sense that something bad might happen. It's hard to be creative when you're afraid that what you create may be misinterpreted at some future date and come back to bite you. In the case of privacy, it's not just the abuses themselves that are harmful but also the looming threat. Never knowing when you're being watched is unnerving. Like a beaten dog waiting for the next blow to land, a future privacy-pummeled society would be characterized by its insecurity; people would be on edge and worried about the future. Like an insecure child, such a society would be driven by conformism; in short—a lack of privacy leads to a risk-averse culture. Although this isn't the general sense right now, well-publicized privacy-related disasters have the ability to undermine the security of our society. This possible future society has its roots in the privacy troubles affecting each of us today.

When personal information gets out involuntarily, it can be embarrassing, even humiliating, always unsettling. Sometimes the exposure of individual facts about ourselves is benign, but the totality of the disclosures feels invasive. For instance, the fact that I bought peanut butter at the supermarket isn't a particularly critical secret; I don't care whether anyone knows when and where I bought it. I don't even mind if they find out that it's crunchy Jiff. I would care, however, if someone saw my whole shopping list for, say, a year. With it, they could derive enormous insight into my personality and health by analyzing my shopping patterns. How often am I sick? Do I drink alcohol and how much? Do I take vitamins or herbal remedies? Do I buy diabetic test strips, condoms, or men's magazines? How have my purchases changed over time? Grocery stores routinely sell and trade customer-preference databases compiled from store courtesy cards without shoppers' permission. The individual instances of exposure have minimal effect, but, in aggregate, a person's shopping lists are revealing. What does it say about you if you're pushing a shopping cart full of beer, *Maxim*, and Similac to the checkout counter?

One negative outcome for society from detailed purchase tracking could be consumer discrimination. Businesses accept that people who spend more money with them should be treated better than those who spend less. But sophisticated data analysis of buying behavior could lead to different kinds of customer segmentation, which might encourage stores to shift their gold-plated treatment from big spenders to a different group. For instance, some people are going to spend the same amount at a store no matter how they're treated. They may need products that are available only there, or

the store may simply be the only one that's geographically convenient. A big chain electronics store near my house has horrible customer service, but I go back there time and again because it carries
the products I need. By cross-indexing my purchases to information
about where I live, the store may decide that it's smarter to kiss up
to a second-tier consumer who might freely shop at a competitor.
Amazon.com actually tried this technique; it charged the best customers more, figuring they were hooked anyway.[2]

Eventually marketers will get good enough at developing profiling tools that they will be able to use shopping information to
create "psychological inducement coupons" on the spot; they will
figure out the best approach for each type of consumer and display
or print coupons as needed in their stores. Although, to some, targeted discounts are an attractive way to save money, to others these
savings imply that a store keeps track of a scary amount of behavioral information that could be used someday for purposes other
than providing coupons. Chapter Ten discusses advertising technology and speculates on what stores might someday do with that
information.

Dorothy Lane Market, an upscale grocery chain in Ohio, already
uses the data from its loyalty cards to determine the value of individual customers. The company analyzes the data it collects and
uses them to identify the customers who spend the most. Customer
Specific Pricing allows the chain to charge different prices to each
segment of customers, with most of the discounts going to the top
30 percent of shoppers.[3] If you're in the lucky 30 percent, this kind
of discrimination is good, but what if you're in the bottom 30 percent? You pay more and may get substandard goods or perhaps infe-
rior customer service.

The Return Exchange is coming soon. Retailers will use this new
service to decide whether a customer can return an item. Besides
needing a receipt, customers will be required to provide identification, even if it was a cash sale. The information will be processed
through a machine that will show the clerk the customer's return

history. If that history is considered suspect, the money will not be returned. The standards used to evaluate customers will be kept secret, and customers will not be told why the return was denied.[4]

Multiple tiers of service based on secret criteria could result in neurotic purchasing behavior. Just like businesspeople who display an almost superstitious fear that a trivial action will trigger a tax audit, some people may act differently if they think they can influence the cost or quality of their purchases or the support they receive from a store by what they buy, not necessarily by what they spend. If the Return Exchange becomes widespread, it could encourage unusual consumer behavior as shoppers try to avoid falling into a twilight zone where they can no longer return items or in some other way get treated by the store as a second-class citizen.

Watch people in a security line at an airport second-guessing what will trigger an embarrassing full-body search. I bet that companies that make shoes with metal inserts and belts with big buckles are selling fewer of these items to seasoned travelers. A small change in policy by a bureaucracy or business can result in the adoption of widespread societal habits long after the original reason is forgotten. Twenty years from now, will anyone remember why airplane spoons are metal and knives are plastic?

Deus ex Machina (God from the Machine)

Computers run almost every aspect of our lives. They decide what the price of a stock is; they announce the winners of elections; by projecting sales, they decide how much steel to ship to which city to make how many cars that should cost exactly so much.

For machines to make competent decisions about consumers, they have been programmed to extrapolate the future based on past events. To a thinking machine, the future is predictive, the past statistical. The most intensive business work that a computer can do is guessing. It's much more difficult than making mathematical calculations, which are trivial in comparison.

To achieve a reasonable amount of success at this guessing, computers need every scrap of information that they can get. The more data that machines collect and analyze, the greater the impact on our culture. Unless a heck of a lot of attention to privacy is built into the software, the concept will be lost in the automation process. We might count on a human being to respect our privacy, but we can never make the same assumption about a machine. It is therefore important that we articulate our expectations of privacy so that they can be explicitly programmed into every software system that handles our data.

The number of inadvertent privacy disclosures could grow to unimaginable numbers as an unfortunate by-product of decision-making software. And these disclosures will be difficult to stop because no one will know how. My experience with large software systems is that organizations quickly become dependent on them as business processes grow around them. Typically, complex software systems have greater longevity at a company than their original designers; most of them reach the point where no one knows how they work anymore, and engineering often becomes a matter of patching.

Businesses are not the only organizations that use decision-making computers. The average citizen knows little about the workings of government, let alone the thought processes behind its software. Indeed, some government functions are no longer understood by any one person; their complexity is far better suited to machine analysis. Yet these same machines have access to numerous intimate details of each of our lives. Although they do not "know" us in a human sense, they can make decisions based on a quick peep into our lives. For example, in big cities prospective jurors are picked by computer analysis of such factors as residency and voting records.

As we turn over more functions of society to computers, the workings become obscure, seemingly random. Eventually rules-based machines will program other rules-based machines, making their inner workings completely inaccessible and the ability to "back-trace" a decision impossible.

The Need for Transparency

Part of the problem are our assumptions that technology is necessarily good because it is new and that because we can't stop progress, we should trust that the opportunities it brings are beneficial. But automated decisions should always be subject to human review because the recommendations made by machines are only as reliable as the accuracy of the information and the stability of the software they use.

A key step would be to demand transparency in all critical automated decision-making systems; such transparency would require human evaluation of the programming. Transparency means knowing the information a program is using to make its decisions, the formulas that are being used, and the weighting or priorities placed on each of the rules. We become transparent in a similar way as our thought processes are observed. Opinions to a human are the same as heuristics (rules) to a machine.

As we become more publicly visible because of privacy exposure, machines will become more opaque. Computers will know more about how individuals think as, conversely, individuals know less and less about how machines make their decisions. The rules that our society operates under will become increasingly obscure as we cede control to our cyber servants. Privacy will be harder to maintain because computers, not human beings, will decide whether private information becomes public.

Transparency is especially important because of the way Western societies currently operate. Privacy is a modern invention and an intrinsic right in a democratic society. People in feudal societies have little privacy—all know their neighbors' business. However, these societies have a rigid code of conduct, usually qualified by age, gender, and class, that defines the acceptable parameters for people's actions. A deviation from the social code is the true crime in these cultures. Twenty-first-century Western urban societies don't have strict cultural rules governing group behavior. But as in every other society, various techniques, like condemnation or, in extreme cases, shunning, can be used on a recalcitrant member.

Legal action aside, we are shunned by our peers only when we cannot explain our actions or when the reasons we give for our actions are not satisfactory. We tend to look for exceptions, extenuating circumstances. We like to give others the benefit of the doubt because we'd like them to do the same for us. The toughest capital cases for juries to decide are ones where there is a believable motive for committing the crime, like poverty. A bad upbringing is a legitimate alibi in our courts, as is outright craziness.

As members of our society, we expect to be given the right to explain. We don't expect to be convicted either by the courts or by the community without being heard first. Unfortunately, losing control of our personal information denies us the chance to explain because, in a machine-driven society, accusations are made in absentia.

How the Loss of Privacy Harms Society

Society is harmed in two ways when technology is given the power to make decisions that are based on or that lead to violations of people's privacy. First, people acquire labels based on personal information that is analyzed by machines, not by human beings. Second, when people are under constant surveillance by machines that have the power to label them, they begin to conform to the rules the machines have been programmed to follow in making those decisions. The creativity and innovation that vibrant societies depend on are then lost.

Labeling

Computer systems cannot make judgments based on morality. They are superb, however, at categorizing. The results of this kind of profiling are labels such as "credit problem," "security risk," and "possible terrorist." Demographic categorization was human-driven by voluntary disclosure; psychographic labeling is assigned by software. Demographics are a person's external attributes: age, gender, race, neighborhood. Psychographics are attributes relating to personality, values, attitudes, interests, or lifestyles.[5]

Involuntary segmentation based on those labels is a troublesome side effect of our loss of privacy. Because categorization software is automated, the assignment is cut and dry, based on objective criteria. For instance, most states have a point system used by computers at their Department of Motor Vehicles to determine when a motorist has crossed the line from being issued a ticket to being forced into a driver-education program. Each infraction is assigned points, and a driver with a certain number must attend refresher classes.

We cannot plead special circumstances when we're afflicted by a machine-generated label, assuming that the label is even public knowledge. Security officers and credit-scoring analysts not only don't want their methodology for arriving at a label exposed; they often don't want the results made public. And the Patriot Act makes it a crime even to notify the subject of an investigation. Although the facts behind the labeling are objective, the causality is not necessarily empirical. It may be true that an Afghan American woman bought a copy of the Koran; it doesn't necessarily follow that she is a terrorist, although a scoring system may very well label her as such. Labels are as human as opinions, subject to the biases and vagaries of individuals, even when printed out by machines.

It's difficult to shake the effects of being labeled, especially when it's done by a machine, not a person. Some people struggle their whole life because of tags they've picked up in school such as "slow learner," "lazy," or the dreaded "troublemaker." People can be similarly pigeonholed when they are labeled by age, race, credit rating, or their job. These labels are impossible to remove, even if the assumptions are factually inaccurate. When the labeling is the result of a computer error, loss of benefits, alienation, and defamation of character can be the legal outcome, but there's a greater harm to society because the democratic ideals of fair process are challenged when we are unable to effectively confront our accuser.

Another harm to society from too many of these categorizations is that people begin to try to "game" the system instead of just doing what they think is right. Like hard-core lottery players, they assign causal significance to random numbers and events, convinced that they can manage their future. They begin to anticipate the machines instead of training the machines to anticipate them.

We could end up living in a world where we walk through life staring at our feet like a person with an obsessive-compulsive disorder, counting our steps, so intent on affecting the outcome of institutional labeling systems that we lose sight of how human beings should make decisions. The resulting society would be at best cautious and risk averse; at worst, completely conformist. Freedom from labeling gives us the space to make our own mistakes based on choice and not expectations.

Conformity

People act differently when they think they're being watched. What will happen when children grow up realizing that every interaction they have with the online world may come back to haunt them? How will they feel living in a world that has them under constant surveillance as soon as they leave their homes? Cameras in schools are becoming commonplace, and they can also be found mounted on lamp posts in neighborhood parks, on street corners, in malls, on school buses, and in most places children frequent. The youth of today will have to contend with a tomorrow in which the walls don't have just ears but also memory. Privacy provides the freedom to make mistakes in solitude. Imagine learning to ride a bike, tie a bow tie, or make love in the middle of a stadium, watched by twenty thousand people.

Constant surveillance can easily lead to privacy violations. Cameras placed in locker rooms in a middle school in Overton County, Tennessee, caught more than a dozen ten- to fourteen-year-old students changing their clothes.[6] Unauthorized people were able to view the pictures because the school didn't change the original access codes on the equipment. The photographs were eventually posted on the Internet; the children were embarrassed and were possibly put at risk of being molested. Citibank security workers in midtown Manhattan monitor banks of video cameras that are placed in and near every branch in the city and suburbs. They also get to watch more than a quarter million New Yorkers who pass by those cameras every day.[7] New York City is said to have more than five thousand cameras on the streets.[8]

This constant surveillance could eventually reinforce behavioral change, as people adjust to the presence of the cameras. It's not clear yet whether people will just ignore them or moderate their behavior so as not to be singled out. Expressing individuality is a strong human need, but an equally strong one is fitting in. Much schoolyard angst comes from this dichotomy. British studies have shown that people who dress differently or somehow seem out of place are monitored much more closely and for longer periods of time than are those who dress and act conventionally.[9] Monitors single out those who do not fall into acceptable, predefined, stereotypical groups, labeling them as deviant in some way. Although it is not a crime to be different, those who are could some day find that for them the hassle factor in public places like government buildings and airports has increased. It is simply a hassle if you experience an isolated instance of this phenomenon. But if it were to happen all day long, every day, it would probably smother free expression. Unless you're an exhibitionist, you probably don't like being watched. The desire to sidestep society's gaze is strong; in many cases it outweighs the desire to be different.

The fear of being observed and the desire to conform are strong motivational factors for many of us. As we adjust to the computer eyes and the analytic brains that track our movements, we will learn to not stand out because it will make our lives easier. We will be hassled less at the airport, stopped less by the police, and experience less disapproval from our peers.

Studies done in prisons suggest that feelings of paranoia, distress, humiliation, apathy, and helplessness are psychological effects of long-term surveillance. Prisoners also get so accustomed to highly visible and external modes of constraint that their internal controls deteriorate or, in young prisoners, fail to develop altogether. Some prisoners become so dependent on external constraints that they eventually stop relying on their own volition to restrain conduct and guide actions. When away from the cameras or when released from prison, these people find it difficult to refrain from self-destructive behavior and committing additional crimes.[10] Always-on surveillance may take the place of civic responsibility and possibly moral guidance because it will be easier to defer to the hidden watchers than to take action as individuals. Chapter Eight discusses the technology that will make the voyeuristic society of tomorrow a near certainty.

The likeliest coping mechanism that might emerge in an always-watched society is a cultural inclination toward conformity. As described above, primitive societies live by a rigid code, rewarding adherents and punishing contrarians. Lack of privacy for its members causes such a society to devolve; it becomes more dependent on rules because it can rely less on individual initiative. We're all a little bit conformist anyway, but because much of our lives happens behind closed doors, we're only "on" a few hours a day, when we're in crowds or interacting with authority figures. As we become watched around the clock, this careful behavior will become our norm. Consider well-known politicians who are under this kind of scrutiny their whole adult lives; they learn to develop a professional "mask" when in public that hides their true selves.

A totally conformist society would be hesitant to innovate because people who are marching to a different drummer look out of step until they reach their destination. Lack of initiative and unwillingness to take risks are fine when restricted to only part of society. When they become the norm, the creative standouts—the inventor and the artist—have a difficult time. Those who are truly different in such a society would be subjected to substantially more grief for their differences than they are now. The damage to a society that drives out its geniuses is incalculable.

The strength of a society is not just the sum of the strength of its members; it's also based on the accomplishments of its few super-achievers. Every history book is filled with the lives of the iconoclasts and the curmudgeons, the Jeffersons, Einsteins, Carnegies, and Warhols, the innovators who dared to be different and survived long enough to prove that they were right. Any society that makes it hard for its artists to prosper will suffer. There are several good examples of cultures that made life difficult for its intelligentsia, such as the Soviet Union. Most of them collapsed within a few generations.

The exceptional are often unusual, especially as children. They are exactly the kind of people who will stick out in an always-watched society. It remains to be seen how much peer pressure will be leveled against them for their eccentricities in this computerized world, let alone how they'll interact with authority figures such as policemen, tax collectors, teachers, and credit analysts. Presumably if they're ground down too much, some of them will conform, and many will run. I question whether any society can afford to lose most of their truly gifted members and still grow.

Privacy Rights Protect Other Rights

Privacy is an enabling right; it creates the foundation for other basic entitlements. For instance, the Second Amendment right to bear arms is diluted when exercising that freedom entails exhaustive gun registration. The Fourth Amendment protects a person against government intrusion and is the basis on which all other civil liberties, such as freedom of religion and speech, are built. Without the Fourth Amendment, a person's activities could be adversely affected by government interference. Freedom of speech is easier to exercise behind a shield of anonymity or at least pseudonymity. Anonymity makes retribution harder and constrains arguments to logic, not vindictive personal attacks.

Privacy protections are the bulwarks against encroachments on other rights. Voting would be difficult without privacy because of the likelihood of retribution. Freedom of religion would be limited if details of religious observances were made public. The press would be unable to use confidential sources without some concealment of their identity. In a democracy, privacy makes possible freedom of expression, of choice, of association, of mobility, of thought. Many totalitarian societies (including prisons) have one thing in common: lack of real privacy, which results in no dignity and no respect for its citizens. If everything we do and say is recorded, judged, and perhaps used against us, there is no freedom.

Privacy is based on expectations that are set by society at large. Computers are not franchised participants in our culture, yet they have a growing amount of control over enforcement of its rules. This authoritarian role for thinking machines is made possible by the enormous amounts of data on each of us that are now available. Chapter Three talks about the advancements in technology that have created this situation and explains why data never really disappear.

Part II

Why Technology Is Key

This part of the book offers a historical perspective on the relationship between technology and privacy by describing some big-picture aspects of the digital world that affect privacy. Chapter Three concerns the important relationship between privacy and technology. It explains, for example, the permanence of electronic data, why it's cheaper to buy another disk drive than it is to erase information, and how the emergence of networks has destroyed our ability to control our own information. Chapter Four reveals new privacy-related crimes that didn't exist before computer technology; some of them are so new they aren't even getting press coverage yet.

Technology Affects Privacy
How and Why

*If you hire a billboard, and you write what you're saying
on the billboard, I don't think it's an invasion of privacy
for the FBI driving by to look at the billboard and read it.*
John Ashcroft[1]

The advances in electronic and computer technology since the
early 1980s have had a drastic impact on privacy. In this chapter
we take a step back to understand why this is. Computers themselves
are not the problem; they've been around for a long time. It's the price/
performance ratio of digital equipment that has obliterated privacy.

Chapter Two explained what might happen to a society that's
had the privacy rights of its citizens dissolved. This chapter starts
out by discussing the historical nature of privacy and then explains
how the concept of "control your environment—control your privacy" has turned into "privacy lost." You might be wondering about
the title of this book and asking whether the loss is inevitable or
whether the clock can be rolled back on technology-fueled privacy
intrusions. The short answer to the latter question is "no."

Historical Privacy

In the past, controlling privacy meant controlling your environment. If you were alone with the window shades down, you could
do whatever you wanted whenever you wished, and no one was the

wiser. If you didn't want to be overheard, you stayed out of earshot. If you didn't want someone to peek at your communications, you burned old letters and made sure that your correspondents did the same. You could easily stop others from knowing what you were thinking—you didn't tell them. And it helped to have money because, at some level, being wealthy meant being able to shape the world instead of having the world mold you. Master your surroundings, control your privacy. It was different if you were poor because you had no expectations of privacy to begin with. The only privacy that a peasant had in the Middle Ages was anonymity, or as the saying goes, there's safety in numbers. This type of privacy lasted right up until the modern era.

Even though much of the personal information contained in electronic databases was available in paper form for decades, it was unusable for institutional privacy invasions because it was paper. Paper is highly susceptible to environmental changes; it gets old and mildewed. It's bulky and is typically stored in hard-to-get places. It's impermanent, hard to manipulate, and difficult to search. The average person who wasn't being targeted by law enforcement was effectively immune from intrusion because he or she would have to be violated purposely, by name, by a human being, which is an expensive process, too expensive for wholesale investigations. Technology has yanked away that veil of privacy and the interwoven sense of personal security that blanketed the average citizen.

Technology Changes the Medium

Documents that were laboriously scribed with quills on vellum or parchment over a period of months or years had their subject matter carefully chosen. Writing materials were costly and hard to get. The invention of the printing press in the fifteenth century and factory-produced paper in the nineteenth greatly increased the amount of recorded information available in the world, although storage quickly became a problem.

Even though substantial information was preserved, the threat to privacy was still minimal for two reasons: the short life of the medium and the incredible difficulty of storing, filing, and searching voluminous amounts of paper. Microfilm was seen as a solution and thrived for a short period, extending the readable life of the knowledge captured on ephemeral paper. Although it solved the problem of longevity, it didn't improve search capabilities.

The invention of silicon-based information storage, however, addressed both challenges. Even though the working life of memory chips and hard drives is probably no more than a decade, moving information onto a backup machine or an automated storage device is easy and effectively creates an unlimited life span for digitally stored information. A new storage or search technique can be applied retroactively to the data with little investment of resources and time compared with the huge investment made by organizations initially shifting from paper to microfilm. Scanning paper is a huge job; moving a database from a 160-kilobyte floppy disk to a 60-gigabyte hard drive is not.

The most privacy-menacing attribute of digitally stored data is enhanced search and retrieval capabilities. Searching paper or microfiche requires an index, which is time-consuming to build or create, so only the minimally necessary ones are generated. For example, consider a newspaper archive, aptly named a morgue. In the antedatum era, the papers had to be stored in their original form, preferably in a climate-controlled environment that would help preserve the paper. Paper takes up space. Picture how thick a one-year stack of the *New York Times* would be. Now let's say that you had to index that pile. The process would be so time-intensive that you'd probably just tabulate the subjects of the stories so that you could look up, say, a person's name and find the right article. You'd have to build another index if you also wanted to be able to search in chronological order and yet another to find articles by the reporters' bylines. Each of these indexes would have to be painstakingly prepared by hand, and they would be big—often bigger than the papers themselves. What if someday you thought of another way to index the articles, say by neighborhood? You'd have to start the whole process again.

Electronic databases are far superior. The cost of storage is low enough that it's easy to store multiple indices centered on any one field (a part of a data record). If the situation changes and a new index is required, it may take a few hours but only a few keystrokes to create it. Searching an electronic database is also much faster than walking through a dusty room and hauling down boxes, looking for the right information.

The technology that's affecting privacy the most on the Internet is improved search. The history of the commercial Internet is locked to the rise of search engines. In the 1990s, nonprofit engines such as WAIS gave way to early technology powerhouses like Excite and Alta Vista as well as directory companies like Yahoo. But now they've all taken a back seat to the eight-hundred-pound Googorilla—Google has effectively locked up the market for search engines. Google is getting too good. The term *googling* has become a publicly acceptable verb, meaning to look something up on the web. It's become trendy to google someone prior to going on a date. Salespeople and reporters have made googling a customer or interviewee a required part of their homework. The total amount of information that Google returns for most well-known people is staggering; for regular people it's illuminating and will be scary when they start to google themselves and find pictures, emails, their home address, and other personal information. Even though this data may be public information and might even be true, its dissemination can still violate someone's privacy.

Search techniques on extremely large-scale databases (for example, the whole Internet) are workable, but the field is still in its infancy. The next few years will see huge improvements in search capabilities on existing data repositories, fueled by the success of Google and the demands of Homeland Security.

Optical disks, hard drives, flash memory—all wired or wirelessly networked together—will provide people in the future with what tar pits gave to paleontologists—a voyeuristic look into long ago, made possible by the perfect storage of perishable things—a slice of a living past, dense as a fruitcake, studded with stories. The digital trash heap that we are accumulating today is orders of magnitude more information rich than any physical artifacts that have ever been left behind by a society. But these waste data are easily accessible now by anyone who cares to look for them.

We have lost control over our selective information environment. The famous have lost their shield and the common their anonymity. Money can't buy privacy other than walled off isolation because technology has made too much information on everyone available to anyone. We all leave a digital trail, no matter how rich or famous. The refuge of the common, their facelessness, is also gone because of automation. Keeping a low profile used to work to avoid attention, but not any more; it's too easy for computer programs to sweep through the database records of enormous numbers of people quickly and comprehensively. One must now take great pains to avoid being electronically spotted; even using cash, hiding from surveillance cameras, or being rich enough to hire "privacy gophers" (who use their own plastic to protect their employers from leaving an auditable trail) is no guarantee of protection. There is too much information on everyone for it to be suppressed. Electronic gadgets shed tens of megabytes of detritus daily from computers, credit-card purchases, and transactional log files. The volume is ever increasing as more analog devices like phones, cameras, and radios are replaced by Global System for Mobile Communication (GSM) phones, digital cameras, and satellite radio. The aggregate amount of cast-off information is staggering. All of it is a threat to privacy because it's outside our control and can be analyzed to reveal personal information about us.

The relevance of this electronic waste to any specific person may not be immediately apparent, but as searches become faster, even routine queries will be able to be directed against not only the obvious caches of information but also the huge heaps of digital garbage. Who knows what might turn up? Candidates for analysis might include repair logs of cars, years-old videos from an ATM surveillance camera, discarded computer equipment, ten-year-old grocery purchases, and even emails we sent while in college.

In addition to the accidental data, the purposeful information available on each of us, often on the Internet, is huge. Almost everyone shows up somewhere in Google, for instance, regardless of how well known they are or are not. Although each item may be true and not terribly invasive of our privacy, the totality of what turns up when you google someone is generally impressive; college papers, work references, amateur sports scores, even candid photos taken by someone long ago. It's as though we've all become celebrities chased by silicon paparazzi. Andy Warhol would feel vindicated as we all get our fifteen minutes of online fame.

Affordable computers aren't quite up to these massive searching tasks yet, but they soon will be because of an observation commonly called Moore's Law. In 1965, Gordon Moore, a co-founder of Intel, predicted that the number of transistors that could be built on an integrated circuit would double every two years.[2] This statement about the short time frame for increasing capacity (popularly shortened to eighteen months) has been generalized to imply a larger truth about the computer industry: the overall complexity and therefore capability of computer equipment will double every one and a half years at the same cost. Many other computer metrics appear to increase at this rate, although most eventually taper off, such as central-processor or hard drive seek speed. Data seem to be accumulating at a commensurate pace, leaving an ever-growing pile of digital garbage for privacy invaders to search through. The proliferation of networked devices has made cross-talk between gadgets common. If private information is on one machine, it's safe to assume that it's accessible by many others. Each action, transmission, or sensory interrogation generally creates extra data for auditing purposes. This cyber chaff contributes to the sediment along with purposeful data files, photographs, videos, text files, sound recordings, and even unwanted and forgotten executable code—the programs themselves.

The more of these kinds of data that are lying around, the likelier it is that they will affect our privacy in some unforeseen way. Anyone who's ever seen forensic television shows like *CSI* knows how much information can be gained from the angle of a wound or a discarded cigarette butt. Imagine what could be figured out from the piles of data available on everyone. Just as DNA is an encoded representation of our physical bodies, this digital DNA models our minds and, in the hands of a trained analyst, can provide incredible amounts of insight into us and our actions—perhaps more than we're comfortable sharing.

Why aren't we drowning in bits? Because the cost of storage media has also been tracking to this curve. The rapid and substantial reductions in the cost of hard drives, CDs, DVDs, and even flash memory has kept pace with and, in some cases, has exceeded the speed of accumulation. Digital data operate under different rules than real-world analog information does. There's plenty of room to store all these data and if there isn't, there will be next week.

Electronic Data Never Go Away

It is difficult to be certain that a chunk of digital information is ever completely deleted. Files can be recovered from hard drives long after they've been erased, restored from backup tapes that no one knew existed, or plucked from network relay machines or caching servers. Easy to collect, cheap to store, and expensive to delete, our personal information accumulates in the world's computers like orphaned socks or dusty *National Geographics* in the garage. But the cost of a spring cleaning of information, unlike the cost of a spring cleaning of the garage, goes up just as fast as the storage cost goes down, and thus it is impossible to contemplate wide-scale data purging. In my more than twenty years of computer experience, I've never seen a company that has created and enforced a data-deletion policy. Many executive managers probably think that they do, but talking to the data-center staff reveals a different story. Often "purged" data are simply moved out of the way.

The operative principle in a data center is that disks are always cheaper than decisions. Systems administrators know that much of the stored information in their care is unwanted, often unlabeled, and unidentified. It would require too much time to carefully pick through and identify which files are safe to delete, either for mission criticality or legal reasons. The gain from freeing up a little disk space is minuscule compared with the potential damage from inadvertently deleting a necessary file. Therefore no one deletes files. The rapidly decreasing cost of storage makes this nondecision all the easier, but it turns every disk drive into a potential Pompeii of rich information for a future data researcher.

The World Is a Single Computer

Here's a secret—there is really only one computer in the world. All the tentacles of the early proprietary networks, IBM, Prodigy, CompuServe, AOL, governments, and intelligence agencies have become hopelessly intertwined. They are effectively a single organism. Some are directly wired to networks. Others use modems to communicate via phone lines. Still others have wireless capabilities like Wi-Fi or Bluetooth. Regardless of the technology, every personal computer sold today has the potential, if not the outright capability, to connect to a network, another computer, or a variety of peripherals like printers. Most of these switching devices and storage systems are also dedicated computers that talk to each other. It's meaningless to say that computers are connected to the Internet. There is no Internet independent of the tens of millions of general-purpose and specialized computer systems that constitute it. All computers and their networks, the one and the many, are the same thing.

Because most computers are linked, a computer-savvy guy sitting in a Calcutta cyber cafe with a laptop can research you by accessing relevant computers even though they're half a world away. He can buy your credit report from Experian in Illinois, hack into your email from AOL in Virginia, read your California-based MySpace web profile and your Google blog. Even if he fails, he's probably untraceable. Now imagine that instead of a hacker, he's a computer programmer. His software can do the same thing against 100,000 people at the same time, and it won't even cost that much. With $20,000 he can buy a roomful of personal computers that can be located anywhere in the world with a fast Internet connection and do what I just described. The intertwining of computers around the globe makes remote information access too easy; the only thing stopping widespread abuse is computer security.

Contrived Security

Even many tech-savvy people have an inflated view of the effectiveness of computer security. Because networks are designed to make it easy to get to information on many machines, it's a lot harder to secure a networked computer than most would imagine, and it requires constant vigilance and thus costs more than most businesses are willing to pay. The many out-of-the-box security solutions all crumble under a determined assault—indeed, security walls are often the primary targets of hackers.

In today's operating systems, security is an afterthought. It takes special software to artificially partition information and regulate conditional access; eventualities have to be thought of and explicitly blocked by the programmer. Any mistake, intentional or otherwise, will allow someone to get in. The basic rule of security is that if there is a vulnerability, someone will exploit it. Anyone who wants to badly enough can get any piece of information stored in any computer in the world, no matter how secure. For example, U.S. military networks have proven to be easy to hack.[3] Software and hardware vendors are now devoting resources to toughening their products' security, yet the value to the hacker of breaking in is increasing just as fast. If there's enough money at stake, someone will find a way in. Notice how often Microsoft releases a major security patch, for instance.

Every moving part in a computer system is a potential weak link. Every place where multiple processes exchange information is a possible back door into the system. Every connection to the outside world allows egress for hackers or viruses as well as legitimate users.

For this reason Microsoft products leak like a porcupine's water bed. The complexity of the programmer interfaces that connect the various processes in the operating system and the provisions for every major form of personal computer input/output make it impossible to test for every anomaly.

Vendors have always been quick to promote the security of their software. Companies like AOL center much of their advertising on the idea that it's safer to browse the Internet through them than to traverse the wild and wooly "raw" Internet. Even Internet Service Providers (ISPs) like Earthlink push security as a sales point. But these companies' products aren't much safer than others, and browsing the Internet is not all that safe—but neither is walking down a city street at night, although many people do it. This false sense of security lulls many people into ignoring what they leave behind when strolling through cyberspace.

Reality Crossover

You can spot the moral weakness in a society by watching what passes for entertainment. The gladiator matches and coliseum games foreshadowed the eventual decline of Roman civilization. What then to make of reality television? Every network on the tube, including most cable channels, have at least one show that has turned invasion of privacy into an art. Whether it is a police ride-along, a video-monitored house populated by drunken has-been celebrities, or an island where couples are encouraged to cheat on their significant others, these unscripted scenes play out for the benefit of hidden cameras and, by extension, for the vast voyeuristic viewing audience. There has never been a more popular genre in television.

The seeds for this form of entertainment were the harmless antics of *Candid Camera* and the not-so-harmless bombastic grudge matches of talk-television commentators like Maury Povich and Jerry Springer. Springer (an ex-mayor of Cincinnati) is so popular that a controversial comic opera based on him played in London to sold-out crowds.

It is difficult to imagine where this trend will take us, given how far such programming has come in a short time. An identity-theft show, perhaps? Or maybe even the ultimate—a being that exists only on television for the amusement of the public, such as the character played by Jim Carrey in the movie *The Truman Show.*

It's ironic and perhaps not entirely coincidental that at the same time that we are experiencing major erosions of privacy in the United States, reality television has become so popular. These shows are made possible by the same hidden cameras that are used for urban surveillance. Shows like *Cops* and *Caught on Tape* are created almost completely from hidden video. Both activities, entertainment and surveillance, will continue to benefit from advances in technology. A good way to visualize what an extreme privacy violation might look like is to watch a reality show in which a whole house is wired, miked, and stuffed with hidden cameras.

Smart-Search Programs

One threat to privacy comes from increasingly invasive manual tools like improved cameras and exhaustive databases, but another threat is the ease with which routine tasks can be batched and automated. The combination of low-cost computing, fully networked databases, and automation now makes wholesale privacy invasion a reality. It's unnecessary to take a special interest in individuals before invading their privacy. Cheap storage and networked, interoperable databases create a perfect environment for artificial-intelligence programs that roam the Internet looking for valuable personal data. Simple versions of these bots (short for robots) are used for simple autonomous searching like comparative product shopping and for more devious purposes such as credit-card scrounging. Computer viruses are a form of these bots with the additionally handy feature of being able to reproduce.

Plain keyword search tools are useful against well-structured databases but are not as helpful for working through large amounts of uncategorized information in multiple databases, as counter-terrorism experts found out after 9/11. A much better strategy is to use profiling software. Possessing limited reasoning capabilities, governed by a programmed rule set, these intelligent routines are the perfect answer to the dilemma posed by predictive intelligence—how to find a certain type of person before he or she commits a crime. Profiling software has two major advantages over simple search: it can search across databases with different schemas or structures, and it can come up with answers given incomplete information by using "fuzzy logic" or heuristic reasoning. This technology, although helpful and perhaps necessary for law enforcement, poses a much bigger threat to individual privacy than any possible damage from a single, dedicated individual with harmful intent. Imagine a fully automated House Un-American Activities Committee with millions of cybernetic Joe McCarthys devoting every second of their existence to every moment of *your* existence. Profiling has removed any vestiges of protection retained by the masses through anonymity. Law-enforcement officials find it useful to be able to target low-profile people who haven't lit up on anyone's radar screen. And, truth be told, doing so might help catch terrorists, although the cost to the privacy of innocents might be too high. This categorizing technology can segregate and segment birth characteristics like gender and race, adoptive inclinations like political affiliation and religion, and thought attributes like opinions or sexual orientation.

As the data world gets more and more populated, the need for profiling systems will grow. They are the only reasonable strategy for navigating the choked, tricky waters of cyberspace in real time. The terrorist problem faced by the Department of Homeland Security brings this conundrum into focus. How else can an intelligence agency spot potential terrorists before they act other than by somehow getting inside their heads, observing their actions, and listening to their conversations? A challenge that our society will face in the coming years is reconciling this need to use automated accusatory software with the desire to protect civil liberties. They are both legitimate needs and must be tempered by ethical considerations and, if necessary, legal guidance.

The Double-Edged Sword

Technology is a neutral medium; it's apolitical and amoral. As with other weapons, the pointy end does not operate independently of the person holding the handle. Some of the violations described in this chapter may not seem like privacy problems, and in today's view they may not be. But as new uses for information technology are found, the potential for damage increases proportionately.

One of our society's great challenges will be to figure out how to create a balance between the harms and benefits offered by global access to universal information. If we wait until privacy intrusion has clearly become a problem, then we're likely to do a poor job of righting the balance because there will be too many entrenched economic interests. It's unclear how we pull all this information back once it's out there. It's unlikely that anyone will ever support legislation banning the use of search technology, which helps us make sense of this growing information space that we've created. The use of profiling software, however, could certainly be regulated and probably should be. At a minimum, the rules and the calculus used by financially and governmentally sanctioned profiling software should be a matter of public record because otherwise it will be impossible to refute. This chapter and the previous one have covered only the privacy intrusions that are already happening and obvious. Many more are now starting to appear, brought about by both technology and an increasing cultural reliance on the Internet. Chapter Four discusses these new harms to our privacy in detail.

New Tech, New Crimes
Fresh Wounds

The fantastic advances in the field of electronic communication constitute a great danger to the privacy of the individual.

Earl Warren[1]

New capabilities brought about by the Internet extend not just our perceptions but also our personas. When you don't physically meet the people you deal with, their behavior becomes more important than their appearance. In the disembodied, yet highly communicative, world online, you don't have your looks, your figure, your height, your gender, or even your race; all you have is your reputation. Lose face and lose your soul; get a new one because that identity is effectively dead.

Wherever there's value, there's crime. As identity and reputation grow in importance, they present new ways for us to be attacked and new ways for others to violate our privacy. Several new abuses are so novel that there aren't even names for them yet.

Some of these new privacy problems will occur because information technology makes it easy to pry into personal lives. Other privacy incidents will happen because most online communication and entertainment web sites require their users to create accounts. These accounts have pseudonymous identities that over time take on a life of their own. There is no universal directory for people using the Internet, so every communication application like Instant Messenger, every online game like World of Warcraft, and every portal like Yahoo has a different "phone book." It's almost impossible to get the same name in every web site, so people are forced to creatively pick different names or variants in each world. Because no one cares whether you use your real name or not, most people have developed the habit of creating unique and colorful pseudonyms. After a while, people get attached to these aliases because they spend a significant and meaningful amount of time living them. An attack against these identities assaults their privacy. In an online world, anything that undermines your identity is a privacy violation.

As each successive generation spends more of their time online using newly networked gadgetry, their identities and, more important, their reputations become essential to the stability and quality of their business, community, and personal life. And increasingly their pseudonyms are becoming equally important. Privacy invasions impugn the reputation and stature of their targets in both physical and online communities. The more time that we spend in cyberspace, the worse the harm to our privacy if things go wrong with our Internet presences and identities.

Avatar Abuse

For many of us, much of our daily interaction with other people occurs online. The identities that we've created there add a whole new ingredient to the already complicated mix of privacy issues because these new identities and aliases are just as susceptible to attack as is our real-world identity. These Internet personas can be simple aliases or graphical interfaces known as avatars (see next paragraph). The damages from privacy violations are converging between the worlds as more "real" functions, like fungible money, are replicated virtually. As an example, a popular online game, Project Entropria, offers a card that works in ATM machines but draws money from the play money used in the world of the game. It works the other way too. Players can spend real-world cash to buy game artifacts. Jon Jacobs, a player of this game, spent 100,000 real dollars to buy a space station, which he intends to develop as an outlet on which media companies can sell music and videos.[2] The line between online worlds and the underlying physical one are quickly blurring, making it increasingly likely that an attack against an identity in one will cross over to the other. Millions of dollars of virtual artifacts used only in online games are sold every year on eBay, including swords, magic spells, and even cyber furniture and digital houses.

The term *avatar* comes from the Sanskrit word *avatāra*, which means descent. In Hinduism it refers to various earthly incarnations of Vishnu, the preserver. It's also become a high-tech term for a visual representation of a person's online identity. Right now, avatars are two-dimensional pictures or animations. As better and more sophisticated display technology is developed, including three-dimensional representations, holograms, and virtual reality, avatars will be some of the first applications using them. Popularized in fiction by Neil Stephenson in his novel *Snowcrash* and in gaming by the PC game Ultima, the term is often extended to the "buddy icons" used by America Online's Instant Messenger (AIM) and other instant-messenger technologies. Worlds Chat (started in 1995) and AlphaWorld (later known as Active Worlds) were the first avatar virtual worlds launched on the Internet. Meridian 59 (1996), Ultima Online (1999), and EverQuest (2000) came later. Online avatar communities have thousands of people working together to design and build huge three-dimensional worlds, such as in The Sims Online (2002). These games started out as pure entertainment, as a logical extension of their single player/single computer predecessors, but they are rapidly evolving into actual communities based on fantasy themes. Participants are free to act in any way they'd like and to represent themselves any way they wish. Many young people use these games as a major part of their recreational life, complete with their own online circle of friends.

Avatars are not bots or agents, which often just mimic human behavior; they usually represent a living being. An avatar may be a realistic rendering of the actual person, a stylized representation of what that person would like to be, or a fantastical model of anything that the person desires to become. The technology will be restricted only by a lack of creativity, programming talent, or funds.

Avatars are used in many different spheres. Companies are using avatars for their corporate training, in part because it is convenient but also because it increases productivity and saves the companies money. Simulators used as surrogates for big-ticket hardware like submarines and space shuttles have long been viewed as a cheap training method. Governments around the world are using avatar technology as part of their planning for the future. The U.S. military has long used avatars for all types of training. Military strategists use them to plan battles and for tactical reflex training. The Marine Corps evaluated using the popular shooter game DOOM for tactical practice. If you want to understand the immersive environments of the future, look no further than computer games. Today's games will train fighters for tomorrow's wars. NASA and Digital Space have re-created the polar conditions on Mars in a simulator; team members enter as avatars to study the living conditions on the planet and also work together as a crew in training exercises. NASA is developing several other avatar projects that will help scientists plan future space missions. Online museums are using avatars as tour guides for their digital collections, and a green-haired avatar named Ananova will even read you the news. The first major appearance of an avatar was in the mid-1980s in the ill-fated television series *Max Headroom*, a show that was doubly doomed because the title character was also the spokesperson for the failed New Coke. Many technologists believe that the ultimate interface to the online world will be via an avatar. This model will be a three-dimensional, dynamic simulation of a living organism; people will see and interact with this model online.

The fashion world will likely adopt avatars, causing the same sort of expensive bare-arms race in the cyber world as in the real one. I expect to see avatars modeled after celebrities as well as normal people—for a price. This modeling will raise the interesting question of who owns a person's likeness. If someone creates an avatar based on your face do you have the right to stop that person from using it? Could a designer trademark an avatar and sue to stop others from copying it? The answer to both these questions is probably yes.

Avatars not only lead to privacy-infringement suits, but to privacy abuses against the individual through impersonation. What would happen if someone adopted an avatar designed to look like you? You might be able to sue if you could find out who was doing it. It seems like a new kind of plagiarism as well as an odd form of privacy violation to have your face and body copied into cyberspace and manipulated by someone else. Just as in conventional privacy attacks, the victims have lost control over information about themselves. In extreme cases, the impersonation is not just a graphic copy but is authenticated so as to appear to actually be the person.

Puppetry

I call an unapproved use of another person's virtual identity *puppetry* because the target's online manifestation is jerked around as if it were on strings. Puppetry is taking over someone else's avatar, possibly damaging that person's reputation in the process. Usually puppetry involves getting a password to authenticate, so it appears as though the puppet is being controlled by the same "operator." Because third parties who know the person don't understand that someone else is running the show, they blame the victim for anything the puppet does. It might express racist or sexist sentiments, talk salaciously, or, far worse, make comments that raise government interest in the puppet and master. Being on the wrong end of a puppetry incident after the puppet publicly announced support for terrorism could quickly bring a knock on your physical door by very real investigative agents.

> The most famous case of online puppetry happened in a MOO (an interactive textual adventure game environment) called Lambda-MOO.[3] An avatar, Mr. Bungle, used a computer command called "voodoo-doll" to force two female characters to have graphic sex with him and each other in a crowded living room of the community. The voodoo command allows someone to take temporary control of another avatar.
>
> The cyber rape caused shock waves throughout the online community. The victims, legba and Starsinger, felt angry, hurt, and humiliated, especially because they were unable to pretend it didn't happen when so many had witnessed the attack. Nor did they want to leave a community in which they had invested considerable time developing their avatar characters and forging friendships that often overlapped in real life. They had lost control over information about themselves, and their reputations were damaged.

As cannot happen in the outside world, a person whose reputation has been damaged can easily walk away from the computer and never return to a specific chat room, but many still find it difficult to forget the humiliation; others worry that their real identity and contact information will somehow be uncovered and they will be forced to look over their shoulder in real life.

Today it's games. Tomorrow these identities will be a big part of our lives. Even now some avatars have been used for several years. When someone loses a ten-year-old persona, it's going to be devastating.

Golem Porn

Sometimes it's not an identity that's stolen, just an appearance, usually for sexual purposes. *Golem porn* is what I call simulated pornography; it can be digitized either with no real person involved or, worse, with someone's face grafted onto another's nude body. The pornography industry has embraced developments in technology with, well, both hands. Some golem porn could affect privacy, especially when real people's faces are mixed in. Advances in affordable digital photography have empowered the voyeur, who can now manufacture custom pornography using your face without your permission or cooperation. I can imagine a cottage industry where someone sends a company your picture and gets back a DVD of what appears to be you acting in a porn film.

Every country has porn, although the definition and the limits change with the time and the culture. The criticism against porn in general is based on the moral argument that the material is offensive to a community at large. This is obviously a highly subjective judgment, summed up best by the famous quote by Supreme Court Justice Potter Stewart, "I can't define pornography, but I know it when I see it."

Like the Court, many average citizens argue over the definition and the restriction or regulation of the material, but one aspect of the subject gets almost universal agreement—child porn. Obscene material featuring children is universally condemned and is at a minimum an invasion of their privacy. Unlike so-called victimless crimes like voluntary adult porn or smoking marijuana, distribution or consumption of child pornography harms society as much as does its creation because it financially supports children who are being hurt. This unassailable argument makes prohibition of child porn noncontroversial. No sane human being wishes to hurt children. In addition to the physical and emotional harm that it causes children, exploiting them in this way is the ultimate privacy violation and one that they will never shake for their entire lives.

Enter technology. It's now quite possible to create completely digitized human actors. The technique is frequently used by Hollywood. Originally developed to create fantastic beings such as dinosaurs, talking toys, and anthropomorphic animals, realistic animation continues to decrease in cost to the point where any determined graphics programmer can do a fair job with home computer equip-ment. *Sky Captain and the World of Tomorrow*, a movie released in 2004, was sold to a studio using a demonstration film that was gen-erated by a single man programming a personal computer in his own house.

So what would happen if someone created a completely digitized child and animated it in a porn flick? Because no child was involved in the production, it begs the question of whether it is indeed child porn, subject to the same laws that govern pornography in the real world. In 2002, the Supreme Court cited the First Amendment in striking down parts of the Child Pornography Prevention Act of 1996.[4] This law specifically banned the distribution and possession of virtual porn—material that appears to depict underage children having sex but in reality does not. The Court said that the mater-ial was not intrinsically related to the sexual abuse of children. The John Ashcroft Justice Department had put the onus on producers to prove that the film did not involve minors; after the decision, the burden shifted to the government. Congress continues to try to overrule the Supreme Court on this issue.

There's a bigger question here: Do the old privacy laws apply to fully digital content? Legal issues aside, it's not even clear what the ethical and moral implications are. There is now a spectrum of pornography in which the actors may or may not be real. Or part of them may be real—maybe just their face or their hands or some other body part. It's quite common to see fake photographs created using Adobe's Photoshop or a similar graphics program. These pic-tures are good enough to fool anyone but an expert. Movies like *Polar Express* use accurately rendered representations of real-life actors. Video games, such as the Godfather game with a rendering of Marlon Brando or the innumerable video games tied to blockbuster movies, now do the same.

People have used Photoshop-like programs to graft surrepti-tiously taken photos of an acquaintance or neighbor onto exposed bodies, usually engaged in sexual activities. In this way they build up a library of fetish porn that is tailored to their fantasies of both the person and the activity. A singer from the Irish singing group The Coors was shocked to find that her head was being used atop naked bodies in pornographic photos and performing sexual acts in animated flicks, all available on the Internet. Tennis pro Anna Kournikova and pop stars Britney Spears, Mandy Moore, and Christina Aguilera have also fallen victim to mocked-up videos and fake porn snaps. Many other celebrities are learning they are sporting the bodies of strangers they'll never meet. Is someone's privacy violated by simulated pornography?

The veracity and credibility of photographs are about to take a severe nosedive. Ironically, the ease with which photos can be manipulated almost serves as a counterbalancing force to the invasive aspect of faked pictures. Because it's impossible to tell that a picture is faked, it's impossible to tell that it isn't, giving plausible deniability to those whose likenesses appear in embarrassing pictures.

> The *USA Today* web site pulled an online photograph of Condoleezza Rice that was altered to look as though the Secretary of State had "demonic" eyes. The editors admitted manipulating most of the images used in its publications in regard to sizing, lighting, and so forth, but said that the photo of Rice was a mistake. Expert Photoshop users weighed in, stating that the distortion could not have resulted from anything but a deliberate desire to depict her as harsh and scary.[5]

Spreading Disinformation

When pictures are created deliberately to damage another person's reputation, they are part of a broader category—the spreading of disinformation, which is an intelligence term meaning to deliberately mislead people by providing false information. Information technology can be used to mislead as well as inform because there's no obvious way to check the quality of the content on any given site. In fact, some of the most popular reference web sites are not authoritative, nor are they under editorial control.

The advent of efficient search engines coincided with the rise of the commercial Internet. As the quantity of data available online increased, so did the need for information tools, ranging from search engines like Google and Excite to directories like Yahoo and commercial databases like the Internet Movie Database and collaborative encyclopedias and reference works like Wikipedia. Unlike print media, which often emphasize accuracy over speed, online sites, because of their dynamic nature and ever-increasing quantity, find fact checking extremely difficult, especially in real time. Inaccuracies sneak in accidentally and, increasingly, on purpose. False information can and has created privacy problems for well-known people like politicians and entertainment figures by besmirching their names. As we have seen, a characteristic of the Internet and electronic media in general is how important a person's reputation becomes once all interaction is remote. Disinformation affects this reputation and affects the victim's privacy. In these cases, there is often a financial harm because celebrities live off their reputations. In some cases, however, violations of celebrities' privacy have enhanced their popularity, such as happened with Paris Hilton and her notorious homemade sex tape.

Web 2.0 is often touted as the successor to the current World Wide Web. One important component of the new web is deep-linked, user-generated content, of which Wikipedia is often cited as a good example. Some of the most interesting reference material on the Internet is created and maintained by a group of people using a collaborative software artifact called a "wiki," hence the name Wikipedia. Because wiki authors are usually anonymous, it's difficult to pin down attribution, let alone seek retribution, for incorrect information or disinformation that damages one's reputation.

Many people have a tendency to believe what they see on the Internet, taking authoritative-looking web sites at face value. This credulousness has caused problems for reference sites like Wikipedia that are collaboratively edited. Other Internet-based information, such as the notorious "swift boat" campaign that seriously hurt John Kerry's election chances in 2004, have been deliberately damaging to the reputations of celebrities and politicians. When web sites damage reputations, it is a privacy violation—regardless of whether the postings are true or not. In these cases the target can usually do nothing. Although someone could sue for libel, doing so is often not worth the effort, and sometimes the publicity over the lawsuit ends up causing the opposite of the desired effect—more unwanted publicity.

Sometimes the disinformation is purposely initiated by the person whom the material is about. In February 2006, Wikipedia temporarily blocked a range of Internet Protocol (IP) addresses emanating from Congress because too many Congressional staffers were attempting to rewrite their representatives' biographies, often distorting the truth. Wikipedia released a request for comments describing the problem, in which it said: "The editors from these IP ranges have been rude, abrasive, immature, and show disregard for Wikipedia policy. The editors have frequently tried to censor the history of elected officials, often replacing community articles with censored biographies despite other users' attempts to dispute these violations. They also violate Wikipedia['s policy on v]erifiability, by deleting verified reports, while adding flattering things about members of Congress that are unverified."[6] Although deliberately falsifying information about oneself is not an obvious privacy violation, not allowing people to make up stories about themselves may be; if privacy is about controlling information about oneself, and some celebrities want to control their bios, then aren't editorial overrides on these articles a privacy violation? In other words, can it be a privacy violation if the person in question wants something false put up instead of the unflattering truth? Intuitively there seems to be a principle that celebrities give up this right when they become famous, but it is intrusive for common people, who probably should have some ability to shade how they are perceived by others, at least a little.

There are several publicized stories of people who have had their reputations damaged from disinformation. A posting made to an online French message board is still creating difficulties for Jeanne Achille, a public-relations executive. Someone used her identity and email address to make racist remarks. She is unable to get the messages removed and is constantly fielding questions about them from potential clients, who use the Internet to check her credentials and learn about her before doing business with her.[7]

John Seigenthaler, a former journalist, had a run-in in 2005 with Wikipedia, because it ran an entry linking him to the assassinations of John F. and Robert Kennedy.[8] He had been RFK's assistant, but presumably wasn't involved in the killings. The article ran for four months on Wikipedia as well as on several related reference web sites that pull information from the encyclopedia. Seigenthaler contacted executives at Wikipedia and was eventually able to have the entry modified, although he was unable to get satisfaction for the slight. Wikipedia had no idea who the anonymous contributor was, and when Seigenthaler was finally able to get the IP address, Bell South refused to tell him who it was. He did manage to track down the culprit—a young man named Brian Chase, working as the operations manager of a Rush Delivery store in Nashville, Tennessee. Chase claimed that he had made the entry as a prank, to shock coworkers.[9]

High school students and even younger children face reputational challenges because of cyber bullying. Internet chat rooms and web sites are replacing bathroom walls as the places of choice for harassing peers and scrawling slanderous remarks about fellow students. The bullying can even include stealing someone else's identity to post malicious statements and to create false profiles that cause embarrassment and humiliation.

Ghyslain Raza is not a household name, even in his hometown of Quebec. But as the "Star Wars Kid" he was responsible for one of the biggest Internet fads of all time. He filmed himself swinging a golf-ball retriever like a light saber and accidentally left the tape lying around at school. Several classmates found it and posted it on the Kazaa peer-to-peer file-sharing system, where it became popular; it was eventually downloaded by artists around the world who "remixed" the video, adding sound effects and music. Ghyslain was horribly embarrassed and, according to a lawsuit filed by his parents against the families of his classmates, had to undergo psychiatric treatment.[10]

A trick known as "Google bombing" is sometimes used to affect which pages are presented for a given search. For instance, typing in the words "miserable failure" will bring the searcher to the official biography page for President Bush, followed by Jimmy Carter's home page and then Michael Moore's. This trick works because, from one perspective, Google has a simplistic ranking algorithm—it counts the links from a keyword into a given web site or page. The more links, the higher the relevance. Because this ranking is generated from third-party sites, it's possible for anyone to affect the search engine's rankings by creating fake references around the Internet. Google bombing becomes a privacy issue because it causes reputational damage, although subtly. This disinformation technique is humiliating, even infuriating, for its victims but is almost impossible to challenge. It is especially frustrating because many people, especially students, don't realize that items that show up on the first couple of pages of a search are not necessarily credible or accurate.

Profiling Discrimination

Disinformation often affects normal people accidentally because they're caught up and miscategorized by intelligent software called profiling systems. Profiling is computer guessing. As digital information continues to pile up at enormous rates, profiling software is the most reasonable way for organizations to find a few people out of the millions of records in their databases, especially when some of the information is missing or of dubious legitimacy. Profiling can be as straightforward as "find all people born in Ohio in 1956 who own a Cadillac" or something more subjective like "Which people on this airplane flight are likeliest to be terrorists?" The terrorist case illustrates the ability of computers to reason with insufficient information and is often called "fuzzy logic." Such labeling is at heart attaching a bias—they're almost synonymous. It's insidious because names carry assumptions and are difficult to refute. Whether the label is accurate or not, labeling is privacy-invasive if you don't choose it for yourself. It can also have real-world consequences for credit, employment, and travel, depending on who's doing the profiling.

Since the mid-1980s, a great deal of proprietary software designed for marketing companies and government agencies is used for people categorization. Assorted data feeds are transformed by rules, and the output is sorted into groups of people. The software is only as good as the heuristics and the data, but the results quickly become authoritative as the source becomes detached, leaving only the label attached to the person's reputation. For instance, "credit risk" may be the only entry carried over from a financial scoring system into a Homeland Security database, but the facts that led to that label may have been dropped in the transfer.

Much of the grief people have with bureaucracies stems from feeling victimized because of having been unfairly or incorrectly assigned to a category. It's usually difficult to shake a label. It's hard enough when you're aware of it, impossible when you're not. The most visible examples of this principle are credit reports and scores. Even with yearly debates in Congress and regulations such as the Fair Credit Report Act, correcting incorrect and damaging entries in these reports is still extremely difficult.

Although not always a crime, specious labeling will become more and more of a nuisance in the twenty-first century. One label will keep you from financing a car. Another will block you from renting an apartment or keep you from flying on airplanes. The more insidious tags will be the psychological ones. How do you fight a label like "irresponsible" or "untrustworthy" or "disloyal"?

The Digital Age provides many opportunities for false labeling, with a new wrinkle added—categories generated by one system can become part of another. Since 9/11, barriers between corporate and governmental databases have been substantially weakened. A commercial label of "credit risk" will quickly find its way into a government database. Even more disturbing, government labels may find their way into commercial databases, especially when government departments and commercial enterprises swap information, such as when JetBlue Airways voluntarily released information on five million passengers to a subcontractor for the Defense Department.[11] In the days following 9/11, the FBI put together a list of individuals it was interested in questioning. The FBI sent the list to utilities, banks, airlines, and many types of private businesses as part of Project Lookout. Most of the people on the list were not considered suspects or terrorists; they simply might have been able to provide FBI agents with important information about the hijackers. That fact was never mentioned when the list was circulated, nor was an updated version with corrections ever sent. Copies of these error-filled lists are still being used to improperly screen job and credit applicants because the original meaning of the list is lost. The continued circulation of these lists has resulted in many people being fired, denied jobs, and turned down for loans and apartments; others have been labeled as terrorists.[12] The risk of such improper dissemination of private information is rapidly increasing and will increase even more as barriers between government and private commercial entities continue to be removed. Government workers also need to realize that adding someone to a suspicion list can make the target's life difficult even if the person being investigated is labeled a "person of interest."

> Steven Hatfill sued John Ashcroft and the Justice Department because he was publicly labeled a "person of interest" in the ongoing investigation into the 2001 anthrax attacks. To date, he hasn't been charged although the several FBI raids of his home were mobbed with accompanying journalists. His lawyer, Victor M. Glasberg, is quoted as saying: "Steve's life has been devastated by a drumbeat of innuendo, implication and speculation. We have a frightening public attack on an individual who, guilty or not, should not be exposed to this type of public opprobrium based on speculation."[13]

Even if the label doesn't become public, it's still out there in a database, looming as a future privacy problem if it gets out. No one has yet created a procedure, either technically or legally, for thoroughly fixing an erroneous database entry, because most databases are linked to many others, making comprehensive cleansing difficult; the data often automatically propagate in other machines. Because the machines are all interoperable, an entry is essentially permanent once it gets into the system. Profiling discrimination is an insidious privacy violation and stopping it is like figuring out who keeps writing graffiti in the bathroom.

> Shortly after the subway bombings in London in 2005, David Mery was on his way to meet his girlfriend for coffee. He usually took the bus but because he was running late that day, he decided to ride the tube instead. As he stood on the platform waiting for his train to arrive, he was arrested under the Terrorism Act. He had a knapsack with him and was wearing a jacket that police guarding the tube considered too warm for the weather. They arrested him under suspicion of being a terrorist because of the jacket, the knapsack, and the suspicious way that they said he had checked his phone messages. Before the day

was over, his apartment was ransacked by police, and his computer equipment and electronic gadgets were confiscated. Mery was finger-printed, photographed, and had DNA swabs taken from his mouth.

Mery made this incident public immediately and appeared on television and was interviewed numerous times by the press regarding his wrongful arrest. He was unable to get the police to expunge the personal information collected as part of the mistaken arrest. Although all charges were later dropped, his fingerprints, DNA samples, and every piece of information collected during the investigation are online and have been shared with Interpol and other police databases around the world.[14]

A Digital Watergate

The new crimes mentioned in this chapter are made possible by advanced technology that, if misused, can invade anyone's privacy. Some violations, especially those that damage reputations, can affect some people more than others because some people have more to lose—politicians, for example.

The U.S. political scene in the early 1970s was dominated by the Watergate scandal. The revelation that the Richard Nixon White House had authorized the break-in of Democratic headquarters at the Watergate Hotel led to disclosures of other crimes: the break-in and theft of records from the psychiatrist of Daniel Ellsberg, the Pentagon Papers whistle-blower; the "enemies list" of peace activists and protestors; the misuse of the FBI and IRS for politically motivated investigations and several unethical campaign activities. The campaign activities were conducted by the appropriately named CREEP, or Committee to Reelect the President. This group was responsible for election dirty tricks such as sending black campaign workers into predominately white areas to ostensibly drum up support for George McGovern, Nixon's major Democratic opponent, and hiring actors to appear at rallies for the Democrat carrying misleading and racist signs. Donald Segretti, the head of the dirty-tricks squad, referred to these political activities against an opposing candidate as "ratfucking."[15]

These types of tricks are still played. In 2005 an active CIA agent, Valerie Plame, was "outed" by an unnamed White House official, presumably because her husband, Ambassador Joseph Wilson, was an outspoken critic of the Iraq war. As of this writing, the culprit hasn't been identified, although I. Lewis "Scooter" Libby, Vice President Richard Cheney's chief of staff, has been indicted by a grand jury. Revealing the identity of undercover intelligence agents is one case where an outing not only is a privacy violation but is also illegal.

Dirty tricksters are usually caught because they leave a trail of their shenanigans. Phone records, credit-card receipts, and other evidence lead special prosecutors to the perpetrators. Enter technology. The Internet is a wonderful venue for anonymous tricks whose potential use in politics has not yet been fully appreciated or realized, although the 2008 election may well be the time. Looked at from one perspective, all politicians have are their reputations, and if they are damaged, careers can be destroyed. Privacy threats are therefore meaningful to a politician.

Imagine that right before an election an email purportedly from one of the candidates goes out to a hundred million Americans espousing a mildly believable but extremist view on a subject such as gun control, abortion, or immigration. Many politicians are careful to straddle the fence on these highly charged issues. Mass mailing of a fake email supporting late-term abortion could throw an election in a red state, while a strong pro-life statement could hurt a candidate's chances in a blue state. It's impossible for most people to tell whether an email is authentic, and it's a trivial operation to forge an email header. Comprehensive mailing lists, categorized in almost every conceivable way, are available for purchase from several direct-marketing companies. Voting lists are a matter of public record, as are political contributions.

Surveys show that many voters depend on the Internet for political information. Gallup polled 596 Internet users in February 2000 and found that 23 percent use online resources to find out information about candidates.[16] During the 2004 elections, the Digital Future Project found an increase in voters accessing online political information; 60.4 percent of users agreed that the Internet is a tool for learning about politics, and 61.7 percent believed that the Internet is important to political campaigns.[17]

In light of these data, using digital tricks to undermine a candidate can have serious consequences. The 2008 presidential campaign will be the ideal proving ground. It will be the first wide-open campaign for both parties since the technology to perpetrate large-scale web frauds has become available. The Internet is the ideal echo chamber for whisper campaigns. Not only will it be extremely difficult to attribute the slander to someone, but it will be even harder to effectively refute the charges. If a negative campaign on the Internet were started right before an election, it would be impossible to undo the damage.

Whisper campaigns are not new. President Grover Cleveland was the target of one in 1884, when Republicans spread rumors that he had an illegitimate child; they chanted at rallies, "Ma, Ma where's my Pa?" After he won, Democratic newspapers added the tag line, "Gone to the White House, Ha, Ha, Ha!" Frequent whisper campaigns were focused on President Franklin D. Roosevelt and often made use of his support for civil rights. Contemporary equivalents include a trick during the 2000 Republican presidential primaries often attributed to Karl Rove. A whisper campaign alleged that "John McCain has an illegitimate black baby." In actuality, Senator McCain and his wife had adopted their daughter Bridget from a Bangladeshi orphanage run by Mother Theresa. Rumors and paper fliers also accused him of being mentally unstable because of his years in a prisoner-of-war camp during the Vietnam War. Allegations that he was a married homosexual and his wife was a drug addict were also bandied about online to undermine his character.

The presidential election in 2008 may be the first in which the war of words will be fought primarily on the Internet, not by the official web sites or by the candidates themselves but by third parties who will use slander, labeling, and outright lying to get their candidate elected. This election could make Nixon's 1972 reelection bid look like a pillow fight.

New technology creates new opportunities; new capabilities mean new violations of all kinds. Each of the privacy sins mentioned in Chapter One will change as cultural adoption of technical innovation both enhances and threatens personal identity and control of self-information. These acts might not yet be "crimes" in a literal sense, because the law always lags behind invention. Chapter Five talks more about the existing legal environment.

Part III

Privacy in Context

This part puts privacy into different contexts. Chapter Five explains the legal basis for privacy in the United States, describes how civil torts are related to privacy, and briefly discusses constitutional case law, federal legislation, and the legal status of private-sector data-collection agencies. Chapter Six examines the relationship between identity and privacy, focusing on newer shades of meaning for identity in the Digital Age such as pseudonymous identities on the Internet. Chapter Seven looks at cultural differences in how we view privacy. The idea of privacy is not absolute; it changes around the world, in cities and in rural areas, and by age.

Privacy and the Law
A Right Ahead or Left Behind?

Privacy is the right to be alone—the most comprehensive
of rights, and the right most valued by civilized man.
                                          Louis Brandeis[1]

Is privacy a right? Apparently most Americans think so. A Gallup
Poll conducted in February 1999 found that 70 percent of respondents believed that the Constitution guaranteed citizens the right
to privacy. In fact it does not. The word *privacy* doesn't even appear
in the Constitution—not once.

State and federal privacy laws are on the books, and you can sue
for privacy—within limits. To understand the impact that technology has on privacy, it helps to know something about these existing legal protections. After all, if the legal system adequately
protected what most of us think of as our privacy and was flexible
enough to accommodate changes in technology, privacy wouldn't
be as hot a topic as it is. This chapter outlines the civil basis for privacy lawsuits, describes constitutional protections and protections
afforded by federal laws, warns about the negative implications for
privacy of governmental outsourcing and the increasingly close connections between government and private-sector data-collection
companies, discusses commercial contracts and privacy policies, and
suggests ways to improve the legal safeguards of our privacy. Bear in
mind that as weak as privacy laws are, they are going to lose even
more ground as technology moves forward, even though there are

precedents that could be extended to cover privacy intrusions brought about by technology.

The gulf between the legal protection of privacy and state-of-the-art information science is growing. Most laws on the books today deal only with the analog world, not its digital equivalents, partially because the law moves slowly and technology quickly and partially because it's hard to write technically savvy laws. Just as lawyers are the ones who understand the law, technologists are the ones who understand technology. In my experience, most middle-aged lawyers, politicians, and staffers are not comfortable with nor do they understand the Internet, especially social applications like AIM, MySpace, and Flickr. My encounters with judges have left me with a similar impression. This lack of understanding on the part of lawmakers coupled with the rapidly moving bull's-eye of technology is responsible for the weak state of today's privacy laws, especially in regard to modern information devices. As a result, wiretapping statutes protect telephones, not cell phones, and postal laws protect paper mail, not email. Even if legislation is crafted to cover the new devices and technology, it will be very difficult to narrow the legal guidelines enough to make them enforceable and at the same time make them broad enough to handle evolutionary technology.

Absent adequate legal protection, the most common way to get relief for a privacy problem is to sue. Unfortunately, suits are most effective where there are clear-cut legislative statues or where case law—previous cases where judges have established guiding principles—applies. There are some privacy precedents, but few deal with topical issues in the Information Age, many of which were mentioned in the preceding two chapters. It will take years for the courts to catch up, but technology will continue to move on.

Privacy in Civil Law: The Four Torts

Civil law is the area in a common-law system that governs relations between private individuals.[2] Although federal rights can come from constitutional interpretation, when people refer to the "right to privacy," they're usually talking about civil law, about suing to protect privacy. The story of judicial privacy goes back to 1890. Lawyer Samuel Warren and his partner Louis Brandeis (before he became a Supreme Court justice) wrote a landmark article for the *Harvard Law Review* entitled "The Right to Privacy," which addressed the legal status of privacy in the United States for the first time.[3] They were trying to address two trends that disturbed them: technological innovations and a growingly intrusive media. Technology, primarily photography at that time, had already stirred up nineteenth-century society. An apocryphal story is that Warren was angry because of unfavorable reporting about his daughter in a society-page article.

Warren and Brandeis defined privacy as "the right to be left alone" and decried innovations such as "instantaneous photographs" and "numerous mechanical devices" that make it so that "what is whispered in the closet shall be proclaimed from the house-tops."[4] These lawyers were worried that technology would make it impossible for a prudent individual to protect himself or herself against bad publicity. They saw privacy violations as the unwanted public exposure of information. Their article opened the door for assorted privacy lawsuits over the next seventy years; most were of the peeping Tom or inappropriate-newspaper-story variety. The article was particularly significant because it provided a solid foundation on which U.S. tort law regarding privacy could later be built. A tort is a private, or civil, wrong or injury. Their right to privacy was different from other American rights in that privacy had no ancient roots or precedents.

Brandeis and Warren took a giant leap in creating the basic right to privacy out of thin constitutional material. It's interesting and timely that they did so as a reaction to their feeling threatened by new technology like cameras and voice recorders. Their view was that privacy was the responsibility of the individual until it became impossible to control by oneself because of technology. They concluded that it was then appropriate for the government to step in as an equalizer. We are in a similar position today—technology has again surged and has once again put privacy beyond an individual's control. This might be another time when it would be appropriate for the government to step in and right the balance.

The next significant evolution of privacy law occurred in 1960, when a legal academic named Dean William Prosser wrote an article claiming that a "privacy tort" is an amalgam of four separate and distinct torts.[5] The four torts described by Prosser are appropriation of name or likeness ("Appropriation"), intrusion upon seclusion ("Intrusion"), public disclosure of embarrassing private facts ("Private Facts"), and making statements that may be true, but are misleading ("False Light"). It's important to note that privacy laws are state, not federal, and therefore an individual's privacy rights vary widely. For example, North Dakota and Wyoming have not yet recognized any of the four privacy torts, while Rhode Island recognizes all four privacy torts by statute. California has some of the most robust state privacy protections.

Each of these torts has been and will continue to be influenced by technology. Appropriation of name and likeness covers domain name squatting. Intrusion upon seclusion can easily be extended to cover computer-augmented eavesdropping. Private facts can cover massive data breaches. And false light can be used to shut down a slanderous web site.

Appropriation

Appropriation is the use of a person's name or likeness for commercial purposes without his or her consent. For instance, selling a breakfast cereal named "David Holtzman's Granola" and putting my picture on the box could trigger a lawsuit from me on two grounds, misuse of my likeness and misuse of my name. The legal issues here tend to revolve around consent; if given, there are no grounds. One of the landmark appropriation cases was *Roberson v. Rochester Folding Box Co.* (1902).[6] A young girl's picture had been used without her consent on advertisements for a flour company. The courts refused to rule in favor of the girl's family. In response, the New York legislature created the first appropriation law (granting a statutory right of privacy) in 1903. The statute stated that without a (living) person's written consent, that person's name, portrait, or picture cannot be used for advertising purposes.

A seminal privacy decision was handed down in 1905 by the Georgia Supreme Court in the case of *Pavesich v. New England Life.* The insurance company used a photograph of Paolo Pavesich without his permission in a print advertisement. The caption read: "In my healthy and productive period of life I bought insurance in the New England Mutual Life Insurance Co., of Boston, Mass., and today my family is protected and I am drawing an annual dividend on my paid-up policies." Pavesich won on appeal. The case was significant because it was the first one to recognize the right to privacy opined by Brandeis and Warren fifteen years before.[7]

At the time, it was difficult to manipulate photographs. Now anyone who owns a computer probably has software to manipulate pictures. In the future, it's going to be much harder for accusers to prove that the accused actually copied their likenesses. Also, it will eventually be up to the courts to decide how much of a person's visage can be copied before it's actionable. There is also the issue of photo-manipulation software, which can distort a picture by a measured amount, blurring it, stretching the shape, changing the colors. Think of Andy Warhol's celebrity portraits.

Appropriation statutes differ based on whether the person is a celebrity. Generally, a noncelebrity can sue only for emotional damage but can be awarded punitive damages. For instance, in the 1952 case of *Eick v. Perk Dog Food Co.*, the plaintiff was awarded damages when her photograph was used without her consent in an ad selling dog food.[8] She claimed emotional distress and humiliation. Damage awards like this one will be important in Internet appropriation lawsuits because without them there won't be enough of a financial deterrent. Unlike others, celebrities can also sue for loss of income in appropriation cases. Protection can extend even to catch phrases. Johnny Carson sued a toilet company for using his catch phrase "Here's Johnny." The company used the phrases "Here's Johnny" and "the world's foremost commodian" to describe their toilets.[9]

Some famous celebrity cases include Bette Midler's win against Ford when the company hired one of her backup singers to sing one of her songs during a car commercial, presumably because it was cheaper than hiring the "Divine Ms. M" herself.[10] Vanna White won a lawsuit against Samsung when it ran an ad featuring a robot with a blond wig turning letters on a game show that resembled *Wheel of Fortune*.[11] In 2005, civil rights figure Rosa Parks settled a lawsuit against the rap group Outkast, which had used her name in one of their songs, including the line: "Ah-ha, hush that fuss. Everybody move to the back of the bus."[12] Tonya Harding, the notorious ice skater, threatened to sue the makers of "Tonya Hot Sauce."[13] Initially Dustin Hoffman was awarded $3 million from *Los Angeles Magazine* because the magazine used his picture from *Tootsie* in a fashion article without his permission, but the decision was reversed upon appeal.[14]

The distinction between the famous and the not so famous was a lot easier to discern prior to the Internet. Andy Warhol's famous comment about everyone being famous for fifteen minutes comes to mind here. Are bloggers celebrities? For a good idea of how stars are likely to be anointed on the Internet, look at reality TV shows like *American Idol*.

Technology has made it much easier than in the past to misappropriate because of the ready availability of digital cameras and, more important, the magnification effect of being able to reach a wide audience.

One of the best known misappropriation lawsuits is *Zacchini v. Scripps-Howard Broadcasting Co.*[15] Hugo Zacchini was a human cannonball who sued a local television station for broadcasting his entire fifteen-minute performance, thereby depriving him of revenue. The case was especially interesting because the TV station claimed First Amendment protection, but the courts ruled that the economic damage to Zacchini trumped the amendment in this case. This case and its prioritization of economic damages over the First Amendment could have interesting applications to the Internet, especially because digital video cameras are now so plentiful and video-sharing services like YouTube are so popular.

Intrusion

Intrusion upon seclusion is exactly what it sounds like, breaking in on someone's private space, either figuratively or literally. It's the only one of the four torts that doesn't require publication of private facts; simple invasion into someone's space is sufficient grounds to initiate a lawsuit. The rule of thumb is that the intrusion is actionable if it would be highly offensive to a reasonable person. Intrusion has two broad categories: an abstract encroachment into private matters or conversations and a purely physical trespass into a private place. Physical intrusion also includes wiretapping and hidden photography. In the modern age we can think of these offenses as trespassing and surveillance.

Intrusion had its foundation in the wrongful entry of private places; in an early case, a man entered an area where a woman was giving birth. From there the law has been extended and has been applied beyond places and spaces to include such intrusions as eavesdropping and using technologies like wiretaps, hidden cameras, and microphones.

Nowadays, the courts have to consider cell-phone interceptions. An example is the 2001 U.S. Supreme Court decision in *Bartnicki v. Vopper*. A radio personality broadcasted a tape given to him by an unidentified person. The tape contained an illegally intercepted cell-phone call between two union members. The radio commentator said that because the recording was newsworthy, it was shielded by the First Amendment. The court agreed (citing the Pentagon Papers, in part), stating that the media are well within their right to air matters of public interest and concern. Further, even if the information in question was collected illegally, it can be used as long as it was lawfully obtained from a third party. Supreme Court Justice Stephen Breyer wrote, "The Constitution permits legislatures to respond flexibly to the challenges new technology may pose to the individual's interest in basic personal privacy."[16]

The public interest is often used as a defense in intrusion cases. For example, in *Davis v. Temple* the plaintiff claimed that her privacy was invaded when she was questioned by a police officer about her husband's part in a criminal property-damage incident at her place of work. She sued both the police officer and the city, but lost when the court held that although intrusion upon seclusion was a viable cause of action, it failed because the criminal investigation was of interest to the public and of concern and therefore could not be considered private.[17]

A 1941 example involved the public disclosure of a debt. A man named Trammell owed money for groceries and was asked repeatedly to pay the bill. When he did not settle the account, his creditor gave him notice that he was preparing to publish an announcement in the local newspaper providing details of the debt and to run the notice until the debt was paid. Trammell asked both his creditor and the editor of the paper not to publish such information about his private affairs, but they did not comply. He sued for invasion of privacy. The court ruled that although the plaintiff did in fact owe the money, both the publisher and the creditor would have to pay Trammell damages and were liable on the grounds that the publication invaded the plaintiff's right to privacy, exposing him and his family to ridicule and public contempt.[18] This example could easily translate to slanderous web sites, even if their information is based on truthful circumstances; examples of such web sites include the many variations of the [fill in company name]sucks.com type.

The intrusion tort makes the media sweat; it poses special problems for reporters in that it questions the way they gather information. A highly publicized intrusion case was *Shulman v. Group W Publications*. Ruth Shulman was trapped in a car on a highway after an accident. (She later became a paraplegic.) While crying and begging to know whether her son, who was in the car with her, was okay, she was filmed by a television crew doing a show on emergency medical technicians. No one asked her for nor did she give her consent. Once she was in the rescue copter, a microphone-wielding nurse taped her as she screamed, yelling that she wanted to die. She later sued, claiming intrusion. The court ruled against her for the television taping, but allowed her to pursue a claim for the audiotaping. The court balanced the fact that she could have been overheard by others while in the car with the expectation that she would have some degree of privacy in her pain and anguish while talking to a nurse.[19] This tradeoff between possibly being observed versus the expectation of privacy is a recurrent theme in intrusion cases. Technology has become a game changer for privacy in part because, as we become accustomed to remote sensing technology like super-sensitive microphones and public surveillance cameras, a violator can argue that we have no expectation of privacy anyway and therefore there's no intrusion. What happens to the expectation of privacy when it becomes common knowledge that everyone is constantly under surveillance?

The guidelines for intrusion are not completely intuitive. Basically anything that happens in a public place can be recorded, at least by citizens (the Electronic Communications Privacy Act places some limits on the government's ability to record in public places). Cameras are okay. Under some circumstances, telephoto lenses are not, nor is sound-enhancing "big ear" equipment. Generally, if you can hear it or see it in a public place without special equipment, it's fair game, even if what you are doing can best be characterized as eavesdropping. Using a photo is, however, subject to some exceptions. Anything that happens in a private place with the expectations of privacy cannot be recorded. Although mail cannot be opened, it is legal to sift through garbage. Why? Expectations of privacy—garbage is thrown out without regard to the contents.

Perhaps the most famous intrusion case is *Galella v. Onassis*. Ron Galella was a paparazzo, a photographer who made his money candidly photographing celebrities. After Jacqueline Kennedy Onassis sued, the court granted her an injunction keeping Galella twenty-five feet away from her and her children.[20]

As in the Bartnicki case, intrusion is where privacy collides with the First Amendment. In *Dietemann v. Time Inc.*, the right to privacy superseded the First Amendment. A. A. Dietemann was a plumber who pretended to be a licensed doctor. A *Time* reporter posed as a client and, with the help of the district attorney, snuck into his home and used hidden recording equipment to prove that he was guilty. Dietemann was arrested and pleaded no contest, but later sued *Time* for invasion of privacy and won. The Ninth Circuit appeals court said, "The First Amendment has never been construed to accord newsmen immunity from torts or crimes committed during the course of newsgathering. The First Amendment is not a license to trespass, to steal, or to intrude by electronic means into the precincts of another's home or office."[21]

The First Amendment and the protection against intrusion are headed for a constant clash in the near future; the combatants will be the media versus private citizens. Former executive director of the First Amendment Center, Ken Paulson, has said, "The challenge is to hold invasive technology at bay without handcuffing the news media. Concerns about personal privacy and a free press are on a collision course, and our nation's priorities hang in the balance."[22]

Think about the *Cops* television show. The Supreme Court has upheld the sanctity of a private home when the police arrive with a media ride-along. In both *Wilson v. Layne* and *Hanlon v. Berger*, the court ruled that it was unconstitutional for the press to enter private homes with the police.[23]

Intrusion will also be the basis for many future electronic privacy law-suits. Liam Youens used Docusearch, an Internet search firm, to obtain the SSN and work address for Amy Lynn Boyer, a young woman he had been obsessed with since high school. Docusearch got the information by calling Boyer and using a technique called pre-texting, which is the practice of collecting information about a person under false pretenses. Youens waited for her until she left work, at the address that Docusearch provided, then shot her and killed himself. Boyer's mother sued Docusearch for invasion of privacy through intrusion upon seclusion. The New Hampshire court allowed the law-suit, ruling that these kinds of services can be liable for what's done with the information they sell.[24] This ruling could have a significant impact on database companies that sell our personal information because of the potential for their getting hit with damages.

Our technology-driven world has created privacy concerns that courts have never had to address; this trend will continue with the proliferation of smaller, cheaper, and more powerful mobile communications and pervasive computing devices. How will personal privacy be maintained alongside freedom of the press and the public's right to know?

In *Lake v. Wal-Mart Stores, Inc.*, three young women from Dilworth, a small Minnesota farming town, took a spring vacation in Mexico. While there, one of them took a picture of the other two in the shower together. When they returned home, they took the film to a Wal-Mart store for processing. The store refused to print all the pictures be-cause of the "nature of their content." Later on, it became obvious that others in the town had seen the pictures that supposedly were not printed, and the girls began to be harassed about their sexual ori-entation. It turned out that a Wal-Mart employee had been showing the pictures to other employees, and the shower shot had been mak-ing its way around the town.[25] The plaintiffs won. This case held a third-party custodian of personal information accountable for its handling of second-party personal data. I would expect to see suits like this brought against picture- and video-sharing services like Yahoo, YouTube, and Flickr if they leak personal information, even though their terms and conditions may state that they're not liable.

Private Facts

In intrusion, the act itself is the violation. In the tort of private facts, the publication of information whose intimate nature would greatly offend a reasonable person, the information that's revealed constitutes the privacy harm. Private facts is the only privacy action that can be defended by proving that the allegation is true. As in the other privacy cases, consent negates the ability to sue. Additionally, if the information is publicly disclosed by the individual, it is no longer a private fact; it's now in the public domain. The published information must thus be truly private for a private-facts lawsuit to be successful, and the plaintiff is required to prove that the private information published is not of legitimate concern to the public.

The issue here is what constitutes private information; the courts have rejected numerous private-facts cases because the disclosed information was contained in a public record. For example, a federal district court in Texas rejected a private-facts claim made against CBS, which had released information about a lottery winner's family, particularly the allegation that one of the daughters was sexually abused. In the 2002 decision, *Green v. CBS, Inc.*, the court stated that because the information was included in divorce proceedings, it was part of the public record.[26] When Oliver Sipple sued Chronicle Publishing in 1984 for broadcasting that he was a homosexual after he had prevented the assassination of Gerald Ford, he was unsuccessful. The court ruled that because Sipple was active in the San Francisco gay community, the information was not private; it was deemed newsworthy and part of the public domain.[27]

Information technology has the potential to make it increasingly difficult to sue using this tort because of the growing amount of information that is now becoming available publicly. The public record today is many times larger than the public record ten years ago. The public record ten years from now will be enormous and will probably include many new sources of information such as feeds from surveillance cameras, tax records, or travel history.

This particular privacy tort is of great concern to many First and Fourteenth Amendment advocates because the invasion-of-privacy claim can be made even if the information is true. The First Amendment guarantees the rights of freedom of speech, religion, and press. The Fourteenth Amendment binds the states to uphold the Bill of Rights. In 1975 in *Cox Broadcasting Corporation v. Cohn*, the U.S. Supreme Court ruled that the media could not be held liable for publishing the name of a rape victim who died in the attack because the news team had obtained the name from public records and therefore did not invade the family's privacy.[28] The high court claimed it was the constitutional freedoms of speech and press that were at stake, principles it again upheld in its 1979 decision in *Smith v. Daily Mail Publishing Co.*, saying, "State action to punish the publication of truthful information can seldom satisfy constitutional standards."[29]

Generally speaking, the courts have held that any public document such as a court record is fair game for the press and is no longer private. As cut and dried as this definition probably looked in the past, it's ambiguous today because of technology. What is a public document in the Information Age? Who are the press?

The social value of the information and the extent to which the individual voluntarily sought public notoriety can both be taken into consideration by the courts when determining newsworthiness. In *Garner v. Triangle Publications, Inc.*, a reporter wrote a story about a woman who was in an auto accident and incidentally mentioned that she was living with a man who was not her husband. The woman sued, using the private-facts defense, and won because the information was not considered relevant to the story.[30] In another case, a woman sued for invasion of privacy when a newspaper published on the front page a photograph it took of her without her consent. The picture showed the plaintiff with her dress blowing up, exposing parts of her body. The Supreme Court ruled in favor of the plaintiff, dismissing the newspaper's argument that the photograph was taken in a public place, because the publication would embarrass anyone of reasonable sensitivity.[31] Several sites on the Internet that publish amateur photos might fall afoul of this ruling.

Medical information is one of the best-protected categories of personal information. There have been some well-publicized breaches, mostly from third-party data handlers. Over the years, many plaintiffs have used the private-facts tort as a basis for successfully winning lawsuits involving the disclosure of confidential medical information.

> One of the leading private-facts cases is the landmark 1942 case *Barber v. Time.* The magazine ran pictures and published a story about Dorothy Barber, a compulsive overeater who checked into the General Hospital in Kansas City. She claimed that her privacy was invaded when a reporter and photographer came to her hospital room without her consent to conduct an interview and to take pictures. *Time* picked up the story and published it with a humorous slant, headlining it "Starving Glutton" because the plaintiff was unable to gain any weight although she ate and ate. When Barber won the case, *Time* appealed in the Supreme Court of Missouri, which upheld the jury verdict. The court reasoned that information concerning an individual's medical treatment is intrinsic in the right to privacy, particularly when collected during a time of illness and without consent.[32]

False Light

Private-facts suits are about the unapproved release of private information; false-light claims deal with information that makes someone look bad. The tort of false light is usually described as publicizing highly offensive information that portrays someone in an erroneous and negative way. False light is often confused with defamation, although for an offense to qualify as defamation, it must meet the more stringent requirement of reputational damage, whereas false light is usually used to cover emotional distress.

> The classically cited case involves a swimming pig. A Texas woman who performed in an aquatic park with pigs sued *Chic* magazine for publishing her picture without her direct consent. Although the pictures were official and true, the article implied that there was something deviant about her performance. She won.[33]

Although the accusation of false light is often used against the press, it could be extended to blogs. Because many people claim that blogs should be treated as if they are press, they might end up being held to a higher standard than they now are. One of the problems with amateur publishers like web sites is that they're likely to fall into these kinds of liability traps because they have small staffs compared with print publications—indeed, the low cost is one of the attractions; as a result authors publish directly to the web without the kind of editorial and legal review common in the print media.

A significant Supreme Court ruling on false light was triggered by a story written by Hollywood wunderkind Joe Eszterhas (*Basic Instinct, Showgirls*) while he was a reporter for the *Cleveland Plain Dealer*.[34] He wrote a human-interest piece about a local tragedy, the collapse of the Silver Bridge into the Ohio River, an accident that killed forty-four people. Eszterhas's story dealt with the funeral of a coal miner killed in the accident, Melvin Cantrell. The story was well received, and Eszterhas decided to do a freelance follow-up story. He traveled to West Virginia to visit the Cantrell house. Unfortunately the mother was not home when he arrived, so he spoke to the children. When Eszterhas wrote the article, he made it appear as though he had interviewed the widow, even describing the look on her face and how she refused to speak to him and made the children talk instead: "Margaret Cantrell will talk neither about what happened nor about how they are doing. She wears the same mask of non-expression she wore at the funeral. She is a proud woman. Her world has changed. She says that after it happened, the people in town offered to help them out with money and they refused to take it."[35]

The article emphasized how shabby the house was and that the family was poor, and it contained many other factual inaccuracies. The family sued both Eszterhas and the newspaper that published the story. Although they initially won, the family lost on appeal, with the court citing the higher need of freedom of the press. However, in 1974 the Supreme Court stepped in and ruled in favor of the Cantrells, stating that the defendant reporter was liable because he knowingly used false statements that put the family in a bad light; the publisher was also vicariously liable because it employed Eszterhas.[36]

Protections in the Constitution and Federal Laws

Privacy does have tenuous roots in the Constitution, although the Constitution is more often cited as a protection for personal decisions, as in *Roe v. Wade*. The Bill of Rights (the name commonly given to the first ten amendments to the Constitution) is interpreted by the courts in such a way as to provide some privacy protection. The First Amendment implicitly protects the right of association. The Fourth Amendment protects privacy in the home by ensuring against unreasonable searches and seizures by government agents. The Ninth was cited by the Supreme Court in its landmark decision in *Griswold v. Connecticut*, which struck down a Connecticut ban on contraceptives; the court found that the state law infringed on the right of marital privacy.[37] Writing for the majority, Justice William Douglas claimed that "specific guarantees in the Bill of Rights have penumbras, formed by emanations from those guarantees that help give them life and substance."[38] The word *liberty* in the Fourteenth Amendment's due-process clause is often used as a general protection for privacy because it obligates the states to comply with restrictions imposed on the federal government by the Bill of Rights. Otherwise each state could create completely different criminal-law environments for privacy; their doing so would be a problem today because Internet companies are rarely in the same states as all their users.

The Fourth and Fifth Amendments often come up in connection with privacy intrusions and new technology such as encryption or DNA mapping because the traditional constitutional requirements for due process, notification, and protection against self-incrimination have been steadily weakened by the courts through increasingly narrowed interpretations, including interpretations of some provisions of the Patriot Act. New guidelines in this act changed the way FBI special agents gather information for terrorism investigations. Agents have always been allowed to collect data from publicly available information, but the Patriot Act made it easier for them to get to email and other private forms of communication as well as commercial databases. They are also able to "review intelligence and law enforcement information from all agencies of government," without probable cause.[39]

The Freedom of Information Act (FOIA) was the first law to give everyone (U.S. citizens, corporations, non-Americans), the right to access records of federal agencies. For example, Vietnam War veterans' groups used FOIA in 1979 to access Department of Defense records for information on the defoliants used in Agent Orange. Under FOIA, federal agencies are required to disclose records when they receive a written request from any person. (Information can be withheld in accordance with the nine exemptions and three exclusions that were added to the statute.) FOIA does not apply to congressional records, court proceedings, or anything held by state or local government agencies. The Privacy Act of 1974 was passed as an amendment to FOIA after the Watergate scandal rocked the nation and other FBI domestic-spying abuses made national headlines. The Electronic Freedom of Information Act

Amendments of 1996 require federal agencies to maintain an FOIA web page.

The Privacy Act requires that individuals be given notice when information is collected about them. Citizens and legal permanent residents also have the right to examine the data that government has collected about them and to make corrections. Government agencies can now legally store only information that is relevant and necessary and can collect only data that are directly relevant to their mission—in principle. In practice, it's become difficult to use the Privacy Act for protection when the government claims that national security is involved. The act contains major exceptions for intelligence and law-enforcement personnel along with provisions allowing government agencies to obtain a variety of information from private corporations. For example, as discussed in detail later in this chapter, if a governmental agency is merely accessing a commercial database, the records are not subject to requirements laid out in the Privacy Act unless the information is subsequently stored in a federal database. This government purchasing of commercial information is discussed in more detail in Chapter Eight.

Some extremely narrow privacy laws have been enacted to cover notorious cases. The Driver's Privacy Protection Act of 1994 was created in response to the murder of Rebecca Schaefer in 1989. The actress was killed by an obsessed fan who had hired a private detective to obtain her address from the California Department of Motor Vehicles (DMV). The law now prohibits state DMV employees from releasing information of a personal nature. Unfortunately, the law was diluted by fourteen exemptions, including use by any government agency; matters relating to vehicle safety and recalls; market-research activities; insurance reports; and, believe it or not, access to the information by a licensed private investigator. The act was amended in 1999, when Congress gave drivers increased control over their information by eliminating the opt-out provision for marketing unless a driver gave written consent for records to be released and sold.

Similar diluted legislation will be passed as technology-based privacy abuses proliferate. Generally, Congress avoids the issue until a high-profile case, usually involving a woman or a child, is splashed all over the media. With fanfare, legislators pass a bill that appears to stop the problem, but somewhere along the way the legislation is watered down with exemptions that often benefit specific industries or, in some cases, the politicians themselves. The highly touted "Don't Call" registry created in 2005 by the Federal Trade Commission (FTC) to stop calls from telemarketers has an interesting exemption—political solicitations. According to the FTC's web site, these are not considered telemarketing.

At its heart, technology is about business. Computer innovation is almost always driven by business needs, not government funding— or it has been since the early 1990s anyway. Companies hire lobbyists and make political contributions to ensure that a particular piece of legislation doesn't gut their business. Because of these special relationships, it's hard to believe that Congress will enact significantly broad privacy legislation without prodding by the public, the media, and the courts.

Government Outsourcing and Connections to Private-Sector Data Collection

The federal government creates, uses, and disseminates more information than any other organization in the country, perhaps in the world. Included in the thousands of databases maintained by the federal government are a huge FBI database containing hundreds of millions of records, a Treasury Department database of financial information with records from thousands of financial institutions, an enormous Department of Education depository that contains the complete educational record for every individual, a "new hires" database in the Department of Health and Human Services that provides the wages of everyone working in the United States, along with names, addresses, and SSNs.

> In 2003, ChoicePoint Inc. and Reed Elsevier Inc., owner of LexisNexis, were sued for violating the privacy of Florida motorists when they bought personal data from the state and resold it. The class-action suit, seeking billions of dollars in damages, began when a Florida man claimed that the companies illegally obtained his DMV records. Both lawsuits were voluntarily withdrawn the same year, although a spokesperson for the state acknowledged that the laws in Florida do not conform strictly to the federal requirements for disclosure.[40]

Controlling governmental use of personal information is a critical part of the privacy-protection process. A disturbing trend is governmental use of a loophole in the privacy laws to increase outsourcing and privatization; as a result commercial firms can now do things that they would have been barred from doing in the past. As far back as 1962, David Bell, President John F. Kennedy's budget director, voiced his concerns about the federal government's increasing dependence on private contractors.[41] Outsourcing of government services is growing faster than ever as federal agencies such as the IRS continue to contract out their data-collection projects in multimillion-dollar contracts.

Private-sector data surveillance is currently big business and is increasingly becoming the means by which government accesses information on individuals. The unfortunate reality is that information collected for one purpose will undoubtedly be used for multiple others. If the records were paper, it wouldn't be a problem because it would be too much work to copy the information elsewhere. Unfortunately most government agencies can now cram all their information onto disks that would fit inside a single briefcase. Consumer and marketing information is considered a valuable commodity. As a result, any and all consumer activities are tracked and documented for the money they can bring in, and the government can buy and integrate into its own computer systems the resulting large, restriction-free pool of information on citizens. The data are so easy to transport and fit into federal databases that any practical restriction based on logistics has been lifted; so, absent any legal barriers, public agencies are free, are even encouraged, to buy outside information and use it along with their own restricted information.

For example, data-aggregator companies like ChoicePoint, LocatePLUS, Seisint, LexisNexis, and Acxiom compile millions of detailed records on individuals that they then sell to other companies and government agencies. The companies acquire data such as birth dates, up-to-date credit-bureau files, current and prior addresses, phone numbers, known aliases, SSNs, military records, voter rolls, motor-vehicle registrations, liens, and mortgage information. The information is collected from both official public records and unverified private sources and is bundled together for sale. Much of the data these companies collect and maintain could be considered illegal for government agencies to have in their databases or at least be considered subject to disclosure. Privacy provisions built into the Privacy Act of 1974 prohibited the government from maintaining information on citizens not considered the focus of a criminal investigation, but that act has now been trumped by the Patriot Act. In addition, the government has no assurance that the data are accurate and is not required to correct errors, as stated in the Privacy Act.

One key advantage for government agencies is the time saved by using commercial databases. For example, the FBI can access the data in real time and accelerate investigations. Instead of taking days to collect information on a case and using up valuable people hours to do it, agents can get the data they need in minutes online. Using private-sector databases to acquire information on individuals allows the federal government to get the data it wants while not actually creating the files itself, an act that would be a clear violation of the Privacy Act of 1974. The FBI is not the only government agency using the services of companies like ChoicePoint.

Many agencies, including the CIA and the IRS along with state and local governments, are also their clients.

The Computer Matching and Privacy Protection Act, with which Congress amended the Privacy Act in 1988, establishes procedural guidelines and requirements for agencies to follow before and after matching electronic records. In 1990, Congress amended the act to further clarify provisions and to address problems that federal agencies were having with implementation. The problem is that commercial companies that collect and aggregate personal information are not restricted like the government. The data-marketing industry is not well regulated, and data companies often provide poor security for their records. The Federal Information Security Management Act of 2002 was enacted as a means of strengthening network security for federal agencies and also for government contractors by mandating yearly audits. The act also focuses on Internet security, which is often overlooked and neglected in many agencies. Security is tightly related to privacy. When security is bad, data can be hacked or stolen, with the resulting negative impact on the subject's privacy.

Government is also entering into partnerships with private companies like Accenture, blurring the public and private lines further. In May 2004, the Homeland Security Department awarded Accenture a ten-year technology contract worth $10 billion to create a "virtual" border around the United States. The project gives the company unparalleled access to the personal information of travelers, yet the company is completely unanswerable to the public for the results, intended or otherwise.[42] Because Accenture is an offshore company with headquarters in Bermuda, it may be out of legal range. The public does not have enough information about these types of outsourcing arrangements and what, if any, penalties could be levied if a lack of security leads to privacy invasion.

The only way to stop such practices is to make them illegal or at least highly restricted. The first step toward achieving this end would be forcing the government to disclose any and all data-sharing or purchasing arrangements that it's made with companies, other agencies, or even other governments. In some special circumstances a deal may need to be protected for security reasons, but extending such protection should be the exception, not the rule, and should be subject to congressional oversight. Another useful law would hold government workers personally liable if they break the rules regarding handling of consumers' personal information.

Contractual Protections and Privacy Policies

Almost all web sites use privacy policies to establish how the vendor will handle customers' data. But these policies are usually written by corporate lawyers, and consequently they are effectively useless as protection against misuse of customer data by the company. Generally speaking, companies do not agree to do or not do anything with the customers' data beyond the minimum necessary to avoid a public outcry. Occasionally, a business slips up and promises to protect a customer's information. In this case, the consumer has the right to sue based on breach of contract. Sometimes a consumer can interest the FTC in getting involved and filing a class-action suit against the offending company on behalf of the user community. The nonprofit group Privacy & American Business is regularly tracking almost 150 consumer privacy-violation lawsuits.[43] The limitations to contractual remedies are, first, the company has to be willing to give up its overwhelmingly favorable position in regard to usage of customer data and, second, a contract binds only the signatory parties, not a third party. Once personal information has gotten out to someone else, that business cannot be held accountable for the information's disposition (although the second party can, for letting the information get out in the first place). It's an odd fact of the database-driven business world that customer information is often worth more sold than used for the originally stated purpose. The multitude of legal cases and press stories of companies in every imaginable business show how profitable selling these kinds of data can be. Networks are fast enough that most of these data can be transported directly across the Internet; because the costs involved in the transfer are almost zero, these sales are pure profit. Every consumer company in the Western world today is also in the database business, whether it realizes it or not.

> *FTC v. Toysmart.com* was filed in July 2000 to block the bankrupt online toy store from selling its customer data to a third party and thereby violating its own privacy policy.[44] Toysmart and its parent company, Disney, listed the database of 250,000 names, addresses, and shopping preferences for sale when it went out of business. A settlement was reached early in 2001, when the company agreed to destroy the customer list. Later that year, Massachusetts Attorney General Tom Reilly prevented the bankrupt Essential.com Inc. from selling the personal information of its seventy thousand Internet customers.[45]

On May 25, 2001, the Electronic Privacy Information Center filed a complaint with the FTC against eTour for selling personal customer information to a third party, AskJeeves.com.[46] In its privacy policy, eTour stated that it would not sell customer data. Sears was sued the same year for violating its privacy policy when it allegedly sold confidential customer information to a marketing firm.[47]

In September 2004, Procter & Gamble, Aventis, Bristol-Myers Squibb, Pfizer, and others were sued along with Albertson's pharmacy division for violating the privacy rights of customers. The supermarket giant had unlawfully used confidential customer prescription data to conduct marketing campaigns on behalf of the pharmaceutical companies.[48] In a similar case, Eckerd was sued for using intrusive marketing practices that resulted in privacy-law violations.[49]

A case involving JetBlue Airways made headlines in 2003. The company provided a Defense Department contractor, Torch Concepts, with five million passenger names, addresses, phone numbers, and flight itineraries. A class-action lawsuit filed against JetBlue and its partners claimed they had sold the information without permission, resulting in privacy violations. The airline was told the information would be used in a study to identify high-risk airline customers. What it wasn't told was that the information would be coupled with demographic data obtained from Acxiom: income levels, gender, length of time at a residence, financial profiles, and SSNs. The resulting passenger profiles were very detailed, and one ended up on the Internet for a short time as part of a conference presentation put together by Torch Concepts.[50] In August 2005, a federal judge agreed that JetBlue Airways had violated its own privacy policy by selling personal customer data to a third party, but the judge dismissed the lawsuit on the grounds that there was no proof that damages resulted from the actions of the airline or that it "unjustly enriched itself" from the sale of the data.

Absent any ethical qualms on the part of selling-company executives, the only effective protection for consumers against misuse of their information and violations of their privacy will be direct legal prohibitions. Too much money is involved to trust industry self-regulation, and too many industries are involved; large companies with many business lines often pool their customer data in centralized databases. Regulation by contract isn't an effective long-term solution because, besides the fact that most privacy policies are written to be ineffective, companies merge, get acquired, and buy each other. Our private information is not deleted during these transactions but traded and treated as a commodity. After the information has changed hands a few times, any original restrictions attached to the data will be long since separated from the information that they refer to and forgotten.

In addition to the malicious misuse of personal data by corporations, poor security often results in the illegal release of customer information. Currently, companies usually avoid informing customers when personal records and credit-card numbers are stolen, unless state law forces them to disclose the breach. The FTC would like Congress to consider instituting a mandatory requirement that all businesses storing personal information notify customers when security is breached. I would like to see Congress go further and levy variable fines for data mishandling that results in exposure of consumers' private information.

Acxiom, the world's largest data aggregator, maintains a database with records on 96 percent of U.S. households. The company has banks, automakers, credit-card issuers, and the U.S. government as clients. Although in the past it kept its servers in firewalled, protected vaults, Acxiom had omitted to encrypt its customer data, a serious breach of security. The company had its servers hacked twice, once in March 2003 and again in August 2004, when millions of records were compromised. The company promptly changed password and access procedures, hired a privacy officer, and began testing encryption packages.[51]

Many other companies have disclosed security breaches, including CardSystems Solutions, Wachovia, and Ameritrade. When Bank of America lost some of its backup tapes containing personal account information, it was able to quickly notify law enforcement and affected customers, flag compromised accounts, and monitor for suspicious activity because it is one of the few companies that has a contingency plan.[52] In June 2005, a class-action lawsuit was filed against Citigroup for a breach of privacy. It had lost nonencrypted computer tapes that held the sensitive personal information of almost four million current and former customers.[53]

In February and March 2005, it was announced that both ChoicePoint and LexisNexis had been hacked the previous year; identifiable information for more that a hundred thousand people had been exposed, including their SSNs, credit-card information, and bank records. Hundreds were defrauded because of the security breach. Customers in California were sent warning letters about the identity theft because at the time it was the only state that required companies to disclose security breaches; individuals in other states initially had no idea their information was compromised. Other states are getting on the bandwagon by passing new laws requiring companies to notify customers when their financial or personal records are lost or stolen.[54] Washington, North Dakota, Arkansas, and Georgia passed laws in 2005, and Montana's privacy law came into effect in 2006. Legislation passed in Indiana (2005) requires notification of individuals if their SSNs are exposed.

Privacy Law Needs Updating

The good news is that there is legal protection for privacy. The bad news is that it doesn't work particularly well. As we have seen, the courts have interpreted some of the Bill of Rights to cover privacy. Some narrow legislation has been enacted, but with loopholes. The most effective way right now to assert privacy rights legally is to either sue in a civil court using one of the four privacy torts or if you're lucky enough to have a contract, sue for breach.

The legal state of privacy is in flux because of technology. Data no longer sit in a lockable file cabinet. They shift, flowing across state lines, moving from computer to computer and network to network. Even when a law is created that constrains a second party's use of your data, a third party can do whatever it wants. As a result, custodial lines are being crossed. The government buys commercial data; companies get access to government information. Our personal information is valuable and, without explicit prohibitions, will be sold. In some cases, the right to privacy is at odds with other rights, such as those protected by the First Amendment; thus consumers are pitted against the press, free speech is pitted against privacy. These balances can be upset when technology makes it easy to eavesdrop or to remotely videotape people.

An obvious place for legal modernization is in regard to blogs and podcasts, or, collectively, the blogosphere. The courts have always been careful to carve out special niches for the media, protecting them from too onerous privacy laws in the general interests of society. The obvious question then becomes, What are the media?

The lines have blurred. Quasi-journalists like Matt Drudge almost brought down a president; amateur political commentators like Wonkette become major voices during a presidential election; and pseudo-reporters like Jon Stewart of the *Daily Show* and Steven Colbert of the *Colbert Report* have become the primary news source for a significant percentage of the U.S. population.[55]

Some technology is easier to address legally than others. Anything that is an improvement over an existing media capability should presumably be protected by the same statutes. For instance, case law affecting live television coverage should also cover live Internet broadcasting. Some technology creates new problems with no existing referents and thus no case law. These will be the tough cases because it will take either congressional action or Supreme Court decisions made on constitutional grounds to lay the foundation for future legal actions.

Many people seem to believe that the government is doing or will do something to protect their privacy, but, in fact, current privacy law is not comprehensive. Privacy legislation coming out of Congress usually has too many escape clauses to be broadly useful. Incremental rulings will not work to create a comprehensive privacy environment because of the fast-paced evolution of technology. Willful violators will easily be able to make some small change in an engineering implementation and thereby circumvent narrow laws and rulings and head us further into legally uncharted waters with this new product. What's needed most are sweeping privacy principles on which to build the next few decades of privacy law. We need a Brandeis of the Information Age who can bring privacy law into the twenty-first century. The U.S. Constitution has the seeds of a comprehensive privacy policy but needs enlightened interpretation by technologically savvy judges.

Chapter Six addresses identity—one of the changing concepts underlying a topical definition of privacy that make writing good privacy laws difficult.

6

Privacy and Identity
The Cult of Me

On the Internet, no one knows that you're a dog.
Peter Steiner[1]

Who am I? Am I just a name or the sum of my background facts, or am I a set of opinions and interests? Prior to the Information Age, these types of questions were not asked or even considered much. Technology makes it possible to tease identity apart, so that I can create an online identity that reflects my beliefs but is disassociated from my real name, address, and other identifying information. The problem is that the more of my self that I invest in one of these identities, the greater the harm to me if my reputation suffers.

Each persona that I create using technology increases the chances that I will suffer such a privacy violation. I've spread my ego across the Internet; I'm such-and-such on eBay and so-and-so on Amazon, and I have a Facebook account under an alias and a page on MySpace, and every game that I play incorporates another incarnation of me. Each of these avatars, virtual representations, is me. This is one of those great generational differences: baby boomers believe that creating these online identities is role-playing, like living in a fantasyland. Gen Xers know better: these alternate worlds are as real as themselves. In some ways, the physical world, where you have to get dressed to go to work and make small talk at Starbucks and pretend that you know something about current events instead of that new CD that you'd really like to talk about, is the fake one.

Each of these online roles that I adopt is another opportunity to lose my privacy. Perhaps someone deliberately outs me. Perhaps my favorite eBay account has gotten so much negative feedback that I'm viewed as untrustworthy. Perhaps someone has trash-talked about me enough on a dating site that I have to start all over again. Technology gives us the ability to have these identities and, in the process, adds new ways to have our privacy violated.

Identities

Email addresses. Instant Messenger screen names. Aliases. Handles. User IDs. Pseudonyms. It's not easy finding someone with many online roles and corresponding in a cyber neighborhood. You have to be memorable to stand out. That's why people with established online identities fight so hard to keep them. Reputation is the currency of the Internet; a guy's well-known and trusted persona is valuable because his blog posts are read, he's trusted in online auctions, his book reviews carry weight, and he gets VIP treatment in multiplayer games. Regardless of who he is in the real world, if his online identity is sullied, he has to start over. Privacy violations related to his identity are harmful because their net effect is to damage his reputation and in the process destroy his persona. He may have many years invested in that identity and would find it problematic to start all over again.

Identities are what privacy is all about. It's impossible to understand the shifting nature of privacy and why it is being destabilized by technology without having an idea of how our identities are also changing in response to technology. Privacy is about controlling information about ourselves, even if what we're trying to protect isn't true, especially if it isn't true. Sometimes our online personas may be different enough from our true self that the real privacy violation would be for someone to expose this anomaly. Some people gender-switch on the Internet, for example. Some people may feel that those who misrepresent themselves in that way deserve the consequences, but the social context is more complex than that. Sometimes people are role-playing, but some people act more real online than they are able to in the physical world. On the Internet, you're only what you say you are.

I've been using the Internet and email for a long time, and I've noticed that people often act differently online than they do in real life. Aggressive people act passively, meek people show rage, superficial people show sensitivity. At first I thought that adopting different characteristics was some kind of role-playing and fantasy fulfillment, but now I think that it's deeper and more meaningful. I think that we're creating new identities on the Net, and technology has made it possible to keep them from intruding on our real life, thus preserving our bubble of freedom.

Privacy for online alter egos involves compartmentalization, so what affects one identity doesn't necessarily affect another. Any erosion of these barriers, such as outing, is a privacy violation. Identity is what is violated when our online privacy is disturbed.

Each of us can be located in different ways, according to different addressing schemes. Look at how the size of a single entry in an address book has grown. The basics of name, address, and work and home phone numbers have expanded to include cell-phone number, home email address, work email address, and AIM, Messenger, web, and Skype numbers. We usually get to choose our own handles, user log-ins, passwords, and aliases on different web sites. Some of these are just numbers and are meaningless. Some are personal and reflect an aspect of our personality that we're proud of.

These names have become part of our identity. The permanent ones last forever, and the temporary ones often become permanent. I've had one email address for fifteen years, and I know people who've had them longer than that. We attach an emotional importance to these labels in direct proportion to how reliant we become on them. Watch people arguing at the DMV when forced to give up their vanity plates. I saw a similar phenomenon while I was the chief technology officer (CTO) at Network Solutions, where I was in charge of the Domain Name System (DNS) during the latter half of the 1990s. We were deluged with phone calls from and sued monthly by people who wanted a domain name that someone else already had. Some of this squabbling was motivated by legitimate business issues, but much of it was driven by preferences—people just liked certain names.

Locating someone in cyberspace is different from locating someone in the real world; there's no comprehensive phone book, for example. As new technology is deployed, new identity schemes come into play, and every new web site requires a new user name. It would be nice to use the same name everywhere, but that's not possible because someone else might have used it first. This need for uniqueness coupled with a lack of a universal naming scheme forces us to be creative when choosing names.

Understanding identity is necessary for understanding privacy because most invasions threaten the target's self: sometimes the target's finances, sometimes her dignity, but often the core of who she is and what she stands for. Our identity is our attributes, our identifiers, our likes, our dislikes, what others think of us, and what we think of them. The Internet gives us the ability to segment these parts of an identity that is aggregated in the real world and to bundle complementary pieces together. If I have an Amazon account that I use only to buy and review books about cooking, the fact that I'm a technologist never has to enter into that identity. It's irrelevant to that persona and how others might react to me. As our years of experience online start piling up, we will, of necessity, start accumulating these special-purpose identities, each of which will be us, but a special part of us. This splitting of a personality has some deep psychological ramifications that I'm not qualified to go into, but it's freeing to play in a computer game where the fact that I may be a writer is irrelevant or to express a political opinion in a forum without anyone making any judgments because of my appearance or my sexuality or my ethnicity or my gender. This is the information about my online self that I want most to control. If I'm outed, it will be by me. Any wresting away of control or abuse or stealing of my information is a violation of my privacy, my virtual privacy.

Virtual Identity Needs Virtual Privacy

Technology has split our identity into many targets that can be attacked. We are at the stage in the evolution of networked computers where our self has become fragmented through the prism of technology and emerges as glints of personality. But each online reflection is just as much us as is our corporeal self, even more so in some cases because we invest these online personas with genuine interests and opinions without holding back for fear of real-world retribution. In the physical world, if we screw up badly enough, our poor reputation will follow us everywhere. Even moving out of town to start over again doesn't work as well as it used to; it certainly doesn't fix a bad credit report. This fear of reputational damage keeps us acting in certain ways in the real world. The online world allows us to emphasize one aspect of our personality, ignoring the rest, and not have any problems bleed over into other personas. This compartmentalization is immensely freeing. At some level all privacy protections, both online and offline, are about freedom: freedom of expression, freedom of speech, freedom to be creative.

This prismatic effect has been a form of protection for our privacy, like anonymity. Many people treated the fledgling Internet as a microcomputer Mardi Gras, where they could dress up and act out secret fantasies to their hearts' content. Many others used these identities carefully, to engage in debate or to expand their social life. Most important, the anonymity provided a freedom of sorts with no repercussions. This good-natured anarchy was the basis for the original culture of the Internet and exists today on the World Wide

Web. The core premise of virtual identities is like the Las Vegas slogan, "What you do here, stays here."

If your name is William and you want to present yourself as a woman, you can hop onto a web site and become Wilhelmina. This ad hoc polymorphism bothers a lot of people. Any guy who's ever talked to a virtual woman in a chat room has a hard time flushing the image of a naked, sweaty fat man out of his mind the first time it occurs to him to question his good luck. Yet one of the benefits of these personas is the lack of real-world impact on the person using them. Wilhelmina can turn off her computer and return to being William, without anyone being the wiser. Technology allows him to gender-change. His or her privacy is protected.

But this alchemy is rapidly changing, partly because of the government's actions in response to security concerns, partly because of commercial marketing efforts, but mostly because the technology has improved. Google can out someone faster than a right-wing newspaper. It's possible to automate cross-connections among various identities and pierce most veils by using search techniques. I've never heard of anyone doing it, but it's certainly feasible for large-scale search and custom-matching software to automatically cross-match and harvest pseudonymous identities. Google could probably do it, as could the government. The government probably does.

As people spend more of their community life on the Internet, they will adopt personas that are appropriate for what they're doing. An online gaming identity shouldn't necessarily be discussing religion, politics, or work. That identity exists only for the universe of the game. Any personality attribute relevant to the real-world person that has no relevance to the game is immaterial. Any reputational or legal penalties levied for expressing an opinion should be limited to that online world, not follow the person into the real one. It would be like finishing a game of Monopoly and being asked to cover the fake dollars with real ones. It takes away the fun of playing. Many social activities available online would take on a more somber, even ominous, tone than they now have if the virtual identities were publicly associated with real names and addresses. In the case of blogs and forums, part of the appeal to many of the writers is their ability to speak their mind without looking over their shoulder to see whether they've jeopardized their job or conflicted with their political party's or church's official line. Any disparity between attribution and retribution will act as a brake on free speech, by threatening privacy violations as punishment. One way to avoid this problem is to be anonymous. The closer the online identity gets to the real one, the greater the potential damage to privacy. A tradeoff on these identities in the coming years will be deciding between having a fully authenticated identity and being completely anonymous. Pseudonymity is the middle ground.

Anonymity Versus Authentication

A dichotomy exists between the opposing positions of anonymity and fully authenticated identity, with vocal champions gleefully taking up each side. Anonymity, it's argued, is necessary to protect freedom of speech. How do you protect the participants of a sensitive support group, such as cancer survivors, pharmaceutical test patients, or disabled war veterans from public exposure or unwanted attention? Anything less than full anonymity leaves open the possibility of full disclosure. Merchants claim that e-commerce requires the full authentication of every person and every transaction. The government insists that terrorism can be prevented only by obtaining complete information about potential terrorists: shopping, travel, and communications.

A privacy battle is shaping up over this conflict between completely public, fully-attributed actions and anonymous activities and speech. There are three broad categories of online involvement, and each treats identity differently: financial transactions, browsing, and communication. Each has different parameters and requires differing amounts of user identification. Much of the controversy and confusion comes from mashing together these areas and trying to wrap them up with a single, convergent naming policy.

Our nascent, yet burgeoning online life needs a spectrum of authentication options. Sometimes, as with financial purchases, we have to give real-world information like our name, address, and credit-card number. Without them, how can merchants charge us, and where will they ship the purchase? Sometimes we want to go on a web site and ask a question or make a quick comment. We don't want to give up any real information because it might be embarrassing, and we don't want to be bothered with making up a lot of fake information just to get a user ID for a one-time use; we want to use the service anonymously. Sometimes when we engage with a site, for some of the previously described reasons, we don't want to use our real name, yet we don't want to be anonymous because we want to establish a history and a reputation. Then we use pseudonyms because anonymity does not enhance our reputation. We need to use each of these schemes where they're appropriate.

Financial Transactions Need Authentication

Full authentication is easiest to defend for financial dealings. As mentioned above, credit-card companies need real information to validate a purchase. The IRS would undoubtedly take a dim view of large anonymous cash transactions. Just as when they haunt Las Vegas casinos looking for winners, IRS agents will insist on knowing who each party is when money is moved.

The technology is available for having anonymous financial activity. Phone calling cards, gift cards, prepaid cellular service, and PayPal to an extent offer at least pseudonymous if not anonymous transactions. I believe that such anonymous financial activity will be developed and deployed regardless of governmental dislike because there's too much demand for untraceable transactions, especially because Homeland Security scrutiny will undoubtedly catch many porpoises in their tuna nets, like tax cheaters and software pirates. Some people have legitimate reasons for using the Internet for financial transactions without leaving a trail; people who place a high premium on discretion in personal matters might not want to identify themselves for certain medical or pharmaceutical purchases, such as contraceptives, AIDS tests, or even something as mundane yet embarrassing as hemorrhoid cream or plastic pants for incontinence. Anonymous or pseudonymous purchases and cash transfers in the future are a certainty. These will increase the impact on privacy of having an online identity compromised. Activities on the Internet that don't require full authentication should be allowed to be performed anonymously.

Browsing Should Be Anonymous

The need for anonymous access to information to protect identity poses a better case than the need for anonymous financial transactions. The only strong argument for authenticated browsing is a governmental one: insight into the minds of potential terrorists can be gained only by watching for evidence of thought patterns: What are potential terrorists writing, saying, reading? The negative consequences of this scrutiny are societal. If people know they are under surveillance, they may decide to err on the side of caution and abandon their interest in some subjects so as not to jeopardize their professional life or, worse, risk incarceration because of misprofiling.

Information browsing, more than anything else that can be done with the Net, benefits from anonymity. Democracies gain when their citizens can educate themselves on a subject without fear of attribution. First Amendment advocates believe that information is politically neutral and that knowing or trying to access publicly available information should never be grounds for suspicion.

Pseudonymity Is Necessary for Cyberspace

Sometimes, however, a person wants to enter into a dialogue or a long-term relationship yet not be tied to their physical identity. This is the middle ground—persistent pseudonymity. Pseudonymity has a long literary heritage. It's often used by writers to disguise their gender (George Eliot), their ethnicity (Erich Maria Remarque), or their number (Ellery Queen), or just to protect themselves from real-world retribution (Publius). On the Internet, pseudonymity is used for all these reasons and more. Some of the activity on the Internet is sexual, political, or just too goofy for many professionals to attach their real name to. Some of them, such as lawyers and doctors, could potentially be sued for malpractice if they gave bad advice. Politicians or political workers might change their position at some future date and not want to be stuck with their written record because musings on the Internet are as permanent as a cheap tattoo. To use the Internet as a social medium, you need to have reputation and persistence. Reputation is critical because otherwise you're just another voice in the crowd. Persistence allows others to spend quality time interacting with you and to build up trust over time, just as in the real world. Anonymity offers neither of these benefits. Authenticated identity does, but the stakes are too high. If your reputation is damaged, you can't just start over. In short, pseudonymity is an excellent method for gaining the benefits of social interaction on the Internet while preserving privacy.

These pseudonyms present new targets for privacy violations. Anything that pierces the veil of these alternate identities by tying them to the physical world or even to each other is a privacy harm. Because the main differentiator of these personas is reputation, anything that damages their characters is also a privacy violation.

Reputation Is Closely Tied to Pseudonymity

An important and oft-neglected attribute of online communications is the reputation of the communicators. When a community-naming scheme is based on pseudonymity, reputational rankings, explicit or implicit, create a bell curve of fame and credibility. Every blog, virtual community, and message board has a pecking order of participants, as do the sites themselves.

Some people have invested considerable time in online identities. Gamers, bloggers, and hackers all put a lot of themselves into their pseudonymous identities, sometimes as much as or more than they do into their real lives. It may seem as though they'd want people to know who they really are, but many of them do not. For many reasons, outing would cause them problems in real life. Still, they have put time and money into their online personas and want to protect them. There have already been a few pseudo-celebrities on the Net, and there will doubtless be many more. I anticipate a time in the not-too-distant future when reality-like television programming moves over to the web, and we will make and break these pseudonymous stars.

Sometimes online stars achieve fame for short periods of time using their aliases. I call them "Warhols" after Andy's famous quote about everyone being famous for fifteen minutes. One such early Internet social pioneer was James Parry, better known as Kibo. An accomplished programmer and graphic artist, he was best known for his identity on Usenet, the early Internet message-board system. His particular twist was that he used automated software to join any discussion on the Net that mentioned his alias.[2] In the future, there will be many more of these Warhols. They're going to be the ones writing reviews of books and movies, giving opinions, and spreading rumors. Hurting their offline privacy means outing. Hurting their online privacy means harming their reputation.

Reputation is fungible, with multibillion-dollar industries built on it. The online auction eBay is the perfect example because feedback scores govern trust on the auction site, and trust is what keeps eBay in business. The core business proposition of an online auction is that an unknown person is going to buy something sight unseen from a stranger. As fraught with chicanery as such a transaction might appear, it works, and works surprisingly well. The element of trust that is critical to normal human business interactions is incorporated into eBay with its feedback recommender system. Buyers and sellers are encouraged to rate each other after every transaction and to leave a short comment about the sale. That rating becomes part of the eBay seller's reputation and is readily available to millions of potential buyers. The higher a seller's feedback score, the more likely that buyers will trust that person and purchase something in the future. The reverse is also true: if you develop a bad reputation as an eBay seller, no one will want to take the risk. Message boards also help members to exchange information on fraudulent activities.

Over the years, eBay has evolved into a huge marketplace, but one where everyone uses an alias. People blithely buy multi-thousand-dollar autographs, jewelry, or even expensive automobiles from people with names like scruffydog321 or bigbonusbill, as long as they have a high feedback score and good reputation. The corporate side of eBay takes no part in the rating systems and limits its involvement in (and liability for) the transactions to facilitation. It is eBay community members who maintain law and order by rewarding the honest and labeling and shunning the crooks. Surprisingly, this system works.

Online communities like eBay police themselves, using decreased reputation as the punishment for bad behavior. But there is a weakness in this system. A scam artist who hijacks the account of a legitimate and well-respected eBay member can then use the seller's reputation to lure unsuspecting buyers to fraudulent auctions. That's what happened to Joseph D'Amelio, who thought that buying a 2000 Porsche 911 for $50,000 from a reputable eBay member was a great deal, not the elaborate scam it turned out to be. He lost his money to a fake escrow company and never saw the car.[3] Typically, the bad guys auction some items, collect their money, and quickly disappear, while the real owners of eBay accounts are left to pick up the pieces.

Identity hijackers use a couple of basic methods. They often create a web site that looks like eBay and then send out a series of spam emails that appear to originate from the company; these emails ask users to follow a link to update their account information or tell them to provide their eBay password so that a recent transaction can be completed. If an eBay user complies with the request, the con artist has the password needed to take over the account and changes the email address associated with it.

Another common method called a "dictionary attack" uses an automated software program or bot to identify legitimate eBay accounts that have been idle for a while. A series of random passwords are then entered in hopes of breaking in. That's what happened to another unsuspecting eBay user. While sitting at home relaxing on a Sunday afternoon, he received an email telling him that his user name and password had just changed. Thinking it was some sort of hoax to get him to enter his private account information to a bogus web site, he ignored the message. Later that day he found out that his legitimate account was in fact hijacked by crooks and then used to set up fake auctions. They had used the dictionary attack to fire millions of passwords at his eight-letter-password account, got in, and locked him out.[4] Kevin Jarrett was also locked out of his eBay account and had fraudulent auctions set up in his name. He found out only when one of the bidders sent him an email. Jarrett said that it "never occurred to [him] that 142 feedback points on eBay is a very valuable item. It means that you're trusted."[5]

As a consequence of the success of the web site, eBay names are indeed becoming valuable commodities that not only are stolen but are bought and sold. Sometimes eBay account names are sold by their original owners. They are advertised as having great ratings and include the percentage of positive feedback attached to the account. Some owners have no intention of selling their highly respectable user names until they are presented with a lucrative offer. A U.K. account owner was approached and ended up selling his highly rated eBay ID for £1000.[6] Others put their accounts up for sale, although eBay says that these IDs cannot be sold or transferred to someone else. In addition to ratings value, some eBay accounts are sought after solely for their cool user names, much as domain names are.

Loss of Pseudonymity Can Cause Identity Theft

Aliases, such as eBay handles, can be stolen and sometimes used to make money in the real world. Each pseudonym that a person uses creates another opportunity for identity theft. The comprehensive mapping of handles or user names to real identities is the Rosetta

Stone for direct marketers. By decrypting references to handles, aliases, and email addresses, they can monitor the activity of people on the Internet, analyze the patterns, and then go after those people where they actually live by using the long-established tools of their trade: telemarketing calls and junk mail.

There's a darker side to this computer code breaking—identity theft. Crooks use a technique called phishing to con financial account numbers out of their marks. Account numbers are simply another form of numeric handles. If you have ever received an email requesting that you visit a web site and update your bank-account information, it was probably part of a phishing scam. The fraudulent web site is designed to closely mirror the legitimate one, using similar content and images to gain the confidence of the visitor. Targets of phishing scams include customers of eBay, PayPal, and many large and small financial institutions, along with those of utility companies that accept online payments from their customers. Websense Security Labs reports that financial-service companies continue to be the target of close to 86 percent of phishing attacks.[7]

Phishing attacks have increased significantly since they came into the spotlight in 2003, and they are growing exponentially. Although it is difficult to find comprehensive statistics on phishing, FraudWatch International reported an increase of 215 percent from April to May 2004.[8] The Anti-Phishing Working Group (APWG) reported a 180 percent increase in attacks from March to April 2004.[9] APWG also reported an increase of 400 percent in phishing scams between August 2004 (2,158) and November 2004 (8,459).[10] MessageLabs, a global provider of email security and management services, confirmed a 226 percent increase in phishing emails from April to May 2005, with the number of fraudulent messages exceeding nine million for a month.[11] According to IBM, eighteen million phishing attempts were documented in 2004, a jump of 5000 percent from 2003.[12]

Phishing attacks pose a definite threat to online consumer confidence and create an atmosphere of distrust when it comes to e-commerce activities. A Gartner survey from June 2005 concurs, stating that there is a direct correlation between the number of phishing attacks and consumer confidence: when phishing increases, confidence dips, inhibiting the rate of growth for U.S. e-commerce.[13]

Because phishing is one of the most common methods of facilitating identity theft, it is a threat to privacy. Any technique that crooks can use to equate a virtual to a real-world identity provides a potential opportunity to make money. Phishing is a blatant attempt to unlock a bank account or get a credit-card number. Although it may not be obvious, these numbers are also identities or at least identifiers. In the world of numeric labels, though, the most powerful and the most damaging to privacy is the Social Security number.

Any labeling system that is mappable onto real identities is immensely valuable to direct marketers and thieves because it provides an opening where the virtual world can bleed into the real one. The biggest threat of this kind and a primary contributor to the identity-theft statistics is the U.S. Social Security system. Although it was never intended to be an identification system (and says so on the card), it has de facto become one. Doctors, universities, and telephone companies all ask for SSNs when you begin a relationship with them. In fact, half of U.S. colleges still use SSNs for student identification.[14] Today, SSNs are also used as the identifier for taxes, filings with the Securities and Exchange Commission (SEC), health care plans, and driver's licenses. And SSNs are poorly protected; they can be found all over the Internet. A simple Google search, for instance, reveals Bill Gates's SSN. Any officer of a public company has to submit an SSN as part of the initial SEC filings. These documents then became public information, searchable on the Internet. In 2001, U.S. law-enforcement authorities uncovered a ring consisting of hundreds of illegal immigrants who were using stolen SSNs in order to obtain airport jobs.[15] Others have used stolen SSNs in order to receive health care. For example, an expectant mother from Florida impersonated a woman from Ohio so that her hospital bills were paid while she gave birth. The scam artist went so far as to register the other woman as the mother of the child.[16]

Loss of control of numeric or textual identifiers leads to loss of privacy and can cause direct and substantial financial harm. The technology trend that will make this loss worse than it is now is search engines. Google and similar products make it too easy to find anything that's on the Net. The web is huge and much of the information on it is poorly indexed, but good search engines work around those limitations. Just as long-dead commoners found their privacy in anonymity, denizens of the Internet did at one time too. It was easy to sink into the murky depths of the cyber sea. Even if a rope existed that would anchor a virtual handle to an actual name, it was hard to find. Now it's easy, and it will get worse. Expect significant leaps in search technology. The success of Google has encouraged venture capitalists to fund many competitive search companies.

Protection for these aliases needs to be a part of the privacy-improvement package. As we pour more and more of our selves into online personas, the damage to us that results from an attack on our virtual Doppelgängers increases to the point of financial harm, political hurt, and at the least personal embarrassment. Baby boomers may place little stock in virtual identities, but their children are spending a lot of their social life living them. The longer people use these guises and the more emotional energy they invest in these personas, the harder the fall when their online identities are compromised. This is the Internet version of a privacy intrusion. As use of these pseudonyms becomes increasingly engrained in our culture, the potential damage from a pseudonymous privacy violation will increase until eventually the harm will be comparable to that experienced in the real world.

The Internet is creating new cultures online that cut across ethnicity, geography, and gender. In the real world, however, these demographic attributes are a strong influence on expectations of privacy, as discussed in Chapter Seven.

7

Privacy and Culture in a Technological World
Shoji Screens

*I dream of wayward gulls and all landless lovers, rare
moments of winter sun, peace, privacy, for everyone.*
William F. Claire[1]

Our understanding of privacy is a cultural abstraction, not a
global absolute. It varies by context—by ethnicity, by locale,
by religion, by age. It's hard to define precisely because it's not uni-
form in meaning or application. It's also dynamic and temporal,
changing constantly in step with our attitudes and the evolution of
our cultures. All cultures have the idea of privacy, even if the subject matter is different.

This book describes privacy as control of one's own data. It's
implicit that the information in question is important, either individually or in aggregate. Some information is clearly valuable, bank-
account information for example. Other information is significant
because of its negative impact if made public, such as embarrassing
facts or humiliating circumstances. What strikes at the heart of our
fears, though, is relative to the culture in which we live and, to
some extent, where and who we are in our society.

The Internet has societies also, but they're not necessarily in
alignment with the ones in the real world. Netizens who frequent
certain haunts have developed their own mores and folkways, even
creating new dialects using acronyms and glyphs like emoticons.

Denizens of these virtual worlds can have their privacy violated, either by the breaching of a particular taboo of the online society or by being outed and having their virtual identity involuntarily connected to either another online identity or to their real-world one.

Technology affects our cultural understanding of privacy by constantly expanding the realm of the possible. Many of the privacy problems mentioned in this book are happening now because they've been enabled by the societies that we live in, both in the real world and in the virtual world. Without the Internet, we would not have developed online cultures. Without ubiquitous access to information, we would have a chance to clamp down on the dissemination of personal information. Our future culture will be formed as technology evolves and our sense of privacy changes commensurately.

Our sense of privacy has always adjusted and accommodated itself to the realities of the world or worlds in which we reside. Take feudal Japan, for example. In traditional Japanese houses, shojis, screens made of rice paper, were used instead of hard walls to divide the rooms. The screens were translucent and were certainly not acoustic baffles. Yet they were used for privacy. In that society, they were as good as sound-proofed concrete because rigid cultural mores supported those imaginary walls. Privacy is a cultural compact to protect the space of individuals, whether that agreement is manifested by a flimsy paper wall or a sealed piece of mail. Shoji privacy was not ensured by a complete blockage of sight or sound but by cultural norms. Even though residents heard and, to some extent, saw what went on behind the flimsy walls, it was verboten to discuss what they saw or heard, and the sense of privacy was thereby preserved. To draw an analogy to our present culture, just because we can see, hear, or know private information doesn't mean that we have to discuss it.

I knew a Scotsman who grew up in a small fishing village populated by fifty families who had lived there for five centuries. Children grew up, left the town, and sometimes came back again with new spouses. I asked him about privacy. I was sure that everyone must know what everyone else is doing in such a small community. He replied, "Sure, but we dinna talk about it."

Privacy is often more effectively policed by culture than it is by the law. As pointed out elsewhere in this book, the law often lags too far behind technology to be an effective stopgap, while cultural mores are always right at the forefront of change. Significant technologies that affect how we relate to others carry accompanying behavioral changes, even though we're probably unaware of this process at the time. These changes often occur years before the legal system recognizes them.

Physical privacy can apply to sounds, sights, and smells and is closely linked to underlying taboos. It often deals with nudity, bathroom functions, sexual habits, or intimate family affairs. Nudity taboos, for instance, vary across the world. Although the genitalia are usually protected from sight, some, like orthodox Muslims, also veil the face. Some, like the Victorian English, guarded the limbs and particularly the ankles. The female breast is on display on public beaches throughout Europe. Yet a glimpse of topless flesh in North America is often considered highly titillating and even shocking because to most Americans nudity is a taboo. Privacy thus has different meanings in different cultures. There is no universal concept of privacy.

The extreme range of views on nudity is a good indicator of what might happen to our sense of privacy in the future. Rather than being a homogeneous global view, the idea of privacy is likely to fragment into clusters based on geography in the real world and on interest areas in the virtual one. Today, privacy is determined mostly by where we live and our age.

Urban Versus Rural Ideas About Privacy

Throughout the Western world, two distinct environments, urban and rural, provide the community context for ideas about privacy. Urban privacy is about absolutes and anonymity. Urbanites value their ability to be faceless. They want to walk the streets buying what they like, eating what they desire, and talking to whom they wish without anyone else being the wiser. Our popular entertainment is full of stories predicated on this notion. Cautionary tales about picking up strangers provide the basis for movies like *Looking for Mr. Goodbar* and *American Psycho;* they make sense only to a big-city dweller. Life in densely populated areas involves a slight tinge of neurotic paranoia; there's a lot to be afraid of in the big city. This code governs big-city behavior. If you leave something unlocked, it'll be stolen by the end of the day. If you give someone an edge, they'll cut you with it. Strangers will use anything they know about you to hurt you in some way. Also, because many lawyers and legislators are urbanites by birth or by education, our legal system reflects this townie slant on privacy laws. Lawmakers legislate to protect anonymity in order to preserve their version of privacy.

Rural dwellers see privacy differently. As in the aforementioned Scottish village, privacy isn't about being anonymous. It's about protecting what is important to you: your reputation and standing in the community.

Online communities are inventing similar mores for themselves; as in the real world, newly invented cultural behavior will mirror the underlying environmental realities. Cultural privacy is about compromise, but negotiation occurs quietly, by unspoken consensus, not by passing laws. Technology has injected changes into the online community that have caused rapid mutations in the online experience. Online multiplayer games are a long way from chat in the mid-1990s. Even so, some norms are beginning to develop, and a sense of privacy will be one. Privacy is just as important to online groups as is any other modern ritual.

Generational Ideas About Privacy

In many cultures privacy is viewed differently by different age groups. In our culture, these differences are driven by familiarity with and acceptance of consumer technology. Each significant advance in consumer technology creates a divide between those who embrace it and those who do not. Often rejection of a technological device arises from a weak grasp of the underlying principles. I'm not talking about science; I'm referring to a basic understanding of a concept. After all, few people today could build a television, repair one, or even explain how one works. Yet most of us think we understand televisions. Rightly or wrongly, we're comfortable with the technology. This comfort zone drives generational adoption of new technology.

Getting comfortable with technology happens when you understand what it's capable of. We all know that microwaves make things hot and that some things like metal or damp household pets shouldn't be put in them. The worst thing that can happen from using a microwave is that something will burn. It won't kill you or steal your money or get you arrested. When people don't fully understand the danger and the harm a new device can cause, however, they are afraid to use it. In this sense, intimacy with technology is not about understanding the science; it's about understanding and avoiding the pitfalls.

ATM machines were a boon to many. By providing twenty-four-hour access to funds and bank services, they revolutionized how consumers interact with financial institutions; people can bank at a time of their own convenience. Yet many older people still are uncomfortable using them. They are afraid they will lose money—they'll deposit cash and not get credit, or if they withdraw funds, they will be charged for more than they received. Those who grew up with cash-dispensing machines never worry about what happens if there's a discrepancy. In fact, they have an overriding faith that the bank will make it right. In a way, ATM machines were the first great in-your-face automation of everyday life. The automophobia demonstrated by the elderly is a rejection of humanless transactions, a distrust of the financial technology that has taken away their face-to-face business community.

The personal computer is many things to many people, with much of the difference dependent on age as well as profession. To some it's a glorified typewriter; to others, a second brain with better memory retention. Those who get the most use out of computers are those who understand their uses and advantages and not just the mechanical things like how to turn a computer on or off or how to hook up a printer or insert a CD. People who did not grow up with these machines have trouble with the underlying concepts of computer technology, such as what happens when you turn one off. Which kinds of information will go away forever and which will come back when you turn the box back on? As silly as that question may sound to some, it is the basis of a real fear for the uninitiated. If you don't understand what a disk drive is, then it is difficult to believe that everything is okay when the computer tells you that it's saved your term paper to one.

When online, newbies often feel overwhelmed. The easy parts are simply a matter of memorizing how to perform some basic tasks like typing in a URL, inserting a bookmark, or looking for the lock icon to confirm that a connection is secure before buying online. Those concepts are easy to grasp. However, new users have trouble with the cultural nuances—how to behave in a chat session or how to use emoticons properly. Conceptual misunderstandings also arise in the workplace. People who use the Internet for daily chores have an unspoken understanding of how they will communicate. For instance, when conversations, say about scheduling a meeting, begin on email, they are supposed to finish on email. It's jarring and unexpected when someone responds to an email with a voice mail; often the results are mixed messages and missed meetings. Sometimes people encroach on others' privacy because they're ignorant of the customs of the electronic community that they've become a part of.

The term that describes the amount of time it takes for new inventions to become part of a culture is *adoption curve*.[2] For most personal technologies, the time between experimentation by the pioneer and purchase by the laggard is around ten years, or half a generation. The early adopters, or innovators, are the first to use the new devices. The younger generation watches these pioneers and sees use of the new gadgetry as status-enhancing. For the older generation, the new device is a nuisance, a distraction, and often a threat to the established order. By the end of the adoption period, the younger group knows the technology, approves of it, and desires it. Their elders, if they have not yet started using the new technology during its infancy, are hardly about to do so now. Your ideas about privacy and new technological devices are linked intrinsically to where you are on the adoption curve for that technology.

Early adopters who are in the vanguard of this curve have their expectations of privacy tightly matched to their knowledge of the capabilities of the technology; they're not surprised by what a gadget can do. Their privacy zone tends to be small because it's based on knowledge. Less technologically savvy people often have huge areas of concern about privacy, much of it based on not knowing the capabilities of the device in question. If a camera might be transmitting, then for them it is. If they don't know when cell phones are "off," then they are being overheard. If they undress in a room with a computer camera, they assume it is recording all the time. But people who are completely oblivious to technology in general can't even contemplate what's possible, and thus they tend to be comfortable around new technological equipment.

Generational differences in the notion of privacy track not only to the technology adoption curve but also to expectations about privacy.

Seniors expect privacy. The oldest group has high expectations for privacy.[3] For them, the horror of runaway privacy invasions is financial harm—identity theft—or emotional harm—embarrassment. A business transaction is not real to them unless a human being is involved. For them, trust plays a key role in customer loyalty. They are most afraid of commercial companies invading their privacy.

> Despite seniors' concerns about privacy, a Pew Internet & American Life Project study found that the percentage of seniors who went online soared by 47 percent between 2000 and 2004, with 22 percent of Americans sixty-five and older using the Internet.[4]

In sum, seniors have wide expectations of privacy fueled by a lack of hands-on experience with technology.

Baby boomers don't trust government. The middle generation is always on the lookout for conspiracies.[5] They understand machine technology better than their parents do but don't get networking at all. This group was young during the Vietnam era and Watergate. For them, invasion of privacy is about spying, peeping, and electronic voyeurism. They grew up with the expectation that as long as they were not famous and were not arrested, they would be able to take their secrets to the grave. They became indignant as the electronic bulwarks holding back widespread access to personal information collapsed under the onslaught of technology.

This group is mostly afraid of government. Although the famous paranoid writers of conspiratorial fiction like George Orwell were published during their parents' era, these baby boomers were the generation who took the Big Brother theme closest to heart. They also had Kurt Vonnegut, Joseph Heller, and Hunter S. Thompson to fuel their suspicions of government.

Gen X has no expectations of privacy. The youngest adult generation grew up with computers. They are adept at using digital cameras, cell phones, and MP3 players and are expert at texting, downloading the latest great song, blogging, and emailing, although they prefer instant messaging and use it most often when communicating with friends.[6] When traveling in the third world, they can be found staring stupidly at dial telephones, pushing the holes repeatedly and shaking the handset. They trust computers more than they trust people. They assume that every computer talks to every other computer. They believe that everything can be found on the Net somewhere and that finding it is simply a matter of discovering a way to "hack" in.

As of 2005, 87 percent (twenty-one million) American teens aged twelve to seventeen had the Internet at home; nearly all households with a combined income of $75,000 or more were using high-speed connections to get online.[7]

These kids grew up being watched by baby minders, talking into clown heads to order food, having their money spit at them from machines, preparing for the business computer world by playing video games instead of dress up, and citing the Internet as a source for research papers. They have created virtual personas that are as real to them as their face in the mirror, have more online friends than physical ones, and, in short, do not see themselves as citizens of their country or even of their world as much as they are denizens of cyberspace. They are the always-on generation, preferring the instant gratification of Instant Messenger and SMS to the drawn-out prose of email. Gen Xers took to blogs like dogs to a pork chop. They know that their gadgets are two-way. It's natural for them to believe that everyone's watching. To them, there's no such thing as privacy.

Technology is the driver of societal evolution. One generation invents a gadget, the next struggles to understand it, and the third grows up comfortable with its uses and limitations. Privacy is both personal and societal, but it stems from our expectations. Generations that grew up before computers have high expectations of privacy because the very nature of devices that can see in the dark, remember every grocery item they've ever bought, or locate a car anywhere in the world is inherently abhorrent. Generations that grew up with computers and the Internet see the world and their place in it differently than those who came to computers later in their lives. Their view of privacy is skewed by their expectations, which are insignificant; they're the generation that watches reality television. They know that privacy does not mean that they're not being watched but rather that no one is looking.

Chapter Eight talks about how technology makes it easier to look.

Part IV

The Technology

Information technology is about data and the software that stores, searches, copies, and analyzes them. In this part, Chapter Eight discusses the machines that are responsible for putting into computer systems important parts of our personal information and activities, such as where we are and what we're up to. These devices are the sensory organs for thinking machines: their eyes, ears, and nose. Chapter Nine explains how the data move from machine to machine—the networks and small locating devices like RFID tags and GPS satellite receivers. In combination, networks and locators can perceive what we are doing and share that information with other computers that mix this real-time information with historical data for analytical purposes. This merging of cameras, microphones, databases, chips, and locating equipment threatens our privacy; because of these devices, we will always be followed. But even if our privacy is lost, we will never be.

Voyeurism
Surveillance Technology

We are rapidly entering the age of no privacy, where everyone is open to surveillance at all times; where there are no secrets.

William O. Douglas[1]

Several of the privacy invasions mentioned in preceding chapters may be surprising to many people—some may even sound like science fiction. Some cases deal with old privacy problems made current with new tricks, but digital voyeurism is a new problem made possible by enhanced sensor technology, which enables visual, auditory, and sometimes olfactory detection at far greater distances than would be possible with the naked senses. For the centuries of recorded civilization preceding the invention of the computer, privacy could be invaded by mechanical means but still be preserved by organic ones. Ensuring that no one was close enough to hear preserved the privacy of conversations, and shutting the blinds meant that no one could see. As innovations in sensing technology increased beyond a range that is detectable by humans, the control of our privacy passed from the subjects to the stalkers because we could no longer stop them from looking.

The Brain

Up until now in this book, when I've been talking about technology, it's been mostly about data processing. But the information has to get into the system from somewhere; it comes in from two places: machines and people. In the first part of the computer age, machines thought but were blind and deaf. Human beings were their eyes and ears and fingers; they reduced the complexities of the world to numbers. New jobs like data-entry specialist were created, and many other entry-level positions, such as supermarket checkout scanner and medical-records clerk, were changed to facilitate feeding information to the machines. Now the trend is for the machines to acquire information on their own by controlling their own sensors. This chapter deals with the world of machine input. Machines are now capable of perceiving the world on their own without human intervention. They can see and detect motion, hear and understand spoken language, and, to a limited extent, "smell" and "taste" organic compounds. Today's world is full of sensing equipment. Cameras, microphones, and bar-code readers are the silicon insects of the digital world, ubiquitous and ignored. Who notices another camera on a highway pole? Sensors are a computer's body parts.

Future legislation on privacy must either take this machine omniscience into account or begin banning certain kinds of technology. Some technologies are already restricted; certain sensing devices like cell-phone-monitoring scanners and audio bugging equipment are prohibited in some areas, reserved solely for law enforcement.

In the early days of the Industrial Revolution, the first step in the march of the automatons was the mechanization of manufacturing. Ned Ludd, of Luddite fame, raged futilely against a sock-weaving machine in the late eighteenth century, but within thirty years most industries had completed the transition from human to machine labor. Once the world of the old is powered up, it's time to invent the new. The progress of technology often starts with a keystone innovation that is then joined by blocks of ideas utilizing the original concept.

Such progress has been happening in the Information Era, but not because of the invention of the computer. Rather, the trigger was the formation of the commercial Internet as manifested by the World Wide Web. I believe that we are in the beginning of an age of innovation centered on new uses for universal information, free global communication, and unprecedented levels of technology-augmented social collaboration.

Rapid invention and social change following a key technological development have occurred before. By the time the Industrial Age was in full swing, Thomas Edison had been awarded 1,093 patents for inventions ranging from the light bulb to the phonograph. Innovation was about doing brand new things, inventing devices that performed services that were genuinely new and not just a Rube Goldberg way of speeding up a tedious manual task; light bulbs were not just electric candles, and phonographs had no mechanical predecessor.

Machines continued to replace human hands, but not heads. The first silicon brains began appearing around World War II. Early computers were general-purpose tabulators used for a variety of activities such as breaking German codes during the war, computing ballistic trajectories, and maintaining tote boards at horse racing tracks. These machines were different from those of the steam-powered era, which relied on humans to completely think a problem through and break it into component pieces before they could get to work. The new era of thinking machines changed all that; computers now did the planning and then turned the answers over to the people instead of the other way around. In their first fifty years, computers were task-oriented, solving explicitly programmed problems like the ballistic trajectory of a rocket or counting things like census information. Now, they're goal-oriented and self-tasking, setting their own problems based on sweeping, abstract goals; and when they need new information about the real world and they don't have a sensor, they ask us.

As machines became event driven, they needed organs of awareness to perceive the real world. This new generation of factory machines not only built consumer goods but sprouted sensory mechanisms to spot what was happening on assembly lines. Feedback loops helped to manage exceptions, such as a jammed paint sprayer, a spoiled chicken, or a mangled worker. The mechanical brains now had ears and eyes that could hear and see across the wide electromagnetic spectrum.

At first these sensors were simple gadgets: tripwires, springs, on-off latches; they were mechanical, then electrical. The big change from reacting to anticipating happened because of advances in electronics, initially transistors, followed by integrated circuits. Generally speaking, a transistor is a tiny electronic switch, and an integrated circuit is made up of many, many transistors. As electronic components became smaller, their capabilities could inversely grow increasingly complex. Instead of just sensing on-off latches, industrial machinery could report shades of gray by digitizing analog input, as in the first red, light-emitting diode (LED) digital watches in the 1960s. This ability enabled the machines to measure the real world that we describe by using words like *fast, slow, big, small*, and *red* and to replace those words with numbers, sizes, wavelengths, and weights, information that computers can work with.

Electronic design advanced just as fast, keeping pace with the rapidly evolving miniaturization of components, which reduced circuitry to transistors, then further shrank them to integrated circuitry. Early in the computer era, hobbyists and professionals experimented with "bread boarding" motherboards. Wires were used to jump the circuits, allowing the programmer to change the firmware (hardware programming) without replacing the motherboard. Because these boards could apply logical analysis on their inputs and "think" through the information, this was an effective method for exploring new programming. Successful breadboard rigs would eventually become manufactured boards, and some ultimately became integrated circuits. The early days of Silicon Valley were heady with the smell of doped germanium as the integrated circuits shrank; next year's chip would always be cheaper and smaller and more powerful.

Digital devices then crossed over into the analog world, first enhancing, then ultimately replacing, their antiquated counterparts. As machines inflated with silicon, they were swept away by the torrents of Moore's Law, doubling their power every year, increasing their speed, adding new functionality, and all the while shrinking in size. They began to be able to sense across the sensory spectrum, sampling the real world and reacting in milliseconds to the changing conditions of the outside world.

Circuitry will continue to get better. It will shrink, possibly to invisible proportions. In a segment of nanotechnology called nanomanufacturing, scientists are learning how to build submicroscopic factories, minuscule assembly plants that can make specific products as well as copy themselves. These factories will reproduce, birthing more and more copies, until they all stop cloning and start building swarms of tiny, networked sensors.

One of the forerunners of this kind of technology was the "spy dust" powder developed by the Russian secret service and put to use during the Cold War as a way to secretly keep track of the activities and location of Western diplomats. Chemically based, the invisible spy dust was often placed on door handles, in vehicles, and on small objects including currency in order to unobtrusively trace the movements of people.

The technologies of digital circuitry, laser-driven wireless communications, and micro electromechanical systems are converging to create a new kind of pervasive sensor called smart dust. Not too far in the future, those tiny specks of dust collecting on your overcoat or footwear may actually be tiny wireless sensors gathering data and transmitting the information in peer-to-peer mode to other dust motes and a base station.

Developed as a surveillance tool to spy on enemies of the United States, smart dust is able to detect everything from vibrations to light. Currently the size of rice grains, the spying devices can be sprinkled behind enemy lines to collect vital information, which can then be relayed back to military personnel. The technology is also perfect for perimeter surveillance as well as for detecting the movement of troops and military vehicles. The technology has numerous civilian applications as well in the fields of meteorology, the geophysical sciences, and health care. It is already being used by companies to track humidity levels and monitor temperatures in warehouses.

The real worry is how smart dust will be used and controlled in the future. Spying on private citizens, tracking employees, and recording the movements of those who protest against government policy will all be possible. The only hindrance to widespread use is the size and price of the motes. Researchers want to get the current five-millimeter motes down to one millimeter, at a price of around $1 instead of the $50 to $100 a single unit currently sells for.

Digitally enhanced sensors are a game changer for privacy because certain physical limits like optical focal lengths can be overcome; an ever-increasing range of surveillance then becomes possible. In the future, it will be difficult to physically hide something so well that it cannot be seen or heard or smelled by sensing devices, yet the devices themselves will be completely hidden from human perception. Disguising things well enough to evade detection will become a new black art. It may be okay for computers to have our personal information if the data can't be used for other purposes. Unfortunately, if machines have access to the knowledge, then other people can get to it too.

The Eye

The one form of privacy intrusion that most people immediately understand and resent is being spied on. With enhanced optical technology the surveillance distance has increased beyond the range that a human being can detect, and the cameras have shrunk so that they are small enough to be difficult, if not impossible, for a person to spot.

Video surveillance has always been a function of optics. The best devices were the ones made by the most skillful craftsmen. Look at the refracting telescope, first invented by the Dutch around 1600. The instrument hasn't changed significantly in the last four hundred years. Improved manufacturing techniques have enabled longer focal lengths, but the principles remain the same. I have a 150-year-old antique sailor's spyglass that still functions perfectly well, better than binoculars, although my arm gets tired holding it up. The difference between Galileo's hand-made, hand-held telescope and the monstrous two-hundred-inch Hale reflector at Mt. Palomar is the precision afforded by modern industrial manufacturing. Better grinding and polishing make a better optical device. We have reached the limit at which a lens can be significantly improved mechanically. Most increases in resolution from now on will be digital.

Cameras are in a similar state. Since their invention in the early nineteenth century, they've gone through a few improvements, generally dealing with the chemical development process that results in negatives or prints. The basic functionality has stayed pretty much the same. The zoom capability comes from the quality of the lenses, usually external add-ons.

But now telescopes and cameras are becoming digital. The innovation that makes that transition possible is the charge-coupled device (CCD), a solid-state image-capture chip. CCDs have proven to be an excellent substitute for optical cameras. CCDs capture 70 percent of incident light, compared with 2 percent for conventional film. These chips are responsible for the proliferation of low-cost digital cameras. These devices, like all computerized appliances, are swept away by Moore's Law and get better and cheaper every year. Soon, the digital versions will be superior in almost all ways, and optical cameras will be relegated to the equipment bag of the old-fashioned professional. These devices aren't limited to the visible spectrum either. They're just as adept at recording infrared as they are human-perceivable light.

The significance of the digital output of the CCD is that binary data can be stored, transmitted, and enhanced using normal computer equipment; in other words, the pictures taken by digital cameras are just data files and can be moved around and manipulated like a word-processing file. Tens of thousands of picture files can easily be stored on a home computer, for instance.

From a privacy perspective, the threat of a digital camera is threefold: convenience, cost, enhancement. Digital cameras are compact and getting smaller. A 5x zoom-equipped model can be slipped into a shirt pocket. It doesn't even have to be a dedicated camera. The cost of the digital-camera component is so low that it's become a standard feature built into most new cell phones. With the trend toward miniaturization, it's not easy to spot a camera. Health clubs are now banning cell phones from gyms because of the growing number of people taking hidden pictures of exercisers in compromising positions. There have also been several widely reported cases of "upskirting," the practice of surreptitiously maneuvering a camera-equipped cell phone underneath a woman's skirt and taking pictures. Digital cameras will continue to shrink until they disappear completely. Expect to see cameras incorporated into jewelry like rings and watches, necklaces, bracelets, and tiepins. The average person will be unable to verify that there isn't a camera in a room if it isn't actively transmitting. It is not inconceivable that cameras could become the size of the head of a pin or could be incorporated into building material. The biggest limiting factor is the power supply. The smaller cameras continue to shrink, but their batteries don't.

As mentioned elsewhere in this book, the cost of surveillance used to be an inadvertent privacy protection. When it costs hundreds or thousands of dollars to monitor someone, the motive to do so gets examined with a critical eye. Photography is the same—film costs money and developing costs more. Digital photography, however, is close to free. Digital media are reusable and transferable to other forms of computer storage. A common way to use a digital camera is to take hundreds of pictures, which are stored on a thumbnail-sized flash card that is then transferred to a computer; the effective cost per shot is reduced to less than a penny. At that price, cost is no longer a deterrent, and anyone can take thousands of pictures of anyone else for next to nothing.

Digital pictures can also be enhanced with tools such as Photoshop. It's still possible for experts to tell that a picture has been tampered with, but not for much longer.

Every few years a great hoax employs a funny or ironic manipulated photograph. Right after the 9/11 attack, the Internet was flooded with a shot of a man wearing a knit watch cap and a backpack. He was standing on an observation deck at the World Trade Center and posing for the camera while a plane was clearly visible below him, seconds away from crashing into the building. Supposedly the camera was found in the rubble and recorded the moment right before the crash. Many people were horrified. However, the picture was shown to be a hoax by analysis of the shadows in it as well as by revelations of its factual inaccuracies; for instance, the observation decks in the tower were always closed at that time of day.[2]

Governments have had video-surveillance capabilities for decades. The National Reconnaissance Office, for many years the most secret U.S. agency, has long controlled tens of billions of dollars worth of spy satellites capable of seeing any point on the Earth's surface either visually or with any other part of the radio-frequency spectrum. In the 1990s, it was claimed that the resolution was good enough to make out a softball-shaped object from several hundred miles away in space.[3] Presumably it's even better now.

Video surveillance has a social bias because even though cameras can record everyone, human beings have to decide whom to monitor; the reasons for their choices may not always be objective; the subjective opinions of the human observer can enter into the surveillance.

Great Britain has become the most surveilled country in the world, originally in response to Irish Republican Army terrorism. Clive Norris and Gary Armstrong of the Centre for Criminology and Criminal Justice at Hull University authored a study of the British experience entitled *The Unforgiving Eye: CCTV Surveillance in Public Spaces.* They found that 40 percent of people were targeted for "no obvious reason," mainly "on the basis of belonging to a particular or subcultural group." "Black people were between one-and-a-half and two-and-a-half times more likely to be surveilled than one would expect from their presence in the population." Thirty percent of targeted surveillances of black people were protracted, lasting nine minutes or more; just 10 percent of white people were the targets of protracted surveillances. One out of ten women was targeted for "voyeuristic" reasons by the male camera operators. Finally, those who directly challenged, by gesture or deed, the right of the cameras to monitor them were especially targeted.[4]

In the future the ironic contradiction will be that even though no one will be safe from stealth photography, it will also be impossible to prove that any particular shot was real; this contradiction will create a culture of disdain for photographic evidence. Baby boomers will probably continue to see all intrusive photography as a privacy violation, even if it's faked. The generation that's grown up with Photoshop will be skeptical of pictures and will probably have a greatly desensitized view of their visual privacy. Tomorrow we'll see everything, but ignore it.

The Ear

People have eavesdropped since the beginning of civilization. They've pressed drinking glasses against walls, crouched outside windows, and hidden under the eaves of buildings in an effort to hear secrets. Humans have always had a fascination with knowing the unknown. Most great con games, stings, and scams are based on this principle. Eavesdropping used to be about hearing sounds, but these days it encompasses the entire gamut of communications, and, as with optical processing, covert listening has been augmented digitally. Computers can hear by means of microphones and can understand by using sophisticated voice-recognition software to translate the spoken words into bytes. Various big-ear listening devices are also available. They are parabolic dishes connected to electronic amplifiers, like a telescope for audio.

Telephone-like devices are fruitful targets for spying. Classic land-line telephones were vulnerable to wiretaps; physical connectors attached to the wires, usually at a junction box or on a pole, enabled listeners to hear everything said on calls going over that line. These worked so well that they were quickly regulated so that law-enforcement officers required a judge's written approval, or a *wiretap warrant*. The warrants were not that easy to get and required detailed information, including probable cause of a crime, names of targets, and subjects of interest, in an effort to deter "fishing expeditions" by police, who would start collecting information in the certainty that they would eventually find evidence of a crime. Police could also use *pen registers* to capture the phone numbers of all outgoing calls from a specified number, or *trap and trace* to record the numbers of all incoming calls. The legal basis of protection for telephone calls comes from interpretation of the Fourth Amendment and a person's "reasonable expectations of privacy." By the way, it's a bad idea to ever joke about a phone call being tapped when you think that the line may actually be monitored; if the tape is later introduced as evidence, your reference to being tapped, whether joking or not, indicates that you had no privacy expectations for that call, therefore no protection.

In 2006, *USA Today* reported that the National Security Agency (NSA) had made a deal with several large U.S. telecommunications companies including AT&T, Verizon, and BellSouth to turn over records of millions of Americans' phone calls. The government begrudgingly acknowledged the existence of the program, but claimed that it was given only the externals of the calls, not the content, and therefore it wasn't violating anyone's privacy.[5] (In July 2006, *USA Today* backed off of its claim that Verizon and BellSouth were involved.) In fact, NSA would have been able to perform a kind of intelligence called *traffic analysis* or *link analysis* on the information. This technique can be far more invasive than most people might think; it involves diagramming a group of people who talk to one another and analyzing their relationship using the resulting graph. Sometimes, however, it's an invasion of privacy to know who's talking to whom; it would be an invasion, for instance, if the government used that information to find the source of a leak.

One of the two sources of legal authority over wiretapping in the United States is the Federal Wiretap Act (Title III of the Omnibus Crime Control and Safe Streets Act), adopted in 1968 and expanded in 1986. The Patriot Act added to the list of crimes for which a wiretap could be ordered (violent activities, terrorism, and suspected hijacking were already on the list), and, since then, the standards for obtaining court-ordered warrants have been relaxed. The other legal authority for wiretapping comes from the Foreign Intelligence Surveillance Act.

Most people don't use corded phones anymore at home, but cordless phones are much easier to tap. Anyone can buy a scanner that will intercept many kinds of cordless phones. Phones with higher frequencies (2.4gHz and up) are slightly more secure. Some of the newer ones use techniques such as *spread spectrum*, which breaks the signal up across several frequencies, making any one communication on a single frequency unintelligible. But such communications can also be intercepted. For every cloaking technology, there is a commensurate decloaking one. This is a recurrent theme in information technology and may very well be the defining one in the years to come: the ongoing war between encryption and decryption. It's worth noting that cordless phone calls are still protected by federal law, and interception by law enforcement still requires a warrant, although the contention of the Bush administration in 2006 was that the president can personally authorize any wiretap.[6]

Cellular calls are another matter. Analog cell-phone calls (older models) can be picked up on a scanner. Newer digital cell phones are much harder to intercept, although this is still possible. European services generally encrypt digital phone transmission; most U.S. telecommunication services do not. Cellular-phone usage was not covered by any legal privacy rights until 1986. At that time the Electronic Communications Privacy Act made it illegal to intercept them. The act covers wire and electronic communications, such as online activities, faxes, email, and pagers, and prohibits the monitoring of cellular phone calls. Law enforcement and government agencies have easy access to digital calls through telephone switching stations that relay the calls back to them. A court order is required before a wiretap is permitted, but wiretaps are almost never denied.

In 2005 the Federal Communications Commission (FCC) mandated that all U.S. cell phones be equipped with locating technology, which enables phones to be targeted within one hundred feet. Ostensibly this feature was required to assist authorities with 911 calls. In practice, advertising companies are already gearing up to take advantage of this new tracking opportunity by beaming unasked-for coupons or sales flyers to passersby as they walk by a store. Another obvious implication for privacy with the use of this targeting technology is that the government will be able to locate most urban Americans to within one hundred feet.

Other privacy problems are connected with cell phones. In the world of electronics, there is no conceptual difference between microphones and speakers. All speakers can be turned into microphones and vice versa. The technology is available to turn any cell phone, even if it's not being used, into an active microphone; listeners would then be able to hear anything said by anyone carrying a cell phone.

Laws prohibiting cell-phone snooping are much less stringent than equivalent rules for land-line phones. In 1994, the FCC ruled that radio scanners capable of picking up frequencies in the range used for cellular transmissions would no longer be manufactured, and the commission made it illegal to import into the United States scanning equipment capable of picking up cell-phone frequencies. In reality, it isn't difficult to acquire these devices from Europe. The Counterfeit Access Device Law made it illegal for anyone to knowingly use a radio scanner to eavesdrop on electronic and wireless communication, and that includes intentional cellular interception. The FCC is currently demanding a new phone wiretapping law to cover the increasingly popular Voice Over Internet Protocol (VOIP) and broadband networks. The Communications Assistance for Law Enforcement Act of 1994 requires telecommunications service providers to design their equipment in such a way as to make it easy for law-enforcement officials to spy on their clients.

Privacy laws vary by state. To check the wiretapping and eavesdropping laws in your state, visit the Reporters Committee for Freedom of the Press web site at www.rcfp.org/taping. The National Conference of State Legislatures has also put together a web page de-

tailing federal and state electronic-surveillance laws at www.ncsl.org/
programs/lis/CIP/surveillance.htm.

In addition to the legal aspects of wiretapping, there are the practical aspects. Interception of wired communications generally requires
insertion of a monitoring device at either one of the two ends or
attached to the wire in between. Practically speaking, this means
putting a device at the target's house or at a central switching facil-
ity owned by the telephone company. Interception of Internet communications is much easier because the Internet is decentralized.
The core technology involves breaking down messages into data
packets that are sent from one location to another through an
unspecified set of intermediaries with enough redundancy to virtually guarantee flawless reconstruction of the original message. All
popular Internet applications such as email, web browsing, and chat
live on top of a packet protocol called TCP/IP.

Covert surveillance of computer usage can occur in the hardware using a *keystroke logger*, a small, innocuous-looking device that
stores every key press for future reconstruction. The logger is
attached to the keyboard cord, a universal serial bus (USB) port, or
some other hard-to-spot place. Electronic surveillance can also be
done right in the software of the target computer by using various
forms of Trojan programs or spyware that hides inside the running
programs, suppressing signs of its presence while monitoring everything that goes on. Any computer on a local-area network can host
a piece of software called a *packet sniffer* to log every data transmission on the network. Various spots on the wide-area network can
host interception gear, usually physical components, although some
of it can be implemented in software. A typical spot is at the physical location of an Internet service provider (ISP).

The Patriot Act has made government spying much easier than
it previously was by forcing cooperation from service providers. The
government can spy on Internet communications at ISP facilities,
and it has admitted to doing so.[7] In 2006, the Justice Department
formally asked the major Internet companies to retain customer

information indefinitely to facilitate federal subpoenaing of the information. In June 2006, the government admitted that it was using financial data obtained from the Society for Worldwide Interbank Financial Telecommunications (SWIFT) computer system.[8] SWIFT is a Belgium-based, international banking cooperative.

The multitude of ways that Internet communications can be intercepted makes it extremely difficult to protect online privacy. To date, the most effective way to protect email and other personal communications is to use personal encryption technology such as Pretty Good Privacy, an open-source encryption capability developed by Phil Zimmerman. Encrypting makes it difficult for anyone to read the transmitted content, even though it's still simple to intercept. The FBI is rumored to have a program called Magic Lantern, which acts like a keystroke logger and is used in conjunction with a program code-named Cyber Knight, which maintains a database of communications from email, chat rooms, and instant-messenger programs. Magic Lantern is targeted at a person under investigation by using standard viruslike propagation techniques that can be hidden inside an email attachment. The Trojan installs itself and lurks, waiting for the owner to type in encryption keys. These keys are then used retroactively to read intercepted communications. Supposedly, several antivirus manufacturers have designed their programs to ignore the presence of Magic Lantern worms, at the government's request. The average computer user would never know that the software was there, hiding and watching everything typed.

The rising use of VOIP telephony like Skype exacerbates the situation. VOIP users can make free telephone calls using the Internet instead of telephone wires. Calls made over the Internet would be easy to monitor, absent the normal legal protections afforded to conventional telephony.

Another form of governmental voyeurism is the interception of emails and the tracking of online activities. In July 2000, it was widely reported that the FBI had developed and was using a packet-sniffing intercept monitoring system it called Carnivore. The software was installed at ISPs as a way to monitor online traffic, including incoming and outgoing email. This online technology provided the FBI with full access to the web activities and email communications of suspected criminals. The agency was expected to comply with existing laws and filter only data traffic and grab packets of information relating to intelligence gathering for a specific criminal investigation. Citing privacy concerns for its customers, many ISPs challenged the FBI over its use of Carnivore, but all cases were subsequently defeated in court.[9]

After 9/11 and the passing of the Patriot Act, the FBI found it much easier to install its controversial software and could do so without receiving explicit permission from a judge. The act greatly increased the FBI's power to intercept communications of all kinds and to collect information when investigating terrorist threats. It eventually stopped using the Carnivore software because it was not effective against encrypted files. Commercially available email and Internet eavesdropping-intercept software is currently the application of choice among federal law-enforcement officers.

The NSA is rumored to have a system that is capable of detecting and breaking most commonly used forms of encryption almost instantaneously, as well as the ability to look for patterns that would indicate meaningful data hidden inside an innocuous file (steganography).

These actions by the government are virtually indistinguishable from those of hackers and software-virus makers. Anything that law enforcement can do is doable by a foreign intelligence service, a commercial company, or criminals. The cost of developing this technology is insignificant compared with the cost of visual spy techniques like satellites, and therefore this form of espionage can be in anyone's hands.

The Nose

The most rudimentary of the sensor forms are organic, electric noses that analyze airborne particles to determine the physical composition of a suspicious item. Interest in organic sensing technology has heightened since 9/11 as part of the effort to spot explosives and bioterror material in public spaces. These sensors pose a subtle privacy threat because they can be used remotely to assess our physical condition, our health, and our genetic tendencies without our permission or awareness. As medical researchers continue to discover physical reasons for mental and emotional conditions, the privacy threat will increase. Some day, these devices may be able to spot people who have schizophrenia or bipolar disorder as they walk through a turnstile in a public building. As in other forms of surveillance by sensing technology, the privacy invasion comes more from the use of the information than from the collecting.

Special-use sensors started appearing in the mid-1980s. An example is the drunk-driving-prevention gear that hooks a Breathalyzer to the ignition of cars; with this device, drivers have to prove they are sober before the vehicle starts. Similarly, smoke detectors spot particulate matter in the air and set off an alarm. Radiation meters are placed in key public spaces in the United States and the United Kingdom to spot dirty bombs. Detectors are used in many airports to "sniff" shoes and bags for traces of chemical explosives that wouldn't appear on an ordinary metal-detector scan. National Aeronautics and Space Administration researchers have developed an electronic nose. It is sensitive enough to detect minute amounts of ammonia in a space ship's atmosphere before a leak poisons the astronauts. It is even able to distinguish between Coke and Pepsi.[10]

Currently, one of the largest commercial markets for electronic noses is quality control and processing in the food industry. The technology will also prove useful in environmental monitoring, such as detecting harmful chemicals. Electronic-nose prototypes are already proving effective for identifying pneumonia, sinus problems, and lung cancer by analyzing exhaled breath. Those with certain diseases have distinct characteristics and smell prints that the built-in sensors can spot. Breath analysis can also detect diabetes, liver disease, infections, and gastrointestinal disorders. Electronic noses will eventually be able to screen for medical problems and diseases by sniffing fluids, wounds, and perspiration.

More than one hundred smelling-device prototypes are already in development, and the technology is expected to be in widespread use and ubiquitous in our society in the near future. Researchers at the University of Cambridge have created an electronic nose that captures and analyzes body odor from unobtrusive parts of the body to identify people by their smell.

It's too soon to say how these devices will affect privacy, but I can make some educated guesses. Electronic noses could be trained to spot human pheromones, which would give deep insight into a person's emotional or sexual state of arousal. They could almost certainly be trained to spot fear. A quick pass could determine which prescription or street drugs a person is taking. Lie detectors based on electronic noses would undoubtedly be much better than the current ones, which measure only galvanic skin response and respiration. Rapid DNA-based probes will prove helpful in diagnosing diseases and will be effective in uncovering bioweapons.

But there is also a dark side. Prospective employers, insurance companies, and government agencies could use them to learn more about us than we might willingly disclose. Researchers are currently experimenting with DNA sensors that would spot certain genetic ancestries. The potential for abuse with this technology is obvious— a device could be built that would detect Arabs or Scandinavians by smell, for instance. It should also be possible to replicate many of the simpler clinical tests that doctors perform by using these electric noses. Although the information may not be precise enough for diagnostics, electronic noses should work more than well enough to determine our state of mind and the condition of our health. Although such sleuthing may not be commonly thought of as a privacy invasion, it is a loss of control of information about ourselves.

The Future of Sensing

The eventual ubiquity and invisibility of sensors will make it impossible for the individual to be assured that spaces are surveillance free. These computerized sensors will increase their range far beyond our ability to perceive. Organic sensors are perhaps the least understood of all the technologies mentioned in this book. Organic sensing devices can provide clinical insight into the inner workings of living organisms. The effect on privacy caused by biomonitoring seems less offensive than the effect of other technologies, but that perception may be due to its newness. The technology has the capability to see much deeper, hear more clearly, and smell more acutely than any animal that's ever walked the earth. In the future, we'll all be naked.

We'll continue to see single-sense devices evolving into multi-sensory equipment. Even new gadgets can seemingly do the impossible. Toasters can smell burnt toast. Cars can spot deer by infrared, monitor road obstructions using sonar, and feel rain and start their wipers automatically. Toilets that can "taste" the sugar in urine and diagnose diabetes aren't too far away from market. The gradual introduction of these technological marvels has perhaps overshadowed the increasingly important facts about the direction in which the machine world is heading: it is waking up, opening its eyes, listening with its ears, and assessing the outside world by its own sensations, independent of any communication by its human handlers. Privacy predicated upon hidden actions is a dream of the past; even if no human ever knows, some machine always will.

Chapter Nine explains networking, how these machines are connected, and how that amplifies the potential danger to privacy.

9

Stalking
Networks, Tags, and Locators

*The personal life of every individual is based on
secrecy, and perhaps it is partly for that reason that
civilized man is so nervously anxious that personal
privacy should be respected. . . .*

Anton Chekhov[1]

Networked computers make it all too easy to violate our privacy electronically. A single computer, toll-road reader, medical device, or cell phone has access to only an insignificant bit of inconsequential personal information. Even millions of these devices aren't a privacy threat because it's too much work for anyone to extract the information out of each of them individually. Few of us are worth that kind of attention. But networked sensors and databases can talk and exchange information automatically, substantially increasing the exposure of our private information as well as the resulting damage.

If every computer were self-contained and isolated, then the threat to privacy would be manageable; it would just be a matter of blocking any one machine's access to information. Because most computing devices are specialized and have only the sensors necessary to get a specific job done, the machines collect only necessary information, use it, and delete it as soon as feasible. Now that many devices are becoming networked, the situation has changed because machines are starting to talk to one another. A license-plate number recorded by a camera on a highway, a hotel reservation in Europe made on the Internet, and an airline-passenger manifest can all be interwoven into a cohesive story of a vacation. Each specialized repository of data contains a minimal amount of personal information, maybe enough to be an annoyance; however, in aggregate the amount of personal information that's disclosed is overwhelming and intrusive. Additionally, the remote-access capability of networks makes it all too easy for hackers to slip into databases remotely and retrieve what they want, often with no one being the wiser. Networking raises the bar on the impact to your privacy. Privacy invasion has become the misuse of the sum of all of your personal information available in any computer or digital device anywhere.

The advent of networked digital devices is as big a threat to individual privacy as is the rapidly decreasing cost of computer storage. Information copied onto a network can no longer be localized because it takes only a second to copy it to another machine. Good information security becomes paramount in a networked environment; unfortunately most organizations don't have security procedures sufficiently tough enough to effectively stop privacy intrusions caused by illicit copying of customers' personal data.

Networking makes locating technology possible. Tiny chips costing pennies can be invisibly embedded into phones, clothes, almost anything and can identify their owner remotely. Other chips can use a satellite signal to precisely locate themselves within two meters, anywhere on the planet. The information gleaned from these two chips is by itself innocuous, but when all that information is combined and the results are accessed remotely across the Internet, a large measure of privacy has been destroyed—the ability to stop other people from knowing exactly where you are at all times.

Networks

Computers that can talk to other computers are a growing threat to privacy because they can move personal information outside of an individual's sphere of control. In the early days of computerized appliances, information entered into a device was locked inside it; if another gadget needed the data, the content would have to be keyed in again. Phone numbers punched into a cordless phone had to be reentered into a computer or a personal digital assistant (PDA), for instance. During the first few decades of personal computing, each computer had its own storage capability and was unable to swap information with other machines except through cumbersome processes, like swapping floppy disks. This localization of personal information locked within a single machine helped preserve privacy because it made consolidation of personal information difficult; the less information that's available, the smaller the privacy invasion.

When software or hardware is able to talk and pass information back and forth, it's called *interoperable*. In the mid-1990s, interoperability was the exception; today it's the rule. Interoperability arose in both the public and private sectors. In the public arena, standards bodies such as the Institute of Electrical and Electronics Engineers (IEEE), Internet Engineering Task Force (IETF), and the World Wide Web Consortium (W3C) hammered out agreements on various computer hard and soft components ranging from modems to hypertext markup language. The rise of the network was lock-stepped to the expansion of the Internet. TCP/IP, the underlying data protocol, is simplistic, able to break information down into small "packets," ship them through a series of semi-random relay points, and restore them at the other end. Several communication protocols were layered on top of this protocol, including Simple Mail Transfer Protocol (SMTP) and Post Office Protocol (POP) for email, HypterText Transfer Protocol (HTTP) for the web, and Internet Relay Chat (IRC) for typed conversations. Networks extend the power of gadgetry because all the circuitry doesn't have to reside locally. Miniature sensing devices like cameras and microphones don't have much in the way of brains. They can sense and sometimes record but by themselves cannot categorize, filter, or send alerts. They need to be hooked to a bigger computer that has long-term storage and sufficient computing power.

Efficient, low-cost, highly interoperable networking is now routinely built into sensing devices, giving them the ability to relay information. This kind of networking provides three benefits: size reduction, shared resources, and improved computation. The devices have gotten smaller because they no longer need dedicated input/output (I/O) peripherals, and the networking pieces are contained on a single, ever-shrinking chip, now a single function on a larger purpose semiconductor. This distributed network allows connected computers to share sensing devices, much as early personal-computer networks shared printers. They have access to significantly better computation because more sensors are available for almost any calculation, and because the central processing unit (CPU) no longer has to be co-located, it can be quite large, very powerful, or part of a distributed processing system such as *grid computing*. Grid computing is a method for using many off-the-rack computers in parallel; they form a virtual supercomputer and thus can solve tough problems. The power of a sensor is no longer limited to what can be crammed into its form factor; its limit is now the sum of the abilities of every machine that it can talk to. Not only can networked devices offload analysis onto other machines, but also each computer has access to all the information available on a network, not just what's stored locally on the sensor. From a privacy perspective, the size of a device no longer indicates its power; when even the smallest camera can be hooked up to analysis engines and storage drives, an intelligence agency can be hidden inside the head of a pin.

The modern world is becoming a mesh of sensors, CPUs, and storage devices, any group of which can be teamed up for a specific purpose. Target candidates include established artifacts like cell phones and also newly digital ones like satellite and cable boxes, personal video recorders (PVRs), security cameras, and even wireless electric meters. Soon this list will also include most kitchen appliances, such as stoves, refrigerators, microwaves, and toasters. Traffic lights, computerized billboards, toll-road booths, building security systems, self-check-out supermarkets, smart-card kiosks, subways, and taxis are all becoming networked. As Wi-Fi chips become cheaper and smaller (remember Moore's Law?), it will be cost-effective to incorporate them into every electronic device. Like Ethernet before it, Wi-Fi is now being incorporated into larger chip sets such as Intel's Centrino. Soon all electronic devices will be innately networked.

Any lingering expectation of preserving privacy by controlling information flow will vanish as this spider web of electronic voyeurism is woven from coast to coast. If one machine sees something, then all the machines can. In a few years it will be impossible to tell whether you're being observed or listened to in any urban area in the world. Lacking sufficient security, privacy will be redefined as acting "outside the grid," somewhere where there aren't any machines around to eavesdrop. Once a networked machine has information, you will lose all control over the disposition of the data. The only way to protect your privacy will be to keep your sensitive data out of computers in the first place and hold important conversations in machine-free locations, if you can still find them.

One of the reasons digital devices are and will continue to become networked is that networks are incredibly useful to vendors because they can update software or firmware remotely. These fixes used to be incredibly expensive for developers because of the cost of distribution media. There was also a substantial time lag before the customer got the patch, which sometimes proved disastrous. The cost for online downloads is substantially less, and therefore programmers don't have to be as careful; and because they can fix problems quickly, substantially less staff time has to be dedicated to maintenance and quality assurance.

The convergence of wireless broadband and network-capable appliances will create a smart "house" inhabited by swarming devices capable of both human and peer-to-peer interaction. These communication capabilities will be a boon for gadget freaks, who will use the devices as truly personal electronic servants; in addition to using the network to always stay up to date on firmware, gadgets and gizmos will operate in concert to create truly intelligent behavior. Refrigerators will send lists of items that are running low or that are past the expiration date to your cell phone when you go shopping, for instance. These gadgets may sound too tech-y for the average person, but soon wireless appliances will move out of the realm of early adoption and into the mainstream.

Absent tough legislation, it will be impossible to maintain a semblance of privacy with so much personal information swirling around the household, especially when internal information is occasionally secretly phoned to vendors by devices embedded in appliances. Many software programs have this capability now, and there's every reason to believe that networked-appliance manufacturers will incorporate it into their products for marketing and intellectual-property purposes. Microsoft, for instance, uses the Internet to validate that every working copy of Windows XP is a legal one.

Some digital devices that have the ability to communicate with their makers are already here. Entertainment hubs like TiVo, satellite and cable boxes, all communicate some information to their maker, with or without the consumer's consent or awareness. At some point in the near future, this "feature" will spread to other digital household machines. Kitchen appliances all have rudimentary computers. Timers and self-cleaning cycles on stoves, temperature probes on microwaves, and self-defrosting refrigerators use digital circuitry, as do mixers, blenders, and toasters. True networking gear hasn't yet made it into the kitchen, with the exception of some high-end novelty refrigerators, but it's coming. Luxury kitchens designed in the last few years often have personal computers incorporated into the design for web browsing and looking up recipes. Many companies, such as

GE and Sunbeam, were early innovators of digital kitchen products but got out of the game when sales were slow.

Automobiles are also becoming networked devices. Initially, in the 1980s, they were designed to plug into a computer for diagnostic purposes. With most states requiring some form of emissions control and some, like California, requiring substantial compliance, automated monitoring of a car's electronics has now become both cost-effective and necessary.

Kitchen, car, and laundry spying may not sound like much of a threat to privacy, but as any intelligence analyst will tell you, the devil is in the details. Most privacy violations are not going to be caused by the exposure of huge personal secrets but by the publication of many little facts, perhaps wrapped up in some opinionated analysis. Maintaining privacy is less about suppression of one or two damaging facts and more about controlling the gestalt of personal information. The best way to suppress the big intrusions is to control the little ones. As with killer bees, one is an annoyance but a swarm can be deadly.

RFID Tags

If the privacy harm from networking were limited to breadbox-sized computers, it wouldn't be that worrisome. But RFIDs extend the reach of computer networks into everyday objects and could increase the amount of personal information available on a given individual exponentially. RFID tags are low-cost transponders used for automated identification of the tagged object, animal, or person. They are simple devices—an antenna and a chip. Their sole purpose is to respond remotely to queries from an appropriately configured transmitter. They are not new devices; variations have been used since the mid-1950s by intelligence services and the military, either to follow a tagged vehicle or to identify friendly aircraft and ships.

RFIDs can be passive, semi-passive, or active. Passive RFIDs have a limited range but do not require a power source; they pull the small amount of electricity that they need from the current induced in the antenna. They can be made so small that they are effectively invisible—less than the width of a piece of paper and smaller than this printed letter *o*. They can potentially shrink even more—down to the size of a period, for example. Semi-passive RFIDs have a small battery for increased antenna range, and active RFIDs have a full battery. The advantage of the internal power source is increased range and on-board memory storage. The maximum range at which passive chips are detectable varies according to whom you talk to; estimates vary from twenty feet (seven meters) to sixty feet (twenty meters). Battery-powered active chips can be detected at a far greater distance, but the price goes up by orders of magnitude. The greater the distance, the greater the threat because of the increased number of places where sensors can be hidden; for instance, sixty feet would cover both sides of a passageway in a mall or the width of a highway.

RFIDs are being used now. They will become more ubiquitous in the business world than the bar codes they will replace. They offer a huge advantage for inventory control because the surveyor has to be only in the proximity of the chip to tally it. Because inconveniently placed inventory doesn't need to be moved for the surveyor, pallets can be stacked deeper and higher. Audits can be run ad hoc and finished in a fraction of the time that a person with a clipboard and bar-code reader would take. The RFID reader feeds the information directly into a computer, eliminating any subsequent data-entry requirements. The packing material doesn't have to be oriented to provide visual line-of-sight for the reader, as it does with bar codes. The RFID chips can even be read while embedded in a product or buried in a box. They may be placed in packaging such as shrink wrapping or possibly even woven into fabric.

Retailers stand to gain a great deal from having RFID-equipped deliveries. In fact, at one point, Wal-Mart had required its top one hundred suppliers to incorporate RFID by January 2005 and its next two hundred largest by January 2006. Although Wal-Mart relaxed the target dates, it has converted enough inventory to start quantifying the benefits. For instance, it can restock RFID-enabled goods three times faster than nonequipped merchandise. The sheer buying power of companies such as Wal-Mart will force adoption of this technology, driving down the price.

RFID is the first low-cost locational technology. In 2005, a chip cost about 50 cents; by 2006 the price had dropped to a quarter. A nickel is the next goal. As the chips hit increasingly lower price points, it becomes economical to use them for different purposes; eventually they'll be cheap enough to be used for "throw-away" applications, like hiding them in packaging.

The first RFIDs that were visible to consumers were speed-pass devices on toll roads. Cars equipped with a transponder drive through the booth without stopping and are noted by a fixed sensor in the gate. The charges are aggregated and billed at a later date.

> RFID toll systems have created privacy problems. Some states note the entrance and exit times of a car and divide the distance by the elapsed time to calculate the average speed.[2] If it's over the limit, the police could theoretically mail a ticket to the car's owner, who is identified by the transponder's unique sequence.

The use of RFIDs is already spreading. Benetton had announced a plan to incorporate into its clothing chips with the customer's personal information encoded. It postponed the idea temporarily after a negative public reaction.[3] The European Union embedded RFIDs in its currency in 2005. At the request of the Secret Service, color laser printers sold in the United States print a small encoded sequence identifying the manufacturer and serial number of the printer on every printout. It's visible under a blue light with a magnifying glass.

The privacy implications of widespread adoption of these chips, which could lead to every store-bought item's being traceable, are staggering. Every item of clothing, including shoes and glasses, will be traced or at least traceable. Books, suitcases, watches, jewelry, and eventually most household goods including food will have the chips incorporated into them or into the packaging. Some people believe that conspiratorial plans are already afoot by large companies to exploit exactly this situation.[4] It would be useful marketing intelligence to track a product through its lifetime of consumer use. Unfortunately, it would almost certainly reveal additional information that the buyer might feel was invasive, such as telling a merchant who the tagged person is when he or she walks past the store.

The rush to reach a 5-cent price point has decreased the security of the chips to the point where they might be remotely readable with a cell phone. Adi Shamir, the S in the RSA encryption algorithms, revealed at the annual RSA conference in February 2006 that he was able to crack RFID tags using a directional antenna and an oscilloscope to monitor and interpret power fluctuations in the chip. He believes that a cell phone could be modified to achieve the same result.[5]

The potential vulnerability of these chips is important because without adequate security their widespread adoption by industry puts all consumers at a privacy risk and an uninformed one at that; it seems unlikely that many people will know or have the ability to find out where these chips are secreted. Any industry action that removes the control of personal information away from the subject is a privacy violation.

Even at twenty feet, manufacturers could keep track of a product after the purchaser walked out of the store by putting sensing mechanisms at major urban intersections, doorways of stores, and public-transportation terminals. By deploying a far-flung web of RFID transceivers, a manufacturer could trace an item with an embedded chip (or anyone carrying or wearing the item) throughout most of the day, every day, as long as that person stays in a big city. The generally stated reason that stores give for wanting to switch to RFIDs is inventory control (in other words, stopping theft); that doesn't mean that malicious third parties couldn't take advantage of the presence of these embedded chips once the article has left the store.

A wide network of RFID-reading sensors coupled with industry adoption of RFID chips embedded into household items leads inescapably to a world where everyone is always locatable, fingered by clothing and other possessions. It's almost as though each of us were tattooed with a bar code and lived in a city of scanners.

It may be difficult for a consumer to remove, or "kill," the RFID tag. First, it may not be easy to find. Second, industry has been considering requiring the RFID tag for returns and exchanges, just as the price tag is required today. The RFID tags would be scanned and matched against the purchase history to ensure that the sale was legitimate.

The idea of a hidden tracking device is not new and perhaps not all that threatening in the abstract. The danger to privacy from these chips is in the aggregate. They're cheap and useful enough that it's highly likely they're going to be hidden in many retail products. Even if the accumulated tracking information never results in a major embarrassment, the thought that everything that I buy may be traceable is, for lack of a better word, creepy.

There may be a technological solution, however, to the RFID privacy problem. IBM announced in 2006 that it had invented a chip with a perforated edge so that consumers can tear off part of the antenna after purchase, reducing the effective range of the chip to one or two inches.[6]

The RFID chips by themselves might not be so bad if the sales history of the tagged item was accessible only to the store where you bought it. It's likely though that companies will band together and link their information in a noncompetitive way, possibly as part of a "marketing cooperative." They might even set it up so the tags can be located and searched on the Internet. . . .

Tens of millions of RFIDs will kick out a heck of a lot of information, but without a means of searching and sorting the mess, it will be hard to put enough individual parts together to get the big picture. It would be as though each of us had a nude picture of ourselves made into a jigsaw puzzle, and then we separated the pieces and swirled them all together. Sure there would be something embarrassing in the pile of pieces somewhere, but try to find it.

The tagging of physical objects with RFIDs is also going on in the online world as a content-tagging exercise, first through ad hoc search engines like Google and now through a tagged Internet, often referred to as Web 2.0. The physical and online systems could be joined together so that real-world tags would be linked to virtual-world content pointers. The combination of structured real and virtual worlds is intriguing, yet frightening. For instance, a Google-like search engine could be built that would attempt to locate people through their tagged possessions.

A gaggle of tags will someday be a reality. The result, a taggle, is a widespread area of networked tags capable of reporting on any object that passes within twenty feet of a sensor and linked to databases that can connect the object to the owner. A taggle is likely to be the ultimate integration between real-world sensors and the Internet. Internet technologies that can be used to read and sort digital information could also be used against real-world objects. For instance, someone could go to a browser and type "David Holtzman Nike shoes" and, if that person had access to enough databases, he or she might be able to trace my tennies. RFID chips might also be encoded with information and placed on landmarks, rocks, and trees to assist in Internet navigation through physical space.

The convergence of tagged content on the Internet and tagged artifacts in the real world will lead to a strange world, one where privacy may be much more difficult to preserve than it is today because the disposition of physical objects, including ourselves, will be public knowledge.

GPS Systems

If we can't be located through tagged artifacts, there are always satellite location chips. GPS systems use satellite signals to locate the receiver on the Earth. The satellites were originally intended for military use, but since the early 2000s they've become widely available commercially, mainly for use in automobile and marine navigation systems. Like other semiconductors, they're also being dragged along by Moore's Law—they're constantly getting cheaper and smaller and, as a result, are being incorporated into other devices like cell phones. As they become integrated into ever smaller digital objects, they become a danger to privacy because we won't know that they're there and they will know exactly where we are. Many people feel that their privacy extends to protecting their whereabouts.

> Employers are using GPS transponders to keep tabs on their work-ers. New York City television station WABC-TV had its news trucks GPS-equipped, allowing the company to accurately pinpoint the loca-tion of its employees in real time. Unions are questioning the com-pany's agenda for the installation and are reviewing how the practice violates the personal privacy of its members.[7]

Regardless of what companies tell their employees, location technology is being used to track employee behavior, as shown when Automated Waste Disposal in Danbury, Connecticut used the technology to accuse one of its workers of speeding, and Metropol-itan Lumber & Hardware in New York City rebuked one of its employees for goofing off.[8] Trucking outfits find that GPS technol-ogy helps them track their drivers, and schools use it to track their bus drivers. Other companies have discovered that a new GPS tech-nology called *geofences* (computer-generated barriers) has greatly improved employee productivity and reduced time wastage. When a traveling salesperson enters a geofenced bar, a tracking chip in his GPS-equipped cell phone sends an email to the company, report-ing on his location and how long he spent in the establishment. Presumably the reporting would take place only during work hours, although there is no technical or legal reason for this restriction. Xora is one of the companies selling geofencing software, currently in partnership with Sprint. As with other applications of locating technologies, the need for companies to track employees is a genuine one; the overall threat to privacy remains to be seen and will be determined in part by whether the companies voluntarily restrict their tracking to the minimal intrusion necessary for their workplace.

> Parents are surfing password-protected web sites to keep track of their GPS-tagged children. Information on where they are and how fast they are driving is available. As a result, sociologists have been led to question the level of trust and privacy in families today.[9]

Law-enforcement agencies have also gotten on the GPS bandwagon by investing in electronic-surveillance devices. Officers no longer have to follow suspects in their cars. Jurisdictions across the United States are considering using GPS technology to enforce restraining orders.

The significance of RFID tags, GPS chips, and low-cost Wi-Fi is that they provide a tight overlay of the real world onto the virtual one. GPSs can be precisely located. RFIDs tell a story, the history of the tagged artifact. Together, they perform a similar function in the real world as log files do in cyberspace—they create an audit trail.

The question of how to address the privacy concerns that locating technology creates is not easily answered. The technology makes too much sense to believe it won't be used, and, in fact, there are many legitimate uses for RFID chips and GPS devices. As with the other technological innovations described in this book, the problem is not the sensors; it's the use of the information. If companies were prohibited from adding the data to other databases or from storing more than a few days' worth of information, there wouldn't be much of a problem. Unfortunately such a prohibition would run counter to the direction of the U.S. government, which, in 2006, formally requested that service companies retain data for longer periods of time, giving agents more information to potentially subpoena. This tension between the government's desire to access large swaths of historical database information and the need for quick purging of unnecessary data to ensure privacy will continue to be a problem. The more personal information that's saved by third parties, the likelier it is that consumers will have their identity stolen and their privacy violated.

The near-term use of RFID chips provides an up-to-the-minute addition to the historical transactional information contained in merchant databases. Not only did I buy those jeans, but I was wearing them when I walked by the store last night at seven o'clock. If you believe that you have the right to disclose or not disclose where you are at any given moment, then these locating technologies are a threat to your privacy. It is inevitable that locating devices will proliferate, and it's likely that each of us will be carrying and wearing so many artifacts that are hooked into the computer matrix that we'll always be found, whether we want to be or not. These tracking devices will soon reach the price and size points where it is easy and cost-efficient to build them into so many gadgets that, simply by driving a car or by carrying a cell phone or even by wearing factory-made clothing, we'll be tagged and tracked, like wildlife. Marketing companies have so many technical advantages when monitoring consumers, as explained in Chapter Ten, that it seems like overkill to give them the extra advantage of marking us with transponders.

In the future, only the naked will have privacy.

Part V

The Watchers

Our privacy can't be lost if no one is watching; unfortunately, they are. Chapter Ten talks about commercial voyeurs: marketers and advertisers. It explains databases and profiling and includes a brief discussion of future advertising technology. The commercial sector will probably continue to erode privacy without some kind of regulatory oversight. Chapter Eleven focuses on the federal government since 9/11, recent legislation, and policies that are detrimental to our privacy including the no-fly list and the Patriot Act. The key part of this chapter is the discussion about the balance between national security and personal privacy.

10

Marketing Invasions
Garbos and Greed

*Law-abiding citizens value privacy. Terrorists require
invisibility. The two are not the same, and they
should not be confused.*

Richard Perle[1]

Privacy has two natural enemies: marketers and the government.
Each group has a job to do that can be done much better with
detailed information on lots of people. Whether the job is to persuade people to buy things (marketing) or to track them (government), the task is easier with more accurate, timelier, and more
comprehensive data on, well, . . . everyone.

Technology makes it easier to keep tabs on millions, even hundreds of millions, of consumers and citizens. Not only is the storage
of consumers' data cheaper and easier to search than with paper, but
also a single person can easily run the whole tracking process. No
conventional business function has been changed as much by the
advent of information technology as direct marketing.

At its simplest, marketing means convincing the consumer to buy.
The most benign interpretation is that the seller has likely customers
out there who want to know about a product. In this view the potential buyer has already implicitly opted in in some way and views the
communication as a benefit. From this perspective marketing is primarily a way of providing information, a form of communication.

At its worst, marketing involves convincing randomly or not so randomly selected strangers that they need to buy a product they weren't planning on getting or don't need; they may not even know that the product or service exists. At it's best, marketing hooks up an interested buyer with the right product or service, pleasing everyone, the consumer and the producer. The key to a win/win marketing situation is to hit a bull's-eye: a receptive, targeted audience or customer. When the recipient of a marketing message resents the communication, then it's an annoyance or invasion; too much of this kind of communication is a serious privacy problem. Undesirable marketing communications are called junk mail, spam, or telemarketing. Technology has helped marketers fix the problem of badly targeted messages by using automated software to categorize people based on information about them. Computer people call this data mining, analysts call it profiling, and marketing people refer to it as segmentation. This sorting process is getting out of control; it sometimes labels consumers in a way that they're not aware of and may even resent. This involuntary branding is also a violation of a person's privacy.

Segmentation

Sellers can be more persuasive when they have information about their targets than when they don't, regardless of whether their communication medium is email, postal mail, the telephone, or a person. Salespeople generally work on commission, and because pestering people doesn't generate a lot of sales, they prefer a receptive audience. For large groups, marketers find a receptive audience by segmenting the customers by demographics. The theory behind this form of categorization is that people in certain age groups and of certain genders and ethnic backgrounds are likely to buy a certain product or service. Marketers know, for example, that if you listen to hip-hop, you are statistically likely to buy a specific brand of car.

In addition, long experience has shown that sales techniques can be honed to fit the subject and thereby increase the likelihood of a sale.

The high-tech way to segment is by psychographics. The holy grail of the marketing industry is to be able to determine the mental state of potential consumers, their possible reasons for buying, and the psychological roots of any sales resistance each target customer might have. Psychographic categorization is best suited for Internet commerce, where there may not be any historical information on the customers, because their identity is unknown. In this framework, any previous association between the consumer and the company is incidental, useful only because it can be exploited to analyze the historical pattern of purchases to leverage the next one. Long-term customer intimacy is less valuable than an immediate sale, regardless of subsequent churn. A consumer's privacy suffers because the vendor has no reason to fear alienating the customer through intrusiveness.

Applied marketing technology functions like an online Casanova. It provides seductive paths for acquiring customers, lowers the cost for each "touch," and can be used to increase the take rate through psychologically derived targeting techniques and behavioral analyses. But each sale is a seduction, not a romance. Increasingly, marketers and advertisers will have the technology they need to specifically target the perfect prospects and hardly anyone else. In the future, marketing will continue to narrow its focus using data-mining technology.

Targeted communication aimed at a specific audience that shares a common attribute is sometimes called narrow-casting. At it's simplest, narrow-casting can be conducted with a targeted email campaign. Modern marketing techniques allow advertisers to run sophisticated programs that use profiling technology to thoroughly segment their lists until they reach the ultimate, an extremely personalized list with one name: yours. The core technology of this capability is good databases.

Databases Drive Marketing

Databases are space efficient and can store information in a computer the size of a breadbox that would, in paper form, fill roomfuls of file cabinets. But databases can do much more than just store the files. The real benefit is searching and sorting. Imagine trying to find a single file in the rooms of file cabinets; it could take a while just to find the right container, then the correct drawer, then the file. If the file is out of place, it may never be found. That's why doctors' offices are so meticulous about color-coding their patients' records.

Even if everything is done exactly right—the file is encoded correctly, the cabinet is found, the dossier is exactly where it's supposed to be—this system works only for a single filing scheme based on a *key*, or *index*, field. Some places file by last name; some, like doctors, may use a policy number; the IRS uses SSNs. It's usually a wise strategy to choose an index that won't change throughout the lifetime of the filing system. Phone numbers and addresses are often bad for this purpose because they change too often. If management decides that it needs to track a second field, such as a phone number, a duplicate, parallel system based on the new index needs to be created. A seriously time-consuming, intensive exercise, reindexing a large filing system can take years.

Computers are superb at dealing with these complications. Commercial database software can instantly search on any field in hundreds of thousands of records, although it is significantly faster when searching on an indexed field. Unlike their paper counterparts, databases are usually indexed on more than one key field at the cost of more storage space (typically one third to one half more). But, as pointed out several times in this book, storage is cheap. Creating a new index field may take hours, sometimes days for a huge database, but this time is still much less than would be required to create a paper index. This indexing flexibility makes searching fast and flexible. A user can sit at a computer and ask for a marketing list of everyone in zip code 20170 who makes more than $100,000 per year and voted in the last presidential election. The results will be on the desktop in less than a minute. Obtaining the paper equivalent could take weeks. The efficiency of storing and searching electronically stored information changes direct marketing from being a nuisance to being a privacy invasion. Many of the marketing functions discussed in this chapter would be impossible to perform with paper records.

Database companies collect immense amounts of information. ChoicePoint maintains about nineteen billion records for nearly every adult American, and those numbers continue to grow exponentially.[2] Since 1997 and its spin-off from Equifax, ChoicePoint has strategically bought up more than fifty other companies and has become a powerful leader in the information industry.[3]

Acxiom is another database powerhouse. In 2004, it recorded $1.01 billion in revenue, and managed more than twenty billion records.[4] Acxiom has purchased direct-marketing agencies, background-screening firms, email marketing companies, international data companies, an overseas data-management company, and several small businesses from TransUnion to continue its expansion into international markets.[5] Acxiom also bought SmartDM, which provides database marketing services to casinos and hotels, along with professional- and college-sports industries.[6] When it acquired Chicago-based MarketsOnDemand, the database firm gave it access to a file of fifty-four million names containing postal and email addresses.[7] Consodata, a world leader in information marketing, was bought by Acxiom, and so was Claritas Europe.[8] Acxiom's InfoBase profiler alone collects information on 95 percent of U.S. households from more than fifteen million sources.[9] In 2004, Acxiom launched Personicx, its customer-segmentation tool, which uses behavioral analysis for increasingly focused targeting.[10] The company says it has found a link between postal codes and behavior. Acxiom plans to compile the information and sell it to marketers and advertisers. Experian, the global information provider, has developed a similar tool called Prime Performance Modeling for targeting prospects through behavioral analysis.[11] Experian reports that it holds data on 98 percent of U.S. households, with more than one thousand separate items per family.[12]

These companies are powerful because they collect, control, and sell information about everyone and, even more important, because they're viewed as authoritative, even when they're wrong. Sometimes they make mistakes and privacy violations occur. In the past, a slap on the wrist and the requirement of a public apology were the only punishment for these security breaches. Those penalties may be changing as this book is written. As with industrial pollution, the degree of corporate responsiveness to publicly unacceptable incidents is directly related to the amount of the punitive fines. The FTC has slapped $15 million worth of fines on ChoicePoint to settle charges that the company violated privacy rights and federal laws when thieves hacked personal consumer information held in its databases.[13]

These database companies are too powerful to not be regulated. An adverse record on any of these services can seriously impact the subject's life. Because they're automated, the potential exists for multiple mistakes. It's easy to imagine a program going haywire and screwing up millions of records or allowing a momentary lack of security that exposes intimate details of every person archived in the files.

The age at which people get their first marketing database record keeps getting lower. It used to be created because of a first job, but now marketing companies pick up children by acquiring their birth announcements. Hospitals sell birth records to any company willing to pay the price.[14] Lucid Marketing is one of the companies that buys birth records and ties them in with email addresses. For example, one of its campaigns has customized birthday messages sent out three days before the birthday of each child in a household. Product-related information is included in the Happy Birthday emails and is targeted by age, location, and household income.[15] This practice continues year after year. I remember being surprised when my first child, Lauren, was born, and I received congratulatory coupon mailings at home from companies like Procter & Gamble. The collection of data about children is growing at a phenomenal rate. The Electronic Privacy Information Center (EPIC) reports that governmental agencies, sports clubs, universities, associations, and many kinds of businesses collect data on children of all ages.[16]

It would be naïve to expect that information to not be stored and used again and again throughout the lifetime of the consumer. The coupon for free Pampers I received when my daughter was born signaled the creation of a new consumer to marketers. The file that was opened that day will continue to be fleshed out until the day, seventy, eighty, ninety years hence, when she will once again be presented with diaper coupons. Companies try to start advertising to children as early as possible because statistics tell them that if the consumer is hooked then, the manufacturer can make an extraordinary amount of money over that person's lifetime.[17] Corporate marketing campaigns are even integrated into our public schools. That's why cola and fast-food companies have posters in school bathrooms and classrooms and why hundreds of them donate money to schools in exchange for the schools' allowing them to run marketing surveys in the classrooms, to create corporate-sponsored teaching materials (commercials inserted into educational videos and names of products into textbooks), to offer free book covers covered with corporate ads, or to give free samples of junk food to the kids.[18] These marketing activities flesh out marketing information on children, capturing not only their vital stats but also some initial sense of their consumptive habits and psychographic attributes. Marketing companies can use this information to continually monitor these children throughout their lifetimes and to spot not only what they buy and what they think but also when they've changed their thought patterns. Often the fact that someone has changed an opinion is more significant than the belief itself.

Children aren't the only ones at the mercy of public-record disclosure. At one time, if you were recently divorced and a woman in

Ipswich, Massachusetts, you might have received an ad from a local health club offering you a special membership. The Probate and Family Court in that town had sold the names and addresses of recently divorced women to the health club.[19] Most data collected from court cases in many U.S. jurisdictions is considered a part of the public record. Realtors can also find new clients using this method. Personal information in public records is rarely sealed, except when the case involves juveniles.

Metromail, now owned by Experian, was using prison labor to digitize information collected from surveys. The convicted felons had access to the personal information of consumers all over the country, as one customer found out in an alarming manner. Beverly Dennis received at her home a twenty-five-page letter from a convicted rapist and thief that contained the personal details of her life. He even knew which magazines she liked to read and what type of hemorrhoid cream she used. More important, he had her home address and wanted to come visit her as soon as he could. The case turned into a class-action suit and was eventually settled. Among other terms, Metromail was required to notify the 2.2 million class members that their personal information had been provided to prisoners. Metromail is prohibited from using prisoners to input survey data in the future. And it must screen its contractors to make sure they do not use prisoners.[20]

Profiling for Segmentation

The fact that companies collect these kinds of data is not necessarily a threat to privacy. The controversy is over what's done with it. What marketers really want to do with personal information is feed it into profiling software to segment and find groups of people who are likely to buy what they're selling.

Psychologists can categorize consumers by watching their financial transactions, such as credit-card purchases. They can label people by personality type or by temporal state of mind. Short-term states like depression can be determined by spotting changes in buying patterns, as can longer-term problems like bipolar disorders. Hidden health problems can be teased out by examining medication purchases. It's even possible to guess at sexual orientation by analyzing the choice of entertainment material.

Labels are the specific instance of a segment, or, rather, a segment is a cluster of similar labels. Once they are formulated, they become part of the target's permanent record. The labels are opinions, not facts; but, like the results of credit reports or background checks, the uncontestable information sticks to the subjects forever, just like birth dates and SSNs.

> Walgreens, the drugstore giant, sent a woman a one-month, free and unsolicited supply of Prozac along with a form letter signed by her doctors wishing her success in recovery. The woman hadn't used the antianxiety drug for years. She filed a class-action lawsuit claiming that Walgreens, three doctors, and Eli Lilly, which makes Prozac, had violated the privacy of patients by means of unauthorized access to medical records.[21]

Labels are easily attached to people, and they are hard to remove. They stick like glue. Lawyers, especially those who specialize in malpractice cases, sometimes buy patient records from unscrupulous health care workers.[22] Medical tests can also get you labeled by your insurance company and your employer. Certain labels in a medical file may decrease your chances of getting hired for a job because businesses often check with the Medical Information Bureau, a central database of medical information.

You could also be inadvertently labeled a terrorist because of purchases you make. After 9/11, federal agents developed a profile of a terrorist using the hijacker Mohammed Atta's shopping preferences and tastes.[23] You could have an increased threat profile if you buy the same sorts of food as he did. The Drug Enforcement Agency also uses supermarket records to find people who buy a lot of small plastic bags because they are often used in the drug trade.[24]

Companies can conduct clinical evaluations of subjects by discovering, predicting, or guessing attributes of which the targets themselves may not be consciously aware. It's also possible to passively administer stripped-down versions of personality tests like the Myers-Briggs and present different web sites to the subject based on the results. A company could serve up sixteen different e-commerce web sites, each one tailored to one of the Myers-Briggs archetypes. Introverts might respond to an ad for a vacation package that emphasizes the cultural aspects of a location; extroverts might respond to one touting the location's nightlife.

This kind of targeted sales approach can easily cross the line from custom to creepy. The analysis could also be wrong. An easy way to experience this phenomenon is to order a few books from Amazon for someone else and then watch the company's recommendation engine begin suggesting other books that are in line with the other person's tastes, not yours. It can take weeks to get the suggestions back to normal for you again. Now think about what would happen if you bought several books of pictures of young children along with a copy of Vladimir Nabokov's *Lolita*. A marketing company might label you as someone overly fascinated with little children, especially if it linked to another database and found that you were a childless, single male. A label of "attracted to children" could land you in a pretty unsavory market segment and subject you to a lifetime of unwanted, unsolicited offers and advertisements.

Technology Helps Measure Advertising

Because the cost of advertising is high and can quickly become astronomical, belief in the campaign or product isn't always enough; the sponsors need a way to measure the effectiveness of their pitches. Segmenting the audience for a product is the most basic way to increase the cost efficiency of ads.

Historically, advertising has been a one-way form of communication. A company has a message it wants to send to a target audience. Advertising execs craft the piece in accordance with the desired goals and the medium that will be used. Some media have special requirements. Television and radio ads need to be customized for length; often the same commercial will be used for ten-, fifteen-, and thirty-second spots. Print ads are sometimes driven by the page size but are more often characterized by the content. The low cost of print production allows companies to experiment with several approaches to determine which one would be the most successful. The Internet combines the broad reach of television with the versatility of print and often costs the least of the three.

The biggest problem is that the selling company generally has to wait weeks or, in some cases, months to find out whether the pitch worked. One way of determining effectiveness, correlating the appearance of ads to a commensurate rise in sales, is often difficult because of the many other factors that could be causing the change. A more common technique is to use panels or focus groups to provide feedback on the ad's reach, persuasiveness, and memorableness. The results from the focus group are then extrapolated to estimate what the population at large might say if interviewed. The demographic composition of the focus group is critical because if the ratios don't match those in the population at large, the result may be skewed by race, gender, or age. It's also important to choose a sample large enough to be statistically significant. Another problem with panels is that they cost a lot of money because the participants often have to be reimbursed. Even nominal sums or free meals add up quickly for a large enough group.

A better way to assess the effectiveness of ads would be to automatically poll all potential viewers, even if they number in the tens of millions. The TiVo Personal Video Recorder (PVR) system, for instance, is potentially more effective than the Nielson television rating system because Nielson is based on an absurdly small panel (five thousand viewers), whereas PVR can report on each and every television set equipped with the company's device, hundreds of thousands of consumers queried passively and in real time.

The marketing problem with such automated evaluators is that they're often set up as anonymous systems that aggregate statistics; as such, they're less valuable than other approaches because they aren't cross-indexed with demographic data. Advertisers don't want the sampled consumers to be completely anonymous. Fortunately for them, technology has made it easier than it once was for them to correlate the background of the individual with the computer gadget. Satellite TV, cable boxes, and TiVo integrated with sub-scriber billing records offer a real-time panorama of viewers, right down to street address, ethnic background, gender, and age.

Increasingly, technology-gadget companies that have an ongoing billing relationship with consumers will have a financial incentive to link personal information with usage patterns in addition to selling aggregate data. This possibility poses a clear and escalating risk to individual privacy. It will get worse because of the transition from formerly free entertainment and communication services to pay-per-view models run by sophisticated technology. PVRs and satellite radio are good examples of this trend. Although these companies all have privacy policies, they're essentially worthless to consumers because they contain too many loopholes. And the companies can change the policy with no notice simply by publishing the new one on a web site.

As companies continue to merge, acquire, be acquired, and form strategic partnerships, these pockets of personal data will be matched with possible cross-connections. Cellular-phone call lists integrated with grocery-shopping history. School records mingled with overseas travel records. Psychological profiling combined with family history. Because data never go away, it's inevitable that every piece of information ever gathered by any marketer will eventually be linked into a monster profile of every consumer, similar to a credit report. Companies like Acxiom and ChoicePoint will become the Experian and TransUnion of consumer profiling. These profiles will describe not just our purchasing preferences but also our personalities, much as credit reports have become the indicator not of our financial status but of our trustworthiness.

As marketers, advertisers, and retailers collect more information on us and as the art of consumer profiling improves, these companies will be able to predict our tastes. Like an old married couple who know each other's arguments so well that they just call out the number, the marketer and the consumer will become tediously intimate.

Customer-Relationship Management

Loyalty cards are key for corporate snooping. Supermarkets not only have all our personal identifying information but also keep a list of everything we buy. They claim to use this information to provide discounts and to ensure that shelves are stocked with the most popular products. A list of supermarket and drugstore purchases is much more revealing than people might think. One of the most effective, although low-tech, methods of information collection used by intelligence agents and federal law enforcement is "dumpster diving." A family's life can easily be pieced together by sorting through discarded packaging, medicine bottles, and food containers. Analyzing the results from store courtesy cards is like going through someone's trash without having to wipe off the coffee grounds.

The situation presented by the use of store loyalty cards is ripe for abuse. Food Lion, a grocery chain based in Salisbury, North Carolina, has been accused by an ex-employee of sending customer purchase information along with contact data to database marketing companies and product manufacturers.[25]

The king of customer-relationship management and data mining is the casino industry. It knows more about its customers than any other type of business does. For instance, Native American–owned Foxwoods Resort Casino has a two-hundred-gigabyte-plus customer database that can tell employees how many children a client has and how much he or she earns every year. But that's just the tip of the iceberg. The casino knows how long a person plays, how much money she drops, and her betting strategies. All this information is fed to casino workers so they know how to handle customers. Most of the information is accessed through loyalty cards, which customers like to use because they get points that are translated into free rooms and other prizes.

The MGM Mirage brags that it can tell you which of its poker-playing patrons eat onions on their burgers. Its databases track nine million customers and hold more than six thousand gigabytes of data. Harrah's has information on twenty-three million people and admits to never deleting any digital data it has ever collected.[26] The privacy impact may be slight compared with the impact of grocery shopping, however; unlike other industries, casinos say they never sell or share customer information because it is too valuable.

The privacy damage caused by merchant analysis of loyalty cards is mitigated by the fact that the consumer generally gets something of value for cooperating. However, few people have any idea that the "discourtesy" cards are any threat to their privacy. Even if retailers' use of the information gleaned from the cards can't be regulated, a full-disclosure statement should be legally required, and it should specify in gory detail the possible uses that the retailer might make of the information, whether it's choosing product lines or devising technology-boosted, precision advertising.

Advertising Technology and the Ubiquity of Ads

Database applications that enable companies to communicate with consumers get better as they get faster. The better they are, the more sophisticated the analyses that can be provided in the same period of time; such analyses tease out many cross-connections between apparently disparate pieces of personal data. They become faster as the underlying hardware is accelerated, a direct benefit of Moore's Law. Advertising applications are in the process of an evolutionary change; they will eventually be able to incorporate the best of new display and information technology to get the attention of people in a digitally crowded and communication-competitive world. The Internet is the testing ground for many of these techniques because it's an ideal medium for trying out new display methods as well as for personalizing ads by drawing on databases of consumer information. Each advance in Internet features has been linked to a commensurate jump in attention-getting advertising techniques.

Although ads appear to be merely annoying, they have deeper, privacy-threatening implications. It's impossible to personalize an ad without a good understanding of what makes the audience tick. As segmentation strategies converge on their ultimate goal, targeting the individual with custom marketing messages, some personal information will have to be brought to bear in order to select the appropriate message. This access to a consumer's personal information for the purposes of dishing up a commercial can easily violate that person's privacy.

The earliest commercial advertising on the Internet was the infamous first spamming of Usenet by Laurence Canter and Martha Siegel, immigration attorneys (who were married at the time). Usenet was an Internet news and discussion forum with thousands of subject areas; on it users could create any discussion subject they wanted to. The two lawyers wanted to let potential clients know about an imminent immigration lottery. Congress had just created the Green Card Lottery to encourage diversity in immigration. On April 12, 1994, Canter sent out the electronic ad to more than five thousand newsgroups. Members were infuriated because many of the bulletin boards targeted were not even remotely connected to immigration issues. The law firm did get one thousand new customers from that one posting and made a good amount of money for their immigration practice, but the lawyers had their Internet access cut off and they received a steady stream of emails, letters, visits, and phone calls from angry Usenet users.[27]

Shortly thereafter, more pitchmen moved onto the Net, adding spam to email and popup ads to web sites, effectively destroying Usenet. The lesson became clear: the usefulness of a communication method is directly proportional to the ratio of content to ads.

As the signal-to-noise ratio becomes smaller, useful content decreases as a percentage of readable material, and people desert the medium for other venues. Advertisers abhor a blank wall; technology provides a write-all paintbrush that permits solitude-busting messages to be painted anywhere. These ads do not appear just in the real world; the trend is to push products in cyberspace; advertising in video games is popular, for instance.

Until the Canter and Siegel spamathon, the community-enforced rule was that there would be no advertising on the Internet. Today, every new Internet company and product is evaluated by investors for advertising potential because, for many companies, ads are still the primary source of revenue. Many online companies, like newspapers such as the *Washington Post*, are experimenting with in-your-face advertising created with Macromedia's Flash. These ads range from irritating animations to obnoxious full-page commercials that have to be watched before reaching the desired content. Although advertising is not inherently a privacy violation, the process of making ever more distracting and eye-catching ads will inexorably lead advertisers to incorporate more personal information about their audience into their messages.

Behavioral-targeted advertising is the new wave of the online world. On a daily basis, Yahoo! logs usage information from 200 million email and instant-messaging users,[28] collecting about ten terabytes of data in the process.[29] It uses this information to improve its understanding of customer behavior, habits, and needs. It's also capable of building an entire advertising profile for each user, as is MSN with its adCenter, which allows advertising clients to choose specific Internet users to show its ads to.[30] Google is doing the same thing with ads in gmail accounts customized to the message's content.[31] Amazon has always been unabashedly straightforward about its corporate intent to refine consumer interest and offer progressively more targeted sales inducements; its business model depends on being able to do so.

Targeted ads will be used to track Internet surfers and their habits and to shoot compelling advertising at them. Advances in technology, like Flash, will be used to make the ads more visually interesting than they now are and also to put ads with dynamic content in places that were never reachable before; such technology is able not only to take into account changing world trends but to instantly personalize the message based on the probable recipient.

A similar advertising trend is taking place in the physical world. One manifestation is the placement of ads on every conceivable flat surface. Advertisers are putting LCD panels on the back of the front seats of cabs, on the walls of subway trains, in sports arenas, on airplanes, on the sides of cars, in elevators, along city streets—in short, anywhere there's a captive audience. As the weight and price of these panels come down, they will appear everywhere, able to turn a whole city into Times Square. Wireless technology enables these ads to be instantly updated; it can provide new pricing schemes, such as time-slicing the display and sharing it among multiple advertisers. Some taxis in New York and in other large cities have their digital signs tied into GPS location sensors so that the signs can provide information on restaurants and businesses the cab is passing. The sheer intrusiveness of these ads has brought what was an annoyance to the level of a privacy invasion; they will soon be intolerable.

Advertising is invading the life of the average person in many new and not altogether desirable ways. Advertisers are using technology to push their wares in ever-increasing numbers of video ads in movie theaters, in mandatory commercials at the front of DVDs (many studios disable all the control buttons while the ad is running), and in popular movies, television shows, and even video games through strategic product placement. Reactrix Systems in Redwood City, California, makes big, promotional 3-D holograms that don't require special glasses to watch.[32] The company projects the holographic images onto sidewalks or buildings, and the images track the gestures and movements of people nearby to make the display interactive. For example, a group of people can kick around a virtual soccer ball or splash in a virtual swimming pool, all the while being covered with the sponsor's logo.[33]

The most potentially menacing future threat will be the incor-
poration of so much intimate personal data into ads that the target
will feel violated. The ultimate goal of narrow-casting is advertising that is immediately intrusive, not because of the physical nature
of the message but because of the truly unctuous intimacy of the
pitch. In the movie *Minority Report*, Tom Cruise's character walks
through a mall in which the walls are covered with animated billboards with characters that seem to reach out and talk to him by
name, trying to sell him products (presumably by reading RFID
chips). In such advertising a quick lookup provides enough personal
information for the pitch to be tailored to the individual. Perhaps
the background of the ad will be the cityscape of the town where
he grew up. Maybe the model will look like him or his wife, child,
or mother. Such pictures are available online from the DMV databases, and it would be easy to morph the model's appearance so that
the target's mother appeared to be telling him to buy chicken soup.
Ads will be further tailored by language, special interests, and
vocabulary. People relate to a level of language that matches their
own. Car salesmen instinctively understand this relationship; they
use a technique known as *mirroring,* in which they match their language including cadence and gestures to their customer's. Expect
tailored pitches to use personal knowledge to mirror the subject,
projecting a cloyingly fake intimacy.

> Brickstream Corporation, a Virginia company, is manufacturing a tech-
> nology that will track customers as soon as they enter a store. Cam-
> eras will follow every move. Pressure-sensitive floor panels will tell
> where they linger, stop, and browse.[34] It's easy to imagine linking this
> technology to face-recognition software in order to track the individual.

Another technology already found in some grocery stores is
shopping carts equipped with electronic tablets. Three Massachusetts Stop & Shop supermarkets are asking customers to swipe these
tablets with their courtesy cards so the store can provide them with
a grocery list based on previous visits. The system also offers tar-

geted coupons when customers turn into appropriate aisles.[35] The electronic shopping cart is just one more piece of the predictive-technology puzzle that is making its way to a store near you.

Outdoor advertising has been around as long as people could chisel messages into stone. The Romans placed a type of billboard along their famous roads. Inscriptions found in Pompeii could be called advertisements or at least graffiti. Billboards in the United States took off in the 1830s. In 1835, Jared Bell of New York was creating posters for the circus that measured nine feet by six feet.[36] 1850 saw the first advertising on streetcars.

Advertising today uses the newest display technology as fast as it becomes available. During the summer of 2004, a Ford Fiesta ad campaign for Europe took integrated, interactive billboards to a new height by integrating text messaging.[37] Yahoo! had a twenty-three-story billboard erected in Times Square to launch a new web site. It was interactive and allowed pedestrians passing by to play a video-game broadcast with their cell phones.[38] Accenture has also designed a high-resolution, interactive touchscreen billboard. Pedestrians and mall crowds can interact with images and characters on the screen, as well as play games.[39] Makers of digital billboards and posters around the country are now adjusting displays to meet the advertising needs of different audiences. Rush-hour crowds will get one type of ad, while young couples hitting the bars and restaurants in the evening will get a different set of displays.

Coca-Cola has erected one of the most advanced billboards in the world in Piccadilly Circus. It is also one of the largest at almost one hundred feet. The board has interactive components that respond to people who look at it as well as to weather conditions. The billboard even knows if someone is waving at it. Soon it will respond to cell-phone text messages.[40]

These billboards are the beginning of personalized ads. Initially they'll be targeted to a segment of the population. As technology gets better at identifying characteristics of the audience and using personal location and identification devices like RFID chips, the size of the audience will shrink to an uncomfortable few until the spotlight is just on you. Mobiltrak started using specialty antenna dishes to detect which radio stations passing drivers were tuned to. The company modified electronic billboards in the vicinity of the drivers, based on the demographics of the radio stations, and dynamically displayed ads tailored to people with distinct profiles.[41] Privacy advocates worry that merging such demographic information with GPS technology or license-plate-reading cameras will expose individual drivers' listening interests.[42] Like other technologies mentioned in this chapter, those that reveal radio preferences are by themselves not such a big deal; merging this information with other bits of private information contained in third-party databases can cause a much bigger privacy problem.

Clickspace Keeps Pace with Brickspace

In the online world, spyware takes the place of RFID chips for tracking browsing and buying habits. Several techniques are used to monitor the whereabouts and doings of online shoppers. The classic technique is to use *cookies*, or small data files that identify the user to the web site and maintain continuity between visits. Newer techniques include the placement of invisible pixels or very small windows that track online activities. Some companies use more aggressive tactics like placing Trojan spyware onto consumers' computers, often justifying this practice as an effort to stop "pirates." Another type of spyware, a root-kit, hides software inside an operating system so that it is completely undetectable by the user and is therefore able to root around with impunity in the owner's data. Root-kits have been around for years but only on UNIX computers. In 2005, they started showing up on Windows.

Sony-BMG got caught using spyware in December 2005. It had put a root-kit into several of its popular audio CDs, including Santana's latest release. This software surreptitiously installed itself onto the buyers' computers, where it monitored how many times the music was installed, restricting use to a Sony-defined number of copies; it also inventoried each user's music and sent a list back to the music company. Unfortunately the software wasn't written well, and Sony ended up opening a back door into its customers' computers, which became vulnerable to hackers who took advantage of Sony's file-naming convention.[43]

Symantec, known for its high-profile Norton Security Suite, became the second commercial company to admit it used a root-kit to hide files on computers. The antivirus vendor decided to incorporate the kit to prevent customers from accidentally deleting important files.[44] Reports that AIM was carrying a dangerous root-kit began to appear in October 2005. The root-kit, named lockx.exe, spread with the Sdbot.add worm, getting installed when users clicked on links.[45]

Root-kits and similar technology are the vanguard for waves of intrusive marketing, hacking, and hybrid incursions that combine elements of both. Spyware and Trojans are enablers of future violators; they open up a weak spot, a path where malicious programs can be entered into your computer, steal your information, damage your equipment, and possibly take your identity. Even if the spyware itself doesn't violate your privacy, it leaves you vulnerable to others who might.

The Future of Marketing

Marketing can go in one of two directions. Taking the less intrusive path, advertisers would build on the concept of "opt-in" and create permissions-based marketing campaigns where the degree of intrusiveness is offset by commensurate remuneration. It's perfectly reasonable to trade loss of privacy for a fee. Consider frequent-flyer programs. They track personal information such as travel, yet the prospect of free airplane tickets more than compensates for the loss of privacy. These kinds of systems are always voluntary and are received enthusiastically by consumers if the reward is right. From a marketing viewpoint, they also enhance the brand.

Taking the second and darker path, advertising could continue down the path of "opt-out" or "opt-never." Starting from the premise that goods can be sold by constantly pitching targeted ads at ad-numb customers, companies that choose this route will exploit each new technological advance to track consumers, monitor their activities, and observe their purchases; they will combine this information with historical personality patterns derived from marketing databases to wheedle, coerce, or intimidate people into buying their products.

The ultimate goal of narrow-casting is to segment the target audience into a group of one—you. Databases of personal information, psychographic profiles, and a history of seller-attempted inducements and blandishments along with their relative success rate can be the basis for highly personal, intimate, and disturbing commercial pitches. At this level of technology adoption and privacy shrinkage, there is no difference between megamarketing and government surveillance. Because marketers and the government are sharing information (see Chapter Eleven), it stands to reason that they should share the same restrictions for data usage—requirements for security, guaranteed purge dates, specific usage statements, and significant penalties for misuse.

Marketing is a necessary evil that at times can even be a guilty pleasure for consumers. It slips into the category of privacy intrusion when the advertising messages are both persistent and inappropriately placed, as in taxicabs, or when they tap into personal information about the consumer that the marketer probably shouldn't have and certainly shouldn't use in that fashion. These shopping data come from many sources, but, these days, the data are most often tracked via loyalty cards, frequent-buyer numbers, or the online equivalents. Although consumers often get something in return for giving up their private information, they rarely understand how the acquiring company intends to, and often does, use the data.

The need for improved segmentation and identification of customers is driving database and data-mining technology. As in the past, marketers will aggressively use new technology as it becomes commercially available to push their pitches and to acquire a form of intimacy with the customer. The desire for a 24/7, worldwide sales environment will induce advertisers to examine nontraditional venues for their ads as innovations in technology make them possible. Whether advertisers overtly intrude and irritate by invading your personal space or do it covertly by working behind the scenes, building a detailed dossier of your preferences, they are intruding on your privacy. This intrusion can have serious consequences when the results of marketing segmentation are fed into government counterterrorism efforts, as we will see in the next chapter.

11

Government Invasions for Security
Mugwumps and Momists

*I never said, "I want to be alone." I only said, "I want
to be left alone." There is all the difference.*

Greta Garbo[1]

National security has never been as important to Americans as
it has been since the terrorist attack on the World Trade Center and the Pentagon in 2001. The S word (security) has become a
mantra that, repeated enough, threatens to overwhelm any other
thought. Many civil liberties have become deemphasized in the
name of security, and privacy was one of the first of these rights to
go. From the weakening of the Fourth Amendment to the Patriot
Act, the White House has not been shy about stating its priorities,
and privacy for the citizenry has not been one of them. In 2006, several domestic espionage programs authorized by President Bush were
made public by various newspapers. These programs involved government wiretapping of domestic phone calls without a warrant and
an arrangement between the NSA and several large phone companies to get copies of all their clients' phone transactions.

This tradeoff between security and privacy today is crucial to the
preservation of our privacy in the future because, as has been mentioned many times already in this book, technology is improving all
the time. Anything that the intelligence agencies can do today
regarding data collection is nothing compared with what they will

be able to do in the future because of the usual technology culprits: cheaper disks, smaller sensors, and so forth. Like most tradeoffs concerning policy, the solution undoubtedly falls in the middle: protecting privacy while preserving security. Unfortunately that is not the current political frame of mind.

The Historic Tension Between Privacy and National Security

It is the nature of governments to want to know things about its citizens that citizens don't wish to reveal. If the need is great enough, the government will get the information, regardless of rights or niceties. The notion that a national need or desire is reason enough to strip away the concealment of the citizenry is the root of the privacy conflict. Individuals want to control the details of their lives as much as companies want to control their intellectual property, yet most citizens are willing to subjugate at least some of their privacy for patriotic reasons. The zeal many Americans exhibit in supporting the higher values and interests of their country has often been abused by political leaders. One of these higher values is national security. It's impossible to adequately defend a country without good intelligence about potential threats. As Sun Tzu, the Chinese military strategist, said, "If you know the enemy and know yourself, you need not fear the results of a hundred battles."

In early 2006, President Bush admitted that he had authorized the NSA to spy on Americans without a warrant. As of the writing of this book, it is unclear how pervasive and deep the unsanctioned domestic espionage went. Also in 2006, various media reported that the Bush administration had subpoenaed the search records of several large Internet companies, including Google, Yahoo!, Microsoft, and AOL. Yahoo! and AOL admitted that they turned over logs of consumer searches; Microsoft refused to comment; and Google refused to hand over the information, citing trade-secret protections, not privacy, as its reason.[2] Actions such as these have destabilized the delicate balance of security and civil rights. It's happened before.

Since its establishment, the United States has had an uneasy time evaluating the necessary tradeoff between national security and its citizens' right to or need for privacy. The ebb and flow of policy is based on events, following the tide of public sentiment. Since 9/11, the onus has clearly swept toward the government, the focus on national security washing away the oddments and residues of long-term privacy entitlements. But this moving dichotomy is not new: it began at the birth of the country with the disputes between Thomas Jefferson and Alexander Hamilton.

Jefferson was an intellectual bad boy. Inventor, experimental farmer, and daring lover, he marched to the sound of a different fife and drum corps most of his life. His political views, like his hobbies, were driven by his passion, frequently putting him at odds with his stolid brethren. His feud with Hamilton over governmental limits emerged as the defining battle of the new country, and it is still being fought today. Although privacy wasn't a hotly contested issue at the time, that omission was due more to weak technology than to a lack of relevant principles. The basis of their debate—the role of a central government in the lives of its citizens—continues to this day and is at the core of the privacy controversy.

The first privacy showdown came when John Adams, a Federalist, began to aggressively enforce the Alien and Sedition Acts. These wartime measures gave the government powers to control dissent. The Alien Act authorized deportation of foreigners deemed hostile to the United States, while the Sedition Act made it a crime for Americans to slander elected officials. Jefferson disagreed with these policies and wrote the Kentucky Treatise, an essay in which he said that states had the right to repeal "bad" laws passed by Congress.[3] This position proved popular enough with voters that he was elected president on the strength of it. This was the beginning of the Republican Party.

The Jeffersonian assertion that the rights of individuals (or of regional groups such as states) take precedence over the desires of the federal government has been invoked countless times to justify many causes. The Civil War, the bloodiest war in U.S. history, was

fought over the most extreme application of this principle: deciding who was and was not entitled to the rights of citizenship.[4]

After the war and the passage of the Fourteenth Amendment,
which applied constitutional protections to state laws, the courts
gradually developed guidelines for handling these issues. Civil liberties, either explicit, like freedom of speech, or implied, like privacy, are entitlements but not absolute ones because they are
subservient to more pressing public needs. As Oliver Wendell
Holmes pointed out, freedom of speech "would not protect a man
in falsely shouting fire in a theater."[5] The legal test that he created was that of a "clear and present danger." Without the fire, the
speech was not constitutionally protected. People like Holmes were
able to use common-sense reasoning to protect the balance between
civil liberties and the public good. Mental tests like "clear and present danger" were sufficient to coarsely indicate where the compromise might lie.

Fast forward to the mid-1970s. The United States had swung
hard to the side of privacy after the Watergate hearings during the
tail end of the Richard Nixon administration. The Church Senate
Committee on Intelligence, convened in 1975, exposed involvement by the CIA and FBI in domestic espionage after revelations
of the Watergate affair.[6] The committee hearings revealed one problem after another, ranging from illegal wiretapping to the existence
of President Nixon's "enemy list." This list subjected celebrities like
Dr. Benjamin Spock and Jane Fonda to an illegal amount of scrutiny
by the government, including auditing of their tax returns as political payback. Nixon was hardly the first president to engage in
domestic surveillance; the John F. Kennedy administration did
something similar, using J. Edgar Hoover's FBI to keep an eye on
prominent Americans like Martin Luther King Jr. through a program called COINTELPRO. Some of the committee's revelations
were purely international in scope, such as the Kennedy administration's attempts to assassinate world leaders like Patrice Lumumba
of Congo and Fidel Castro of Cuba. Many were eye-opening expo-

sures of formal government programs that invaded the privacy of citizens. Government agencies were opening mail, conducting illegal wiretaps, and breaking into private homes. It also became clear that the government had crossed several previously sacrosanct lines such as using the military to monitor Americans and employing the IRS as a partisan weapon.

One of the fallouts from the Church Committee hearings was a strict adherence to the requirements imposed on intelligence agencies when it came to domestic surveillance, which affected privacy. Rules were in place regarding sharing of information between intelligence people and law enforcement. For example, collection of information on Americans required a court order for a wiretap, even if only one participant on the telephone call was an American. The NSA adhered strictly to the requirements, forcing its operatives to sign an annual statement vouching that they had read and understood U.S. Title 18, which laid out the ground rules for domestic spying.

The Destabilized Balance After 9/11

Some people allege that the policies that grew out of the Church Committee hearings were directly responsible for the 9/11 attacks because they hamstrung the intelligence agencies and compartmentalized the information they acquired. Much has been made of the necessity for better intelligence collection against domestics and residents as a way of averting future terrorist attacks. In fact, the government did have enough information to identify the terrorists and reconstruct the events after the fact; it did not have a process that would have enabled it to spot the attack beforehand and to be sure enough of the intelligence to act. This gap between punitive and predictive intelligence is the killing zone of protected privacy in the United States. Although the government was unable to anticipate the 9/11 attacks, the amount of citizens' personal information that would have been necessary to preempt them would have been beyond the amount that I, at least, would have been willing to tolerate. Civil liberties, like privacy, are what we're protecting in a democracy, not just lack of casualties. Life, not merely living, is the goal.

Today, the balancing act between individual freedoms and protection of the state is a much more difficult one and is a multidimensional, not a simple linear, problem. Technology makes what were previously intellectual abstractions like the idea that hurting the privacy of a few might help the many quite feasible and financially reasonable to implement. Holmesian reasoning doesn't apply very well to problems like deciding whether it's reasonable to analyze domestic phone calls to try to stop a terrorist attack, especially while still living in the shadow of the last one. Also, technology is excellent at depersonalizing targets. Like videos of smart-bomb attacks, large-scale privacy invasions brought about by technology seem as impersonal as shooting tin ducks at a carnival. If the victims of privacy invasions were addressed as individuals and as human beings, it would be easier to make these tradeoffs without enacting restrictive laws.

This conflict between the rights of the one and the needs of the many is the perpetual-motion machine of democracy; it generates energy by bobbing alternately between fascism and chaos. Governments, although often referred to as the mythical "they," are composed of individuals who by personality tend to champion the opposing sides of this debate. Some, like libertarians, come down squarely on the side of individual rights; others are inherently contrarians, mugwumps who, although they believe in strong national security, will break ranks to preserve the right to privacy; and others believe that a strong government knows what's best for its citizens, regardless of individual preferences. These momists will gladly eradicate privacy out of a misguided desire to protect the masses. Sometimes this privacy debate seems to boil down to a quality-of-life consideration. At what point have so many rights been lost that preservation of the state is a meaningless concept because the individual citizen is miserable? Socrates put it best 2,500 years ago: "Nor was civil society founded merely to preserve the lives of its members; but that they might live well: for otherwise a state might be composed of slaves"

The 9/11 attacks quashed any public objections to increased intelligence collection, even of domestic targets. This destabilization of the previous privacy status quo was driven by the most powerful of human emotions—fear. To provide national security, the guidelines for determining that someone is a threat moved from probable cause to probability, as the Department of Homeland Security used the results derived from computerized hunches as sufficient evidence to trump civil rights. It became a numbers game, where no one was presumed innocent or guilty but was viewed as a threat according to his or her score. Because everyone was being constantly evaluated and scored, a great deal of personal information on every American was needed for the computers.

Bureaucratic and Technical Changes

To facilitate intelligence collection, sharing, and analysis, the U.S. government was reorganized, and the Department of Homeland Security (DHS) was created in one of the greatest bureaucratic restructurings in U.S. history. On the technical side, another privacy threat was developing as the Bush administration's E-Government initiative called for a move toward interoperable computer systems and databases.

This initiative, combined with the creation of DHS itself, has eroded a traditional if obscure protection for privacy: computer heterogeneity. The towering federal Babel of technology had always made it too difficult to inexpensively conduct comprehensive background checks against anyone because government computers didn't talk to one another easily. Another subtle, unintended protector of American privacy has been the competitive nature of the government itself. The CIA watched the FBI. The FBI monitored the White House. Everyone watched the military. The tearing down of these partitions compartmentalizing intelligence information may have destroyed a needed check and balance on runaway government power. The increase in the interoperability of the computer systems will make it difficult to reinstitute this protection in the future. Regardless of any future laws that may be enacted when the protection pendulum swings back, permeable databases will make enforcement of those laws difficult, perhaps impossible.

Several programs designed to look across multiple government databases have already been implemented. The most public of these is the Computer Assisted Passenger Prescreening System (CAPPS), a counterterrorism system designed to identify terrorists before they board aircraft. The original program, CAPPS I, was started by President Bill Clinton in 1999 and implemented by the Federal Aviation Administration as a reaction to the bombing of TWA flight 800 and other presumed terrorist activities in the late 1990s.

The current system, CAPPS II, was put in place in 2004 and is managed by the Transportation Security Administration (TSA). This system is much more comprehensive than its predecessor because of advances in technology coupled with a relative disregard for privacy concerns. All airline passengers are examined, not just the ones who check bags. CAPPS II is a profiling system that looks at data from several databases and applies rules to create a "threat score," similar to a credit score. It works by examining the Passenger Name Record (PNR), the personal information that the airline collects on each passenger. The PNR is cross-indexed with several government databases including the FBI's most-wanted and TSA's no-fly lists. A color code and numeric score are assigned to the passenger and encoded on the boarding pass. Most travelers will get a "green," or no-risk, code; 8 percent will get a "yellow," subjecting them to further searching; and 1–2 percent will get a "red" and be prohibited from boarding. "Reds" will also be questioned by police and possibly arrested. The boarding pass may also have a "***" or "SSS" designation, guaranteeing the passenger at least a full-body wanding before being allowed to board. Many mostly unknown and purely subjective factors can contribute to this designation.[7]

The disturbing part of these practices is that the rules formulated to identify terrorists are not publicly disclosed. The rule makers could use strategies that are racist, such as automatically flagging anyone with an Arabic name, regardless of citizenship, or they could use some other socially unacceptable or illegal method of determining risk, as happens in credit-scoring systems. This program will be a constant problem for privacy seekers until the process used to calculate these scores is revealed. The nature of intelligence work is such that the successes are often kept quieter than the failures, so it's impossible for an outsider to say how effective these new profiling procedures have been at stopping actual terrorist events. It's probably safe to say that law enforcement can do a better counterterrorism job with these new computer tools than they could before 9/11. The issue isn't that privacy is always paramount any more than it is that national security always is. The tradeoff between privacy and national security is a monochromatic landscape painted with many dreary shades of gray. Government counterterrorist policies, however, are necessarily black and white: you either are or are not on a list.

No-Fly List

Another program instituted after 9/11 that affects privacy is the no-fly list maintained by the TSA. Although the government initially denied reports that such a list existed, it publicly acknowledged its existence in 2002. The list is populated with names of suspected terrorists or aliases that suspects have used in the past. No one knows just how big it is, although news reports put its size between 30,000 and 120,000 names.[8]

In 2003, the American Civil Liberties Union (ACLU) sued the TSA to find out how many people are on the list and how it's administered. The ACLU also filed the suit on behalf of two journalists from a San Francisco–based antiwar magazine. Rebecca Gordon and Jan Adams wanted to know whether their being on the no-fly list had anything to do with their history as social activists.[9] The case was finally settled in January 2006, when the federal government agreed to pay the ACLU $200,000 in attorney fees and make secret government records about the no-fly list public; according to the ACLU, the no-fly list is now believed to include tens of thousands of names.[10] The list itself, however, has never been made public. Little information is given about how a person ends up on it. A spokesperson for the TSA has said that revealing those reasons could "jeopardize national security."[11] More than thirty thousand people in 2005 alone contacted the TSA because they were having problems flying.[12] Although there isn't enough information publicly available to ascertain what the effectiveness of this restricted flying program has been in stopping terrorist incidents, it's certainly true that many average citizens have been affected because of "false positives" in the computer system. They've not only had their privacy invaded as an abstraction but have concretely been inconvenienced by being unable to use commercial aircrafts.

The airlines are required to cross-index each passenger's information against the no-fly list and to bar those on the list from flying. Senator Edward "Ted" Kennedy was harassed for three weeks because a terrorist had once used the name T. Kennedy. In this case, the Senator was able to call Tom Ridge, the then-director of the DHS, and get off the list.[13] Actor David Nelson (Ozzie and Harriet's son) and others have been harassed when traveling by air, questioned by FBI agents, and pulled off airplanes because they were on the list.[14]

Barbara Olshansky, the assistant legal director and human rights advocate for the Center for Constitutional Rights, was attempting to depart from Newark International Airport when she was searched and then told to remove some of her clothes in front of fellow passengers. Olshansky was embarrassed and annoyed, but she complied. However, when she was continually flagged for special attention every time she flew, she began to demand answers. She questioned her status but was told only that the computer had spit her name out.[15]

Ever since the federal government instituted the no-fly list, rumors and stories have circulated that it is sometimes used as a form of intimidation against certain categories of people, such as social activists and antigovernment political writers. Even if this rumor isn't true, the secrecy surrounding the program in general guarantees public distrust and suspicion.

An official of the Green Party was grounded and labeled a terrorist while attempting to travel to Prague on business. Art dealer Doug Stuber was told that no members of the Green Party were allowed to fly overseas on that particular day; yet when he returned the following day, he was questioned by police and interrogated about his family, friends, and political associates. Justice Department documents shown to Stuber labeled Greens as possible terrorists, although the party lists social justice, nonviolence, and participatory democracy as key values.[16]

Members of the military also land on the no-fly list, an odd circumstance as they presumably have been cleared in some other way to be able to serve in the military. Air Force Master Sgt. Michelle D. Green is on the list and is unable to get her name removed. She sued the government as part of a class-action lawsuit filed by the ACLU, requesting that there be a fair and quick process in place to remove her name and those of others. The suit is ongoing.[17]

Sister Virgine Lawinger, a seventy-four-year-old nun from Milwaukee, is an activist with Peace Action, a Catholic advocacy group. When attempting to travel to Washington, D.C., Sister Lawinger and a delegation of young students were stopped from boarding their flight and were questioned by sheriff's deputies and airport security. They were on their way to a demonstration against sending U.S. military aid to the Colombian government.[18]

These cases highlight one of the key problems with the TSA security system: it doesn't work very well. The software is English language–based and doesn't do a good job searching Arabic or

Middle Eastern, Asian, and other languages because words get converted into the Roman alphabet using different systems that can potentially result in hundreds of different spellings.[19] In addition, once someone gets on the list, it is virtually impossible to get off. The Associated Press, citing figures obtained from the TSA, reported that at least eighty-nine children are attempting to get their names off the list. More than a dozen are younger than two years old.[20]

Critics of the TSA state that it secretly collected data on more than 250,000 people, compiling approximately one hundred million records that were bundled with information obtained from commercial data brokers to create files or dossiers.[21] If so, this was a clear violation of the Privacy Act, which prohibits the government from compiling information on American citizens without their knowledge.

For a long time government spokespeople denied there was a no-fly list. The TSA now has a contact form on its web site for lodging grievances. However, putting up a digital complaint box isn't sufficient to quell many peoples' privacy concerns. The fact that the TSA has not made public the process for getting on and off the list, coupled with the general air of secrecy surrounding the program and, frankly, the lack of public trust in the motivations of the Bush administration, makes a high degree of accountability necessary. The no-fly list may have a legitimate spot in the counterterrorism toolbox, but there needs to be government recognition that mistakes happen, lots of mistakes happen, and there needs to be a swift and efficient on-the-spot mechanism for fixing them, even for those of us whose last name isn't Kennedy. However, the no-fly list is an inconvenience compared with some other privacy-busting programs to come out of 9/11, such as the Patriot Act.

The Patriot Act

The first few months after the terrorist attack on the World Trade Center and the Pentagon were confusing ones. The United States was not used to being on the defensive, and we became culturally cautious, even paranoid, acting like a newly mugged victim walking through a darkened parking lot. We looked over our shoulders, doubting our intelligence abilities. Worse, we revisited the old debate between individual rights and national interest. Rights lost.

On October 24, 2001, Congress passed the Patriot Act (officially the Uniting and Strengthening America by Providing Appropriate Tools Required to Intercept and Obstruct Terrorism Act of 2001). In the House the bill passed 357-66. In the Senate there was one dissenting vote, by Senator Russ Feingold; Senator Mary Landrieu did not vote. President Bush signed the bill two days later. The assumption behind the Patriot Act is that the 9/11 attacks occurred because of inadequate intelligence collection and flawed communication between intelligence agencies and law enforcement; these inadequacies created gaps in our national coverage that allowed terrorists to use our system against us without being detected.

The Patriot Act attempted to address these issues by making it easier than it had been in the past for agencies to collect information on foreigners, resident aliens, and, worst of all, citizens. Coupled with the subsequent reorganization of U.S. domestic agencies, it was supposed to create a streamlined, governmentwide system that would protect Americans from future threats by providing the rich intelligence information necessary for making predictions.

Many provisions in the Patriot Act are benign, and several are unquestioningly useful, such as providing benefits to victims of the attacks and monitoring foreign students in the United States. Several privacy-related provisions in the act have disturbed civil rights advocates, and they became an issue repeatedly during the congressional debate over extension of some of the Patriot Act provisions. Some parts of the act were permanent, but many have "sunset provisions" attached that forced Congress to review them in 2006. Most of them were renewed, and now all but two provisions, "roving" surveillance (section 206) and the authority to request production of business records under the Foreign Intelligence Surveillance Act (FISA) (section 215), are permanent. These provisions are set to expire in 2010.

Two of the most controversial parts of the legislation are sections 213 and 215. Section 213 deals with sneak-and-peak searches and

215 with store, business, and library records. *Sneak-and-peak* is a term coined by the FBI for quickly obtained secret warrants used for search and seizure of private residences. Although provisions for this kind of investigation existed before, there were checks on governmental abuses; currently most of the civil safeguards previously in place have been diluted or swept aside. The government can indefinitely delay notifying individuals that they've been investigated, for instance. The fundamental difference between these searches and those conducted before is the justification. Previously the litmus test was "probable cause"; today it's "reasonable cause." The only authority required is a warrant from the Foreign Intelligence Surveillance Court (FISC) as required by the Patriot Act's predecessor, FISA. This court is appointed by the Chief Justice of the U.S. Supreme Court and its actions are secret, its warrants private. Even though law-enforcement professionals have usually considered getting these FISC warrants a rubber stamp, it became public in 2006 that President Bush considered the process too slow in many cases and had authorized a procedure whereby the FISC could be circumvented: federal agents could wiretap U.S. citizens solely on the president's direct or delegated say-so. This authorization process has become quite controversial as of the time of this book's writing; it's expected to be the subject of several congressional investigations in 2007.

Section 215 is often called the "librarian provision" because a controversial side effect is that law enforcement can go on a library (or a bookstore) fishing expedition, even though the language seems directly targeted at business records of retail companies, telephone providers, and ISPs. The law allows the FBI to get a secret warrant from the FISC on the simple basis of the subject's being "connected" to an ongoing investigation of spying or international terrorism. The act perpetuates secrecy because it specifies that it's a crime for anyone or any business to notify the targeted person. The 2006 renewal of the act made it slightly more difficult for law-enforcement agents to get library records by exempting them from the Patriot Act if the libraries are not also functioning as ISPs. Federal agents can, however, show up at a library at any time and request the names of everyone who has checked out a particular book. The standard of proof has been changed in the 2006 renewal from the original 2001 requirement that the records were "sought" for an authorized investigation to the slightly tougher requirement that the agents must show "reasonable grounds" to believe that the records are "relevant" to an "authorized investigation."

Both libraries and bookstores balked at the idea that federal agents could come into their establishments at any time and request the personal information of their clients. Some, like Bear Pond Books in Montpelier, Vermont, are taking a stand by destroying customer records.[22] Bookstore owners and librarians believe that their customers should be able to read whatever they want without fear that a government organization will be peering over their shoulders. Many people believe that intellectual curiosity is not an indicator of a person's intentions—reading a book about Ted Bundy doesn't make me a serial killer any more than reading a bio of Castro makes me a Communist. Having our privacy invaded by the revelation of our choice of reading material is bad enough; the possibility of being placed on a no-fly list or being subjected to further physical surveillance or extended government harassment creates real damages.

This isn't the first time that a bookstore has taken a stand for privacy. Kramer Books in Washington, D.C., went to court to prevent Kenneth Starr from seizing Monica Lewinsky's sales records.[23]

On June 8, 2004, at the Deming branch of the Whatcom County Library system in rural Washington, an agent, who arrived without a subpoena or a warrant, requested a list of the people who had borrowed a biography entitled *Bin Laden: The Man Who Declared War on America*. A library patron had contacted federal officials after noticing something suspicious written in the margin of that book. The annotation was "Let history be witness that I am a criminal," which apparently is a quote from a 1998 interview with Bin Laden. When librarians refused to cooperate, the agents served them with a subpoena, which the library fought. Eventually, the FBI gave up.[24]

Some provisions of the act have been struck down by the courts when contested, most notably section 505, which allowed the government to demand customer records from ISPs without any judicial oversight. An alternative procedure, National Security Letters, which is not part of the Patriot Act yet is often confused with section 215 of the act, is a subpoena issued by the FISC. According to a study conducted by the American Library Association and released during the summer of 2005, federal agents had used subpoenas and National Security Letters to formally request information from libraries over two hundred times since October 2001.[25] In 2005, the *Washington Post* reported that the federal government is issuing at least thirty thousand National Security Letters a year, which is one hundred times the number it issued before the Patriot Act.[26] The act put a gag order on recipients of the letters, although the 2006 revision weakened this requirement somewhat. The provision keeping the letters secret, even from the target of the investigation, is disturbing from a privacy perspective. It's hard to vigorously defend yourself against whispered accusations.

One major criticism of the Patriot Act is that the information derived from using the law can be used for constitutionally dubious purposes, such as clamping down on domestic dissenters, or even for a perfectly lawful purpose not intended by Congress, like fighting organized crime.

The Patriot Act has been used to track antiwar protesters. In 2003, *New York Times* reporters obtained leaked FBI documents that proved the bureau was monitoring antiwar demonstrations and compiling information on the protestors.[27] The next year, Drake University in Des Moines, Iowa, was ordered to surrender all documents concerning an antiwar conference held on campus. The subpoena was fairly comprehensive; it requested all records pertaining to campus security officers, attendees, and organizers of the event. Additional subpoenas were served on the local chapter of the left-wing National Lawyers Guild, a sponsor of the conference.[28]

The Patriot Act has been used to investigate people who've gotten abortions. It was invoked to subpoena at least six major hospitals in

New York, Chicago, Philadelphia, and Michigan and to demand that they hand over hundreds of private medical records of patients who had undergone certain types of abortions.[29]

The Patriot Act has been used to fight organized crime. A Justice Department report refers to more than a dozen cases in which federal authorities have used the act to investigate private citizens, order surveillance, use wiretaps, and seize assets in nonterrorism criminal cases. Officials said that the highlighted cases were just a small sampling of the hundreds of cases that the federal government was pursuing under the law.[30] Money laundering, drug trafficking, blackmail, and white-collar crimes are just a few of the areas where the law is coming into play. The Justice Department used the act to obtain information about the financial dealings of Michael Galardi, a strip-club owner in Las Vegas who was the target of a corruption probe.[31]

The Patriot Act has been used to go after pranksters. The Justice Department is prosecuting David Banach of New Jersey as a terrorist under the Patriot Act for interfering with pilots and lying to the FBI. He pointed a hand-held laser at an airplane.[32]

A twenty-year-old woman from California received two years in a federal prison after leaving threatening notes on a cruise ship; she didn't want to go on vacation with her parents because she missed her boyfriend. Provisions in the Patriot Act were used to give her the tough sentence; she was charged with terrorist threats against mass transportation systems.[33]

The Patriot Act has been used against the homeless. A homeless man from Summit, New Jersey, was arrested under the Patriot Act and called a terrorist because he was loitering in a train station.[34] This case is important because it is an example of a municipality invoking the Patriot Act. If this becomes a trend, there will undoubtedly be a great deal of confusion; each local government will apply its own local standards, even standards of morality, by wielding the huge studded club of the Patriot Act. The act could presumably be used to beat other pesky federal laws into submission at the whim of local governments, undoing years of court work in constitutionally protected areas.

The Patriot Act has been used to protect big business's intellectual property. The FBI invoked a provision of the Patriot Act to obtain financial records from Adam McGaughey's ISP in order to file federal charges against him. As the creator of a popular fan web site dedicated to the television show *Stargate SG-1*, McGaughey allegedly engaged in criminal copyright infringement and trafficking in counterfeit services. Because he had contact with fans around the world, his connection to them was represented as an international conspiracy against the Motion Picture Association.[35]

The Patriot Act was used to deport an ideological undesirable. Sami al-Hussayen, a student at the University of Idaho, was arrested and prosecuted in connection with his work for the Islamic Assembly of North America, where he was employed as a web master. As part of his duties he added links to the web site that directed visitors to external web sites. Some of these links provided information written by Muslim scholars; others advocated criminal activity. Al-Hussayen and his attorney argued that he should not be held responsible for the content of the linked sites; he had never visited many of them himself, and he was in the dark concerning the material. Section 805 of the Patriot Act made it a criminal offense for him to provide "expert advice and assistance" to a terrorist organization. He was eventually found not guilty of terrorism, but in exchange for that verdict he agreed to be deported.[36]

The Patriot Act has been used to reopen old domestic cases. The FBI has used the act to interrogate, monitor, and label defendants in old cases, such as the case involving the Black Panthers. Former Black Panthers are considered terrorists under the Patriot Act, even though the case against them is decades old and is closed.[37]

The Patriot Act may be being used to target Muslims. The act was also used in the Brandon Mayfield case when the FBI used secret warrants to collect information about him and intercepted his emails. Agents also searched his property without his knowledge and without a court order, and National Security Letters were used in the case. Mayfield, a Portland, Oregon, attorney, was arrested and held for two weeks because of incorrect fingerprint data. He was mistakenly arrested on suspicion of being involved in the Madrid train bombings. FBI forensic analysis led the police to his door. The Spanish national police eventually realized an error had occurred during the FBI examination of fingerprints and stated that if a more rigorous identification process had been used, the mix-up would never have happened. In the end, it was found that the fingerprints were those of an Algerian national, not Mayfield. Mayfield wonders whether religion was a factor as he'd recently converted to Islam.[38]

The *New York Times* reported that thirty-four credible human rights complaints were made by Arab and Muslim immigrants over a six-month period in 2003. All charges involve physical abuse and beatings while the prisoners were held in federal detention centers.[39] The *Washington Post* reported that the material-witness laws are being abused to detain at least forty-four witnesses connected to the 9/11 attacks, half of whom have never testified before a grand jury.[40] The laws were never intended to indefinitely detain individuals who are not charged with any crime. Racial profiling is also cited as the reason fifty thousand Iraqis have been questioned and more than eighty-three thousand immigrants from the Middle East have been specially registered.[41] Interestingly enough, none of them are Saudi Arabian.

The Patriot Act has been used against students. Children are also sometimes the target of government investigations. A twelve-year-old student researching information for a paper on the Chesapeake Bay Bridge was the focus of an FBI Joint Terrorist Task Force investigation. The student used the Internet to conduct some of the research on how the bridge was built but found the information lacking. His teacher provided him with the addresses of a couple of good web sites, and he submitted questions to the Maryland Transportation Authority site, thereby raising the red flag that led federal agents to him.[42]

The Patriot Act has been used against artists. A sad case is that of Steve Kurtz. When his wife of twenty years did not wake up as usual one morning, he called the paramedics. Later, it was established that she died of heart failure. But while the medical authorities were inside his home, they noticed that he had laboratory equipment and contacted the police. Unbeknownst to them, he was a university professor who used the materials to build sculptures to integrate into educational art exhibits. Kurtz is internationally known for a collective he founded called the Critical Art Ensemble. The next thing he knew the FBI had sealed off his home, and he was not allowed inside. His office was also searched and cordoned off. Everything was confiscated, including his wife's body. He was held for questioning and labeled a bioterrorist by the FBI. Even though Kurtz drank the contents of the questionable Petri dishes to prove they contained nothing that a bioterrorist would use, he was unable to convince the investigators. He had been testing food bought at the supermarket for contamination and genetic modification. He was finally indicted for "mail and wire fraud" instead of bioterrorism and faces a possible sentence of twenty years in prison.[43]

The Patriot Act is one of the most controversial pieces of legislation enacted since World War II. It's unfortunate that Congress was so quick to pass the bill in 2001 as a reaction to the horrors of 9/11. It's even more unfortunate that the bill was so quickly renewed in 2006. As the Church Committee hearings showed in the 1970s, intelligence work conducted in an oversight-free environment can quickly get out of control. Incidents such as Nixon's putting Dr. Spock on an enemy watch list because he was an outspoken critic of the war in Vietnam leave many people incredulous. It's all too easy to transform the definition of an enemy from "someone who is against my country" to "someone who is against my beliefs" to "someone who is against me." It is naïve of Congress to blithely entrust the privacy of their constituents to the good faith of millions of government workers, no matter how well intentioned most of them undoubtedly are. As some of the stories related above show, the digressions from the expected uses of the Patriot Act have already begun. Worse is sure to come as domestic surveillance becomes less abhorrent to the newer generation and it becomes the norm to couple domestic surveillance with advances in surveillance technology.

Domestic Surveillance

I served in the Naval Security Group throughout most of the 1980s, working at the NSA among other places, and I remember how scrupulous my colleagues were about not spying on American citizens. Not only were there laws against it, but also most people whom I had the privilege to work with upheld the spirit as well as the letter of the law as a matter of pride and principle. This institutional nausea at the idea of spying on Americans must have been given a healthy dose of Dramamine in the last few years because such spying has clearly become standard operating procedure.

In 2005, the *New York Times* ran an article revealing that President Bush had signed a secret executive order in 2002 authorizing the NSA to conduct warrantless wiretaps of Americans. Vast quantities of international telephone and Internet communications were intercepted without court approval. The president claims that the NSA wiretapped only subjects who had some connection to al-Qaeda, although since then other evidence has come out that contradicts his claims.[44]

The controversy surrounding this admission stems from the fact that the president's actions may well have been constitutionally illegal and curiously unnecessary, in the sense that the FISC is widely believed to rubber-stamp almost all requests.[45] Immediately after the revelation, Judge James Robertson, one of the eleven members of the FISC, resigned from the court.[46]

As of this writing, the Justice Department had initiated an investigation, not directly into the NSA's actions but into the leak because the existence of the program was deemed classified. Both the ACLU and the Center for Constitutional Rights filed suit against the NSA for violating the Constitution with its no-warrant wiretapping program. The lawsuit also claims that President Bush exceeded his authority by authorizing the domestic eavesdropping.

From an intelligence-collection viewpoint, the post–Cold War world is very different from its predecessor because of the lack of predictability. The Warsaw Pact was just as bureaucratic as NATO, and the resistance to change made it easy to spot the truly anomalous events that had intelligence significance, such as missile launches or preparations for war. Space-based reconnaissance and warning sensors were especially adept at this kind of surveillance. Unfortunately the effectiveness of intelligence satellites as early-warning mechanisms has decreased greatly since the fall of the Iron Curtain because third world terrorists are not moving big enough things to be seen from space. The most valuable intelligence sensor today is human intelligence (HUMINT).

An effective alarm system will monitor the people, not the things. The unblinking eyes of U.S. intelligence must of necessity be refocused onto the locations and actions of human beings.[47] In fact, the watchers need a third eye that can see through the surface layer of *what* into the murky depths of *why*. The unit of measurement in the new world of espionage is not a tank, a plane, or a ship; it is a thought. Technology has been redirected from monitoring the movement of big metal things to understanding the future actions of human beings. However, even the development, to say nothing of the use, of this kind of technology is a threat to privacy, no matter with what integrity it is applied. As of now, it looks as though the tolerance that the public willingly shows a wartime government will be involuntarily and indefinitely extended. This long-term extension of tolerance irrevocably upsets the peacetime balance between individual rights and state security and blurs the legal line between vigilance and violation.

Finding a Counterbalancing Force for Privacy

The real question here is, Does the desire to protect civilians from an outside threat universally trump individual privacy? The technical question is, Can predictive intelligence work without violating privacy? Technology may have weakened the privacy immune system, but terrorism is the infection. This is not a war in a conventional sense; it cannot be won by making it too expensive for the other side to continue fighting. The economic rules that govern this type of conflict are antithetical to those that governed engagements in the last century. Each action taken by a superpower costs orders of magnitude more than it costs the smaller opponent.[48] It took only a couple of hundred dollars' worth of box cutters, flight lessons, and plane tickets to inflict $35 billion of direct damage to the United States.[49] The poorest country in the world can gain leverage against the United States either directly by using American artifacts as weapons or indirectly through sabotage.[50]

The war on terrorism will end when there are no more terrorists—either because they're satisfied or because they're dead. These are the only outcomes for any group of disaffected people willing to step over the threshold of civilized behavior and use violence to advance their cause. Nothing less will remove the threat that the United States will become the target of an attack. The false sense of inviolability that characterized this country's adolescence is gone; it has been replaced by the obsessive self-examination that is the hallmark of the middle-aged.

Terrorism is the war that will never end; technology may appear to help, but it scores so many privacy hits on innocents that technology's ultimate contribution toward the goal of preserving a democratic lifestyle is doubtful. Combatants can be citizens as well as foreign nationals because terrorism is based on ideology, not on ethnicity. The bombing of the federal building in Oklahoma City was a part of terrorism, as were the Unabomber's love letters. Tracking them means tracking every single American because any one could be the next Timothy McVeigh, the next Theodore Kaczynski.

Law-enforcement professionals are good at reconstructing disasters after the fact. They can tell who did it and how it was done by using forensic analysis and old-fashioned shoe-leather investigating. These postmortems help to punish the guilty but are useless for prevention. Stopping these attacks from happening requires predictive intelligence. The breadth of information that this knowledge system requires is at odds with how privacy is viewed today. From the perspective of the average American, the *creepy* factor of this outcome will be off the charts. I use this term to refer to an act that is distasteful enough that, regardless of its legality, it makes most people's skin crawl when they find out the details. Anticipating terrorism demands unrelenting vigilance, which means less privacy. Conventional law enforcement operates by assuming innocence and dealing with the exceptions; counterterrorist professionals treat all acts and actors as suspicious unless proven otherwise.

The planning and plotting tasks of a terrorist are indistinguishable from legitimate behavior if taken out of context. In the hands of a farmer, a truckload of fertilizer is a business necessity; in the hands of an anarchist, it's a bomb capable of leveling a building. Effective intelligence requires collateral knowledge to establish the context in which information should be interpreted. Establishing the context requires collecting the personal, even trivial, attributes of everyone in the United States. Context is everything. The amount of information that needs to be collected and analyzed to establish context for every American is staggering. Analysts will want behavioral profiling tools, like the ones used by credit-card companies to detect fraud. These systems work by building up a transactional history of the subject and creating a baseline of "normal" behavior. The resulting profile is constantly reevaluated as more data become available and quickly becomes enormous.

Psychological profiling uses both contexts and trends to reverse-engineer behavioral makeup. For instance, a person who refuses to go to a hospital after a minor car accident may be viewed in a suspicious light unless it is known that she is a Christian Scientist. Changes in lifestyle patterns reveal changes in thoughts and provide insight into decision making. Knowing affiliations is also critical. Often the only indicator available that a person might be a terrorist is association with others who are under surveillance. Intelligence agencies will want to perform *traffic analysis* on routine communications to discover social groupings and guilt by association.[51] The NSA made arrangements with U.S. phone companies to get the records of calls in order to perform traffic analysis, which can yield a lot of information solely from the externals of the messages. Of course, some of the analysis will be about innocents. In the process of trying to spot terrorists, the computer systems used to scan these phone records will diagram the social networks of pretty much everyone who's considered a target, which could be as small a group as all people under suspicion and as large as the population of the United States plus its visitors.

The final key is the content of communication. The actual messages themselves, whether sent by email, phone, or instant messenger, will yield the critical details such as who, when, and where. If the content is encrypted, the subject's background information can be leveraged to create an automated and highly effective password-guessing scheme.

Preventive measures against domestic attacks require all four kinds of personal information about the targets: details of their lives, a historical trail of their activities, a listing of their social and business acquaintances, and what they talk about. Although there is no general consensus about what privacy is, it's hard to imagine a definition that doesn't encompass these four areas. If all four were collected against an innocent nonterrorist, it would be hard to say that his or her privacy hadn't been invaded.

Unfortunately much of today's new intelligence and preventive measures are designed to stop Arab terrorists from boarding planes with box cutters, commandeering them, and flying them into landmarks. We are not any safer against other kinds of threats created by tweaking one of the attributes of a threatened attack. Change "planes" to "trains," and we're unprotected. Change "Arab" to "white supremacist," and we're undefended. Change "box cutter" to "biological agent," and we're exposed. It's a big world out there, and although the subject is too broad for this book, many security experts believe that it is impossible to be completely safe.

No sane human being wants another terrorist attack on U.S. soil. Americans, indeed any Westerner, would be foolish to claim absolute protection against privacy invasion while still demanding relative safety. Something has to give. It seems as if people are more comfortable with the wide-scale privacy invasions since 9/11 because most of them are confined to the realm of technology. I wonder how Americans would feel if the data-mining technology were replaced by the hundreds of thousands of agents it would take to accomplish the same investigations.

A civic danger to watch out for is a too-comfortable reliance on technology. It often seems that the impersonal nature of science confers confidentiality on private information, sanitizing privacy violations for our protection. It's less embarrassing for some people to order personal things on the Internet, for instance, than to buy them from a human being. But the sterility of a computer interface can easily lead a user to a false sense of security. The information that's being collected may be in a virgin database today but will someday be looked at by a human being along with other information collected on each of us. Some suggestions for righting the imbalance between security and privacy are offered in Chapters Twelve and Thirteen. Information technology in no way protects our privacy; it just pushes the embarrassment, humiliation, and financial damage off to some future date and diffuses responsibility for the collection so broadly that no single person will ever be held accountable for your discomfort.

Part VI

What Can Be Done?

Our privacy may be on the verge of being completely lost. What can we do about it? Chapter Twelve discusses several strategies, ranging from ignoring what's happening to active efforts including vigilantism and acting curmudgeonly—arguing against each encroachment on our privacy. Even if none of these approaches works by itself, together they, and we, can slow down the erosion long enough for our society to adjust to the new kind of privacy in the Information Age. Chapter Thirteen summarizes the main technology trends that are irrevocably changing our view of privacy and speculates about what the future may hold—a tomorrow where we're always being watched and watching.

12

Fighting Back
Gandhis, Curmudgeons, and Vigilantes

*We are all interested in the future, for that is where
you and I are going to spend the rest of our lives.*
The Amazing Criswell, Plan 9 from Outer Space[1]

The premise of this book is that privacy as we know it is lost. It
can be found again, although we will be unaccustomed to, and
perhaps uncomfortable with, its new form. It's too late to revert to
the way our society was prior to computer technology; barring a
tidal wave of Ludditism, it will never be that way again. In the
future, there will always be invisible watchers. Every piece of public information will be recorded somewhere, somehow, whether
we're aware of it or not. We can't stop the coming of what David
Brin calls the Transparent Society, where we'll be always under
computerized surveillance, without destroying or inhibiting too
many other good things in the process.[2]

We probably can't stop the data collection. We can, however,
regulate any sanctioned conclusions that others might draw from
observing us. Knowing something personal or private about us is one
thing; talking about it is another; acting on it is a violation. As a
society, we can agree that some actions, such as unwarranted labeling, are repugnant, and we can integrate this principle into our culture. Prior to the invention of digital gadgets, people could spy on

each other if they wanted to by simply drilling holes in walls, but this type of voyeurism was socially offensive enough in our culture that anyone who did it thought long and hard before bragging about it.

As mentioned in Chapter Eleven, the sterile quality to computers seems to exempt them from the normal offensive stigma that would be associated with human-generated privacy violations. In the same odd way that cartoons like *The Simpsons, South Park,* and *The Family Guy* get away with jokes and even plots that would be highly controversial if performed by live actors, privacy violations by computers don't bother people so much.

It's important that we see computer surveillance for what it is— voyeurism. Allowing the institutional use of euphemisms to disguise privacy intrusions is aiding and abetting the enemy. Spying by the government is spying, peeping, intruding; it's not counterterrorism. The best way to fight being labeled is to label in return. Innocuous names are a great way to control public opinion. If the Patriot Act had been called the Extremely-Scary-Screw-Your-Privacy Act, there might have been more than one dissenting vote when it was approved.

Each of the three major institutions in the United States— government, the media, and the corporate world—have a stake in any privacy solution. But, ultimately, we will have to work individually and as a group to manage our personal information by assessing our options and choosing the role that we feel most comfortable playing. I list five possible personas later in this chapter: the ignorer, the avoider, the deceiver, the curmudgeon, and the vigilante. Whether being a peaceful curmudgeon like Gandhi, or taking matters into your own hand, vigilante-like, the strategy on how we deal with the loss of our privacy is a personal choice. In a democracy, we have some control or influence over the actions of our institutions. If their members hold office, we vote them out. If they're appointed, we throw out their boss. If they're in the public sector, we regulate them. If they're the media, we make it clear that we don't read, listen to, or watch their products, destroying their ratings. If all else fails, we take the situation into our own hands. But the first line of defense is rational regulation, and that's why we have a president to propose a vision, Congress to enact legislation, and the judiciary to interpret the laws and reconcile them with the Constitution.

Why Can't the Legislature Protect Our Privacy?

The legislature is not able to protect privacy on its own because it represents the people, who in general don't spend a lot of time thinking about privacy. Lacking sufficient push-back from constituents, our representatives are left to examine their own consciences, while being influenced by lobbyists representing commercial entities and special interests, to whom strong privacy legislation would mean a weakened business environment or cause. Data-marketing companies, for example, have a vested interest in blocking the passage of an omnibus privacy bill that could make their database business unprofitable almost overnight.

Privacy is a hard subject to deal with as an abstraction; it's much easier to grapple with when considering real-world examples. It's easy to get a congressperson worked up about a privacy issue as long as it is narrowly defined and involves an identifiable person like a powerful VIP, a missing young white woman, or someone from a protected class, like children. It's more difficult to create interest in sweeping debate on an ill-defined subject and to achieve practical, enforceable laws.

Take the case of Judge Robert Bork. During his Supreme Court confirmation hearings, the press got and published his video-rental records (which luckily for him were harmless and included titles like *A Day at the Races* and *Ruthless People*).[3] The Congressional outcry led to the 1988 Video Privacy Protection Act (VPPA), which establishes fines for video-rental stores that reveal private information. This kind of bill has less impact on the privacy of the average Americans than a gob of spit in the ocean, but unfortunately it is the kind of privacy legislation that we're likely to see, narrowly targeted and effectively useless—pork-barrel privacy politics.

Sometimes a well-meaning Congress attempts to pass privacy legislation on a larger scale, as it did with the health care privacy bill, the Health Insurance Portability and Accountability Act (HIPAA), which, although well intentioned, was heavily diluted by special-interest lobbying and has resulted in minimal consumer protection. Enacting legislation almost always means compromising, and it doesn't take much to water down a privacy law. The greatest impact of HIPAA, for instance, was to require all patients to sign annoying waivers, essentially acknowledging that doctors can do whatever the heck they want to do with private information. That's what Sally Scofield found out after she underwent surgery on her knee. She was astounded when contacted by a marketing company that knew all the details of her medical procedure. Scofield learned that under HIPAA she had fewer rights and less control over personal medical data than she thought. Anything she told her physician could now be used without her consent.[4]

> An offhand remark to his doctor about being a sporadic pot smoker two decades before landed a gentleman named Martin in hot water. The information found its way into his permanent medical record in the Medical Information Bureau database, and, as a result, an increase in his life insurance coverage was refused.[5]

The problem with most privacy bills is that they are too narrow and have too many exclusionary clauses protecting special interests. These clauses reflect the reality of Washington politics—laws are made in collaboration with special-interest lobbyists because they provide funding for political campaigns and sometimes pick up incidental, discretionary expenses. As of the writing of this book, K Street (the location of the most powerful lobbying firms in Washington, D.C.) was in turmoil because of the investigation of Jack Abramoff, a prominent Republican lobbyist, but I have no doubt that the storm caused by the scandal will pass, and we'll soon be back to business as usual.

The best thing that the government can do is to deal with the worst threat to privacy—itself. Revelations that the government had domestic activists under surveillance made the headlines in 2005.[6] Like the old saw about every weapon that's ever been invented being used, each power granted to a leader will someday, somehow be exercised. The government can best help protect privacy by deliberately limiting itself legally, not by resorting to subjective "trust-me" arguments, but by respecting the natural and legally imposed boundaries between the branches of government. The constraints imposed on the government by the Church Committee in the 1970s were not bad ones—they worked well as citizen-privacy-protecting guidelines for almost thirty years.

Patriot Act legislation probably would not have stopped the attack on the World Trade Center and the Pentagon if it had been enacted in 2000. It will most likely not stop the next terrorist attack, by either al-Qaeda or some other group, because predictive technology is not good enough and will never be good enough to anticipate and stop an attack that hasn't been seen before. The only way the invasive measures made possible by the Patriot Act would probably ever help stop the next attack is if it is executed by Muslim terrorists who hijack some airplanes and fly them into buildings . . . again. Most precautionary measures being taken today, no matter how invasive, will be powerless to stop an innovative act of terrorism that might happen tomorrow. A total sacrifice of privacy will not prevent another attack, so why should we give up our solitude?

By repealing key provisions of the Patriot Act, or at least putting more checks and balances into the system, Congress can help. Ignoring administration claims about the sensitive nature of collected information and legally mandating full disclosure on some key issues are musts. Procedures like the no-fly list are more than just routinely administrative; they are draconian, especially because there is no avenue for redress. Any prejudicial action taken against a citizen in a democracy must have a means for review and appeal. Not everyone has Senator Kennedy's access to the DHS director to get taken off the list. They need another method. They need control. Fundamentally the best thing that the government can do is to empower Americans with the tools necessary to manage their own privacy by mandating full disclosure of all information contained in government or commercial files, by providing appeal procedures, and punishing anyone who takes one step more than is legally permissible in invading anyone's privacy. These measures will make it possible for people to know that they're in a database somewhere, give them the right to look at that information, and, if necessary, provide a process to correct faulty information.

Congress can also make it difficult, if not impossible, for law enforcement to get or disclose individual medical, financial, psychiatric, library, and Internet records. Heavy fines for individual disclosures and escalating ones for large-scale problems (usually computer-related) will encourage investments in security and discourage sloppy handling of consumer records. Tough penalties and jail time for government officials caught selling information send the right message; this is not a white-collar, victimless crime but an invasion of the rights of the individual.

The long string of data breaches by commercial companies must be stopped. Instituting fines that are tied to the number of individual records affected and are increased by the sensitivity of the subject areas would spark an overnight stampede to hire security consultants to shore up the leaky computer systems of most companies, similar to what happened to corporate auditing and corporate governance after the passage of the Sarbanes-Oxley legislation. Those who casually violate our privacy by their sloppy handling of our personal information should be punished, whether they work in the public or the private sector. A sensible piece of national legislation could be modeled after laws in enlightened states like California that force every company that experiences a data breach to report it to the affected individuals.

The pendulum will swing the other way again, and privacy will be a politically palatable topic, just as flag-waving contests are now. Possibly foreshadowing one of the issues that will be debated in the 2008 presidential election, in June 2006 Senator Hillary Clinton introduced a Privacy Bill of Rights that supports most of the concepts mentioned in this chapter: fines for data breaches and granting citizens the right to view their data files. Most important, Congress must fulfill one of its key and sometimes neglected functions—it must monitor the actions of the executive branch in open review.

Why Won't the Executive Branch Protect Our Privacy?

It is probably naïve to expect the executive branch to exercise restraint in using its wartime powers to sweep aside civil liberties. Regardless of the official rhetoric, it's hard to escape the belief that the Bush administration has little regard for the protection of these liberties. In 1999, Bush was famously quoted as saying, "There ought to be limits to freedom," when commenting on a legal complaint that he had filed against the operators of a web site parodying his presidential campaign.[7]

The post-9/11 government has shown some restraint so far in how it uses the powers granted by the Patriot Act, but it may not always be so. Although there have been hundreds of horror stories, some of which I have highlighted in this book, it could have been much worse. The argument that the administration uses in defending the act is that authorities haven't acted egregiously yet and never will. Like President Bush's defense of domestic surveillance in 2006, the argument comes down to "trust us—we're only after terrorists." There are several problems with this position: the lack of a definition of a terrorist, possible procedural mistakes, the permanent nature of digital data, the unintended reuse of surveilled information at some future date, and the deliberate heavy-handed use of the legislation by the current or a future president against a different target, such as political dissenters. Granting the government extraordinary powers to break down civil protections for privacy is dangerous and should be reserved for times of national emergency and limited in duration. Granting these powers to the government and making them permanent, especially as a reaction to a temporary problem, is foolish.

There has been a steady degradation of ethical reasoning in U.S. society, probably attributable to the proliferation of lawyers and the substitution of legality for calculated fairness. An ideal, probably idealistic, solution would be for the government to champion ethics and tout it as a decision-making strategy in both the public and the private workplace. It's ironic that it seems unrealistic to even mention ethics as a legitimate way to resolve complex problems such as the protection of privacy, considering that logical reasoning about ethics was taught in schools and practiced by statesmen for generations. Most people with whom I've discussed this idea have been cynical; they don't believe that corporate executives or elected officials would even understand ethical reasoning, let alone advocate or practice it.

There is an enormous difference between legality and ethics. The use of ethical decision making has fallen out of fashion in corporate America and Congress. Instead we substitute legality, its bastard cousin. Ethical consideration means reasoning from a generally agreed-upon set of principles. Legal arguments are derived from case law, which often has little connection to commonly held beliefs. Privacy problems are not about legal interpretation; they are about fairness, equity, and dignity. The Constitution is not just a convenience for lawyers and judges; it is a statement of principles. If the United States were a corporation, the Bill of Rights would be a mission statement. Ultimately, the ideal solution would be to amend the Constitution to add privacy to the set of protected entitlements.

In addition to thoughtful inaction, most government departments could help protect privacy by paying more than lip service to the idea and creating internal watchdog functions. One useful change would be to institute a whistle-blower program for reporting privacy violations by the government or its contractors. Although several government offices do have privacy advisory groups and privacy officers, many do not. They should all be required to create these positions. In fact, it's amazing that there isn't yet a privacy officer for the country. (Senator Clinton's privacy plan calls for one.) In my opinion, privacy officers should not be lawyers; lawyers approach the problem from a single perspective. Privacy ombudsmen should be designated for every government agency along with clear instructions to all government workers on how to report violations, all of which should be investigated. Privacy considerations are about the sensitivities of the common people, who deserve elected representatives who understand their concerns. The wealthy can avoid most consequences from these incidents.

The executive branch is composed of elected officials who, although they are compelled to say certain things when running for office, are more or less free to do what they want after they've won. The only time we can count on them to protect privacy is when they have a strong personal view on the subject or a clear majority of the voting population supports their position. Privacy policies will almost always be at odds with other policies a president might want for foreign policy, intelligence collection, and law enforcement. It will cost him or her political capital each time he or she champions privacy over a special interest. It will take a deeply committed public official to support civil liberties in the face of overwhelmingly powerful opposition, and therefore it is unlikely that the savior of privacy will ever come from the executive branch.

Can the Judiciary Protect Privacy?

The judicial branch was for many years the primary champion of privacy. From the legal inception of the concept by Justice Brandeis to landmark decisions like *Griswold v. Connecticut*, the courts have been proactive about protecting privacy. Ultimately the courts must continue to be the champions. Congress is far too influenced by special-interest groups, and White House residents frequently have their own agendas. Once appointed, federal judges own the job;

they are free to change a lifetime of public opinions. Even the worst of them have their moments of impartiality, which rival and usually exceed the best displays of congressional objectivity.

One problem is the age of judges. Many of them are in their late sixties and seventies. They did not grow up with computers, don't really understand technology, and probably never will. They tend to avoid taking significant positions on highly technical issues, eschewing the creation of case law because they don't want to be reversed. Younger judges, who do understand the issues, will have to be in the vanguard of protectionists.

Chapter Five describes how the judiciary has gotten involved with privacy in the past. It may not be possible to protect privacy in any other way. Because privacy as an issue is not historically associated with either the Democrats or the Republicans, there's hope that the strongest statements for privacy will continue to come from the bench, regardless of the administration that's currently in power.

Privacy is a good area for judicial activism. Privacy-protecting justices like Brandeis, Holmes, and Douglas were intelligent, articulate, and thoughtful individuals who had strong personal opinions about civil liberties in general and privacy in particular. Their belief system existed before their appointments, and they were able to project their opinions into their rulings in a persuasive enough manner that some of their colleagues were also convinced. Without activist judges willing to take a stand on an issue that they believe in, such as privacy, it's unlikely that any landmark rulings will be coming from any Supreme Court. It remains to be seen whether the newer, younger appointees to the court will reveal a deep desire to protect privacy, but at this time the prospects for a Supreme Court privacy champion to appear are bleak.

The Media

The media are often too willing to wrap themselves in the First Amendment when reporting strays into personal areas. Broadcast journalists are often the worst offenders because their voracious

need for visual imagery often causes them to feature normal people at the worst moments of their lives, when they don't want the
exposure. In the world of television, the rule is that it's not news
unless there is video. Television reporters are less interested in comprehensive coverage of the issue than they are in getting a "good
shot" or "sound byte" that sums up the story in a tear-jerking or
shocking way. This narrow reporting can get them into trouble
because of the tunnel vision they develop when looking for a great
visual. Television stations will not deliberately keep stories that
their competitors will show off the air simply because of privacy
concerns not covered by the law. Television news today is highly
aggressive, always eager to push the envelope to the edge of the
First Amendment. The media could help by backing off, but they
probably will only when faced with lawsuits and hefty financial
penalties.

There is almost certainly a mismatch between ordinary people's
perception of their rights to privacy and the actual legal situation
known all too well by the television networks. One good solution
would be the creation of a privacy advisory board of prominent and
knowledgeable citizens from different parts of society who would
advise each network on ethical issues.

Print journalism is generally pretty good at ethical self-regulation.
Privacy violations by newspapers are much less prevalent than those
by their broadcast brethren, perhaps because print journalists have
had a longer period to work out their code of professional ethics,
perhaps because they don't need a video, sometimes not even a
photograph, to build a story. Because their reporting is textual, they
tend to emphasize empathy for the affected individual instead of
selecting to portray them at only the most photogenic moment.
They also have a much longer time frame in which to find out the
whole story than do television reporters.

Internet-only news reporting is too new to predict how it will
turn out in relation to privacy issues. The first problem is finding
where the line is between a blogger and a "real" journalist. Historically someone with press credentials was Press, but that's less true

and certainly less obvious now that reporting is often conducted using remote technology. The distinction between professionally trained journalists and Internet amateurs will continue to blur as various flavors of quasi-journalists like Matt Drudge and tyro political commentators like those writing for Wonkette (www.wonkette.com), myDD (www.mydd.com), Michelle Malkin (www.michellemalkin.com), or the Daily Kos (www.dailykos.com) are created. The First Amendment seems to cover these new types of reporters as much as the old ones, if not by the freedom of the press then by the freedom of speech clause, but that assumption remains to be tested in court.

> In May 2006, Apple was on the losing side of a ruling from a California appeals court; the court refused to overturn a lower-court ruling protecting bloggers from being forced to turn over the identities of their sources, in effect affording the bloggers a protection previously reserved for accredited journalists.[8]

Privacy is threatened only marginally by the media, except for the fact that overly aggressive newspapers often go to court, creating the potential for landmark First Amendment decisions that might be detrimental to privacy. It's too early to tell what the privacy impact of blogger-journalists will be, but my hunch is that it will be a mixed blessing. Although blogs are excellent forums for whistle-blowers, the motivation of many bloggers is suspect, and I fully expect to see as many privacy-damaging blogs as privacy-advocating ones.

On another level, unlike real blogs, media firms are companies and are subject to boardroom decisions that may make sense to a parent company such as Disney, which owns ABC, but that may have a detrimental effect on the privacy of their viewers. The complicated intertwining of business interests and news reporting makes media firms an unlikely choice to lead a successful privacy crusade.

Commerce

Corporations are every bit as big a threat to privacy as is the government. The existence of some of them, like direct-marketing companies, is based on making profits by intruding on their fellow citizens. The activities of these marketing companies are legal, but that's not as straightforward a statement as it may sound. The direct-marketing and advertising industries lobby aggressively when their livelihood is threatened, and the state of the law reflects their influence. Corporate lobbying is the reason the United States continues to have huge problems with consumer credit. Congress has passed bills like the Fair Credit Reporting Act, which sound good but don't work because the fines are small and the laws are hard to enforce. The thousands of infractions reported annually are generally ignored by the credit bureaus. Many tens of thousands of other people suffer from unfair credit treatment and don't do anything because they believe that it's futile to try to beat the credit bureaus.

Based on past performance, companies that make their money compiling databases and lists of personal information can never be trusted to do the right thing for privacy without outside oversight. They will have to be regulated by Congress, watched and punished for infractions. Foreign equivalents that collect information on U.S. citizens should be subject to the same regulations as U.S. companies. Nothing can be expected of these companies without legal sanctions. Industry self-regulation is a bad joke dreamed up by lobbyists. We need an oversight agency for the marketing and advertising industries. Having a department like the Securities and Exchange Commission with the power to levy fines and authority over any company, foreign or domestic, that maintains consumer information would make a huge difference.

Even companies in other market sectors like retail and technology can help by increasing corporate awareness of privacy issues. Boards of directors should manage companywide privacy. Empowered privacy officers can be a big help, as can a written policy stating that the company has to listen to and investigate privacy complaints. Such policies should be initiated at the board level, preferably through quarterly or annual privacy audits reported to the directors by third-party consultants.

Directors must monitor their company's security policies as well as its privacy strategy. Profit-and-loss managers don't get their annual bonuses by keeping customers' information safe. Like privacy, security suffers from the "out of sight, out of mind" syndrome. Either no one cares or everybody does—there's no gray area. Better security for a company means greater privacy for its customers. Tightened security coupled with random external audits should be required of every public company. Too many firms have been hacked, and sizable portions of their customer records have been dumped on the open Internet or quietly sold to identity thieves. The more customer data that a business keeps on its computers, the better the security that it should have.

Some simple precautions like the evaluation and auditing of personal information stored in corporate computers would help. No company should ask for, let alone retain, SSNs, yet many cellular phone companies use them for identification, as do universities and even video-rental outlets. The rule of thumb is that companies should keep only absolutely necessary information. The less they have, the less that can get stolen and misused.

A good data-retention policy is critical. More specifically, data-purging criteria should be stated and enforced. If the information isn't there, no one can steal it. It's amusing to see how many companies, some of them with well-known privacy problems, make a big deal about protecting customer privacy with silly and meaningless gestures. For instance, I travel frequently, and my assistant often deals with credit-card companies and utilities on my behalf. They almost always refuse to talk to her because she's not me but will do so when a male voice tells them it's okay. They don't ask any identity-verification questions, they just want to hear someone they think is me assuring them that I'm really me. This kind of silliness touted as security exacerbates the problem. Outsourcing, which often leads to call centers being located on the other side of the Earth from corporate headquarters, perpetuates the detachment of executives from the privacy concerns of their customers.

At the corporate level, privacy is about security. The worst problems are inadvertent, caused by sloppy handling of valuable personal information. Intentional large-scale privacy problems could be handled by class-action suits or by legislative actions targeted at the offending industry.

Five Strategies for Resisting Privacy Violations

Ultimately privacy must be the responsibility of the individual. Both as persuasive members of our community and as unique people, we must proactively safeguard our personal information the way that we lock our car, safely dispose of our credit-card receipts, or monitor our cholesterol. The best strategy is to minimize the amount of private information given out to anyone, government or company. Privacy violations cannot be prevented once one's information is in the system. Any fines levied by the government will not compensate for the embarrassment and personal consequences that will be suffered by the victim.

We can also fight back. Barbara Joyce of Maryland fought back using a federal law, the Telephone Consumer Protection Act of 1991. People can demand to be taken off telemarketing phone lists. If that doesn't work, they can demand financial retribution from the offending company, although they may have to go to court to get it. Ms. Joyce has received over $5,000 in settlements and has gone from having two intrusive calls each night to one a week.[9] If everyone fought back, even the lightweight existing laws would have some teeth in them because the accumulated amount of the fines would become big enough to get the marketing companies' attention.

Government can help best by providing citizens with more powerful tools than they now have to resolve problems that arise. If it doesn't, drastic actions by the individual may be called for.

People can employ five strategies to tackle the privacy problem. Each requires adopting a role, or combination of roles, and playing out the associated attitude. The characters are: the ignorer, the avoider, the deceiver, the curmudgeon, and the vigilante.

The Ignorer

Ignorers pretend there is no problem. They know better; they are not ill-informed and they're not stupid—they're just in denial. Ignorers don't usually ignore as a conscious strategy; they ignore as a way of handling an increasingly complex world, made more so by technology. Sometimes they convince themselves that giving up their privacy is a sacrifice that they need to make for their freedom and security. Sometimes, they swap their privacy for convenience. Ignorers think that the discounts offered by supermarkets for using their cards is a good deal, even if they have to give up some personal information.

Ignorers give their information out when it's asked for, sometimes volunteering it when it's not, especially if they think they are getting something of value in return. Signing up for shopper discount cards is a good example. Security technologist Bruce Schneier once stated that "if McDonald's offered a free Big Mac for a DNA sample, there would be lines around the block."[10] Ignorers don't think about the effects that RFID technology will have on consumer privacy. They don't flinch when asked to provide biometric data when visiting their local gym or tanning salon.[11] They probably offer their fingerprints without hesitating, maybe even blood samples. A lot of people are careless in this way about their personal information, not realizing its value. Consumer ignorance is one of the biggest problems for privacy.

Ignorers won't argue that problems like identity theft don't exist; instead they profess faith in the mythical "them": "they" wouldn't misuse our credit reports; "they" will take care of our medical files. The indeterminate "they" could be anyone with authority—teachers, police officers, creditors, or the government.

Ignorers usually haven't had a problem with privacy personally and don't know anyone who has. They tend to act horrified when they do run into a privacy violation, and their indignation often causes them to shift to one of the other approaches to resisting privacy violations. Like ex-alcoholics who are often the worst temperance bottle-thumpers, ex-ignorers quickly become converts after the first major violation.

Ignoring is not an effective long-term strategy.

The Avoider

Avoiders duck situations where they have to give information. Every good avoider knows that a credit card leaves a trail that can be read by anyone with the wit and will to do so. A good tactic used to be paying cash, but that's gotten more difficult. We are not only becoming a paperless society, but a cashless one. Hotels and rental car agencies, for instance, make it awkward, sometimes impossible, to be paid in anything but plastic. Plane and train travel requires identification now. International travel, even to Canada, leaves a record. Moving around a big city means passing in front of the unblinking eye of video cameras and the auditing of toll transponders.

Apparently you even need a photo ID to stay at some hotels now.[12] A New York Ramada Inn requests identity papers with photographs and retains copies of them for their files. Attending a conference in the city turned into a nightmare for a hotel guest who refused to pass over a photo ID. He had already provided three other pieces of identification, but it wasn't enough for the hotel. Mike Stollenwerk was eventually allowed to check in, but shortly afterward he received a voice mail from security saying, "I'd like you to come down and present some picture ID. Otherwise, the next knock on the door will be the police terrorism squad. Thank you."[13]

Avoiding is an easier strategy for the wealthy and powerful. They've got a long history of trying to avoid media attention anyway. Some of them use "gophers," assistants who pay with their own credit cards, thus saving the celebrity from leaving a trail.

> With $30 million in the bank, John Gilmore, of Sun Microsystems fame, is a model avoider; because of his behavior he is grounded and unable to ride Amtrak or get a room at most major hotel chains. He considers himself under regional arrest but refuses to comply with post-9/11 regulations that require him to show an ID before flying because no one at any airport can show him the rules in writing. He sued on constitutional grounds and lost.[14]

Effective avoiders try to duck situations where they will be forced to use plastic or to present identification. They also use web sites that show how to get through a city without being caught by video cameras; the Observing Surveillance Project (www.observing surveillance.org), run by EPIC, details where cameras are located in the nation's capital, for example.

Avoidance is a legacy strategy that worked well before the computer age, less so after its inception, and not well at all after 9/11.

The Deceiver

A reasonably effective strategy is to lie. I'm amazed at the number of people who employ this strategy to protect their personal data and even more amazed at businesspeople naïve enough to believe that most people tell the truth on forms. It's no accident that the most common sign-in names entered into web sites that require them are Mickey Mouse and Superman. With a few clicks of the mouse, you can digitally transform yourself from an educated forty-year-old woman living in suburbia to an elderly man living on social services. Research done by Forrester Research, Harris Interactive, and the Pew Internet & American Life Project points to the fact that online surfers avoid providing accurate information about themselves on web sites.[15] Many use multiple email addresses as a way to protect their privacy. Truth is slippery on the Internet; hardly anyone tells the truth about themselves now. Approximately 40 percent of the more than nineteen thousand Georgia Tech University students participating in a survey about online privacy said they sometimes lie.[16] Almost 70 percent decline to register when sites ask for their personal information because they worry about how the information will be used.[17]

Lying takes two forms. The first is thoroughly changing the correct information to something else. This is a great strategy for forms, on the Internet and on paper, less so for something important, like hospital admissions. Most of these questioners don't need the right information, but they try for it all the same because marketers are compulsive data pack rats. The second kind of deception is more subtle, but often more effective, and it has the added virtue of providing plausible deniability. Instead of just making information up, obfuscate. Spell your name differently or use a fake middle name. Write illegibly. If you have to give an SSN, transpose a couple of digits. Give an incorrect phone number or add a false area code to the mix.

The motive behind this madness is to create two or more data records instead of one, making a unified view difficult. Each small change in a key field will go into a separate database entry. Because technology is improving, some of these mangled entries can be automatically fixed; but, still, it's worth the attempt.

Doctors sometimes lie to protect patient privacy. A survey undertaken by the Association of American Physicians and Surgeons found that physicians are responding to federal privacy rules that require them to share medical records with the federal government without patient consent by withholding information.[18] Nearly 78 percent of participating physicians admitted to omitting medical data because of concerns about their patients' privacy.[19]

Another popular deception strategy some people use for annoying telemarketers is to say that if they give you their home phone number, you'll call them later and tell them your decision. Variations of this work pretty well with store clerks who ask for personal information. If not, lie.

Deception is a pretty good strategy right now. Its effectiveness is short-lived, however, because databases are becoming cross-linked and soon the liars will be caught by technological double-checking and forced to authenticate themselves with the real info.

The Curmudgeon

Curmudgeons are the cranky complainers who flat out refuse to give information to anyone without a good reason. Often they get away with it. Although most doctors' offices ask for an SSN, I consistently refuse and have yet to be denied service. Curmudgeons could lie, but they're principled. They'd rather not. Curmudgeons could duck difficult situations, but they don't. Curmudgeons don't deceive themselves any more than they would lie to others. They understand the situation and have made a conscious decision to passively resist the encroachments on their privacy.

Sometimes people think that curmudgeons are paranoid. Sometimes they are. But like the old joke, just because you're paranoid doesn't mean that they aren't out to get you. It is easy to be paranoid about your kids. Some Oregon parents were. When their daughter's photograph, grade level, teacher's name, and schedule were posted on her grade school's web site, the parents asked that the information be removed. They also requested a copy of the policy that enabled the school to post the picture without permission. The Oregon school provided them with a list of "directory information," which stated that a range of information can be released to the general public. As a result of their trying to protect their daughter, she was excluded from school activities and denied the opportunity to receive Valentines and treats or to be named student of the week or month.[20]

To be a curmudgeon, just say no. Refuse every unwarranted request for information and begrudgingly acquiesce only if necessary. Refuse, just like the booksellers and librarians who have refused to provide law enforcement with the details of their patrons' reading habits. Seriously question every request for an SSN. Never, ever put your SSN on a form, unless it's a mandatory government one, like a passport application or tax return. Negotiate by offering an alternative identifier, such as a driver's license. But when stores tell you it is their policy to ask for your license in order to process a return, consider it a violation of your privacy rights and refuse. Many outlets not only look at your driver's license but also type it into their computer. It also doesn't hurt to throw in a few of the other tactics from time to time, just to keep them guessing. Transpose digits once in a while, for instance.

If you don't want to be located, avoid advanced technology. Don't use a cell phone, a GPS, or a toll-road transponder. Delist your phone number and have Caller ID disabled for outgoing calls. Curmudgeons know that the first line of defense is to muzzle the stool pigeons, automated identification systems.

If you don't want to be spied on, don't use wireless Internet, any kind of cordless phone, or unencrypted email. It's too easy to monitor electronic communication. A readily available program called PGP does a pretty good job of encrypting email. Services are available that obfuscate TCP/IP addresses, hiding your machine's network address when you're surfing. Speaking of surfing, configure your browser to not allow cookies to be stored, and think long and hard about allowing plug-ins like Flash to be loaded into your browser. Check for spyware, and don't download anything on the open Internet. Use cash when you can. Never, ever use a convenience or a courtesy card. If you have to lose some of your privacy, fight for every inch.

Being a curmudgeon is a way of life. It's embarrassing sometimes to refuse to give out a telephone number to a store clerk, to always be the wacko who doesn't have a supermarket "courtesy" card, to be the whiner, the spoilsport, or the crank. It's not always fun to be a contrarian, but it's better than being timidly acquiescent.

Being curmudgeonly as a response to privacy erosion may not work, but it makes it easier to sleep at night.

The Vigilante

For some people, protecting all their rights online has become an obsession. Some are taking matters into their own hands; vigilantes fight a personal war. Consumers sick of online retailers and auction sites not helping them fight fraud are taking a stand when they feel that no one in authority is listening. Sometimes called cyber vigilantes, they are filling out police reports and tracking down scam artists on their own instead of remaining passive. They are also being vocal in warning about unscrupulous merchants; they put up web sites where they talk about their experiences with vendors. They even have sites for sharing information about bad first dates.

If legal protections aren't forthcoming, expect to see the American spirit of self-help applied to the privacy problem. In addition to the previously described strategies, it wouldn't be that hard for like-minded individuals to band together to jointly attack perceived privacy pigs. Vigilantes are popping up in other high-tech areas because the idea that technology moves faster than the law applies to more than just privacy. For instance, the group Perverted Justice (www.perverted-justice.com) uses online volunteers to entrap pedophiles. Their motto is: "As long as our children aren't safe from predators . . . predators aren't safe from us!"

Schools are opposing Department of Defense measures that target students for recruitment into the armed forces, claiming invasion of privacy. Under the No Child Left Behind educational legislation, schools are required to submit the names and personal information of all students to military recruiters in order to receive federal money to support curriculum and programs.

The superintendent of Fairport Central School District in Fairport, New York, has refused to provide to the military the information on his kids because the school board has a policy of not sharing student information with anybody. Superintendent William Cala wants to make sure he has parental permission before sharing student data with the military, and many parents are opposed to having the information released. He does not intend to back down, saying, "Every aspect of No Child Left Behind is based on the threat concept of if you don't follow what we say, we're going to take your money away. Someone has got to stand up to that."[21]

In another ploy, groups around the country are getting together to have "swap meets," where they trade "courtesy cards" back and forth so that they get the benefit of not being overcharged for not having one and yet retaining their privacy. Because the cards are used by many people, the marketing analysis of their buying habits is rendered invalid or inaccurate.[22] One website, www.cockeyed.com run by Rob Cockerham, even offered stickers with barcodes copied from Cockerham's own Safeway Club card that could be pasted on the recipient's card, protecting the shopper's purchase privacy and in the process creating a "supershopper" with apparently enormous buying power.[23]

Several security companies offer variations of the "honey pot" trap to catch the unwary hacker. There's a growing, yet quiet belief that it's best to deal with hackers privately because of the inattention of law enforcement coupled with the likelihood of unfavorable publicity for the victimized company if the hack is made public. The counterattack can take the form of piercing the identity veil and following up with a phone call or threatening legal letter; it can be *smurfing*, directing a flood of packets against the hacker's network, or it can be outright destruction, like formatting the hacker's hard drives. Dealing with hackers in this way is not that different from what Sony/BMG did with its root-kits, as described in Chapter Ten. If SONY/BMG can do it, why can't we?

Ever since the early days of the Internet, the time-honored approach to heavy spammers has been various kinds of email bombing, now replaced by denial-of-service (DOS) attacks. Known privacy pirates may find bad things happening to their computer systems. They should certainly expect DOS attacks, viruses, spearphishing, or other forms of digital retribution. The industry approach to stopping spam is that spammers should pay off companies like AOL to let their junk go through, sort of like getting a truckload of cigars out of LaGuardia airport. A better approach that many technical people have used for years is collaborating on "black hole" lists, barring the routing of traffic from network addresses of notorious spammers.

Protecting Our Privacy

Ultimately each of us must protect ourselves. Privacy is a private thing and must be protected in the first instance by each of us as individuals and not relegated to authority figures and institutions; their interests in this area are not our interests. Complaining is hard on the complainer and the complainant both, but it is a necessary first step. Like other forms of pain, privacy intrusion is personal and hard to describe other than by screaming.

Institutions won't be receptive to change if they don't see the groundswell of discontent. Enough pressure on Congress from advocacy groups can result in meaningful legislation that requires the appointment of watchdogs for commerce and guardians for government. There is a serious lack of regulatory oversight on the government regarding our privacy. Citizen groups organized to put pressure on legislators would be helpful, especially if the protests were targeted against particularly privacy-unfriendly legislation. If enough citizens had complained about the Patriot Act, its renewal would have provoked a much tougher fight in 2006. Legislators have polls to support their belief that most people don't care as much about privacy as they do about security.

The march of technology is inexorable. Although the government can't or shouldn't stop innovation and it's unlikely that we can create a completely privacy-friendly environment, a compromise is out there somewhere. A combination of vigilantism, regulation, judicial oversight, and vocal advocacy can restore the balance that's been lost.

We need a new kind of privacy advocacy group that comes from someplace other than the left wing. It's too easy for government critics to ignore the actions of the ACLU because, rightly or wrongly, it tends to be perceived as firmly ensconced in the liberal wing of American politics. Conservative or moderate grassroots groups advocating privacy would have a great deal of influence and help convince those in power that the desire for privacy runs across the political spectrum. Protecting privacy should be equated to patriotism instead of being lightly painted with the mark of treason by the manipulative hands of Machiavellian politicos.

The worst thing that we can do is to be complacent. Although some changes are inevitable, cultural acceptance of privacy invasion is not predestined. Technology has accelerated the conflict, government takes advantage of it, industry profits, but we, as citizen-consumers, are the ones who lose. Privacy is about expectations; as they disappear, so will our privacy. It takes our inactivity to cede the fight and accept that privacy's lost. Chapter Thirteen talks about what it means to live in a society of lost privacy.

13

The Panopticon
See the Bars, Rattle the Cage

*Civilization is the progress toward a society of privacy.
The savage's whole existence is public, ruled by the
laws of his tribe. Civilization is the process of setting
man free from men.*

Ayn Rand[1]

The premise of this book is that privacy, as we know it, is lost because of technology. Chapter Twelve mentioned a few strategies for fighting back, ranging from cultivating the bliss of ignorance to mounting an aggressive counterattack. But the inherent problem in this situation is immutable: technology is too valuable to discard flat out, the value and the violation are too hopelessly intertwined to legally disentangle. Some of the characteristics of computers and of the cyber world make it exceedingly difficult for us to control information about ourselves to safeguard our privacy. These characteristics are described in Chapters Three, Eight, and Nine. I recap them below to show the big picture and conclude by giving some suggestions for fighting back.

Technology Is Eroding Privacy

There are five characteristics of the technologies that with and without human manipulation are responsible for the deterioration and loss of our privacy.

Manipulating Bits Is Cheap

Cheap information is the true legacy of the Internet. Although the initial cost of acquiring data with sensors and human input is high, replication and automation introduce economies of scale that drive down the price. Duplicating information, whether on hard drives, networks, flash memory, or futuristic solid-state devices, is inexpensive. Computers are superb at searching. With the assistance of intelligent software, they are able to connect seemingly unrelated facts instantaneously. Governments and industry are ideally positioned to benefit from wide-scale information acquisition.

All Computers Are Interconnected

The tangled, cross-connected nature of the Internet makes restricting access to information stored on any one computer a difficult, never-ending task. Computer security is one of the fastest growing fields in both government and the technology industry for a reason: restricting information is a losing battle. If everything is stored on computers and any computer can be compromised or attacked from anywhere in the world, then there is no truly private information. Once it's stored in a database somewhere, it's effectively public knowledge.

Data Never Disappear

Information can be moved anywhere around the world with no noticeable delay and can be copied an infinite number of times with no degradation in quality; as a result, locating every copy of a piece of information is impossible. The low cost of replication combined with the interconnected nature of modern computers makes it physically impossible to guarantee that a digital object has not been made, copied, and moved somewhere else.

Everything Public Is Recorded

Digital information is not just purposeful recordings made by a human being. It is also the musings of machines. It is log files from household appliances, video from surveillance cameras, records of financial transactions, supposedly deleted love emails, and last year's tax returns. This computer dream world springs from the silicon minds of our digital devices like toll-road sensors, vending machines, cell phones, surgical implants, car dashboards, computerized tennis shoes, observant billboards, taxicabs, television sets, elevators, and coffee pots.

Tagging Links the Silicon and Physical Worlds

The real and the virtual universes are being organized and cross-connected to each other by tagging, typified by RFID chips in the real world and content tagging in the virtual. Taggles are wide-flung webs of low-cost sensors that monitor tags and that are synchronized at the back end with online searchable databases.

Privacy Is About Striking a Balance

The leading edge of technology in the last several decades has been information and computer science. Whether it's genetic engineering or industrial processing, the country's most valuable assets are its information factories. We are now a data-rich society. Our innovation and creativity come from free and unfettered access to information as well as from a democratic society that has, at its core, the premise that anything not illegal is permissible. Capitalism stems from this cultural imperative: businesses renew their competitiveness by reinventing themselves as knowledge companies; multimillion-dollar start-ups raise their cash on a concept. Our economy is not based on guns or butter but on ideas.

The freedom of democracy combined with the open marketplace of capitalism makes it easy for hostile groups to get from the United States whatever information weaponry they need to attack the United States itself. It's like robbing a gun store with one of its own guns. Maintaining our economy means protecting our access to plentiful information. But if we can use it, so can terrorists. That is one of the risks in a democracy.

Just as the country can and should manage information important to national interests, we, as citizens, should control information about ourselves by ourselves. In the Information Age, if we lose that mastery, our privacy is lost. However, we need to avoid another 9/11 at almost all costs. Managing the tradeoff between privacy and security requires an accomplished and trusted hand. It also requires a willing acceptance of risk by the populace and by the government. Maintaining some privacy means tolerating some risk. A democracy is said to be willing to let ten guilty people go free to avoid convicting an innocent person. Likewise, there are private places that we must protect, even if one might be the rat hole that a killer could slither down. For instance, in order to maintain our ability to exercise intellectual curiosity and awareness without penalty, we could preserve our libraries by agreeing as a society that the limited risk of a terrorist's gaining information by using a library for research is an acceptable one.

This is what we need a national debate about—risk. An absolute position is not what we want or need: neither complete surveillance nor total anonymity. The United States must discover the middle ground after a lengthy and necessary debate that hasn't been started yet. The president does not have the right to take away our privacy; only we can do that. As a nation, we need to find the balance between privacy and security that we can live with. The biggest mistake that we can make is to trust those in power to do what's right for us.

Just as the privacy pendulum has swung in the direction of misguided security at the moment, with the presumption that everyone is guilty until proven otherwise, it will once again swing in the other direction and assume that everyone is innocent. What's needed is a well thought-out balance, to moderate the current extreme while preventing the swing to an opposing one.

Too Much Privacy Is a Threat to Our Security

The ultimate in privacy is anonymity. At this point in our country's history, guaranteeing that degree of privacy is an unacceptable proposition. Clearly our safety depends on effective counterintelligence, and therefore some of our information is going to be tracked. We should be willing to give up some of our information but protect other areas that are more sensitive. For instance, it's probably a good idea to be required to show identification when we cross a U.S. border. We should be tracked when we travel. It's reasonable to impose administrative procedures as an obstacle against purchasing clearly dangerous commodities like virus samples, dangerous chemicals, and some weapons.

I can even see why some other purchases should be traced—say, buying two tons of fertilizer, a coil of wire, and an alarm clock. But I'd draw the line at reading material, music, and personal communications. Speaking for myself, I'd rather take the unlikely risk that another plane is going be hijacked than to live in a high-tech police state.

Some people should be exposed to greater scrutiny, but we should legally limit the number of people who are on government terrorist watch lists. It seems reasonable, for instance, for five thousand resident aliens to be on a watch list, but it would be unreasonable if that number were three hundred thousand or three million. Just because we have the means to watch millions of people doesn't mean that we should. There should be a legal restriction on how many people are subjected to thorough scrutiny and put on no-fly lists, for example. Many privacy advocates have grave concerns about the secret Bush administration data-mining programs; their fear is not that a few terrorist suspects are being watched but that the government is going on massive, electronic fishing expeditions, trolling for anything it can find. A target quota would force law-enforcement agents to prioritize and do more due diligence while still giving them the tools that they need to get their job done.

Too Little Privacy Is Economically Damaging

Excessive protection of individual rights leaves the United States vulnerable to external threats, but ignoring our privacy has risks too. One of them is that a privacy-hostile environment will encourage the development of private technologies to counter government or other kinds of surveillance. Just as DVD and CD encryption spawned numerous free "cracking" programs, there's already been a rise in shareware anonymity tools for privacy-protected email, text messaging, and web browsing. Unfortunately, enemies of the United States as well as its citizens can use these privacy-protection programs.

As the sanctioned weakening of our privacy continues, an anonymity arms race is the likely result. Resourceful and clever people will have strong incentives to encourage and create identity-hiding and privacy-preserving technologies, using strong encryption and other means. There will always be some people who will circumvent the system, either out of need or perversity, but a privacy-hostile Internet environment may push adoption of such private technologies into the mainstream.

Common use of encryption presents a quandary for the government as to whether to make its usage illegal. If it is not made illegal, the people who need to be watched will be invisible because terrorists and their like will certainly use encryption. However, if the United States does outlaw the use of cryptographic materials and the rest of the world doesn't follow suit, domestic industries will be handicapped because their products will be seen as noncompetitive in the global market and possibly dangerous. Non-Americans will be leery about using our services if the security provided in the United States is substandard compared with the security offered in other countries.

There is a fortune waiting to be made in providing privacy and anonymity services. Just as prohibition gave birth to organized crime syndicates to feed the public demand for illegal liquor, excessive government monitoring will gestate a new kind of organization that will fulfill the need for untraceable transactions, not just for black-market activities like prostitution and drug dealing but also for legal but embarrassing activities like the buying of sex toys and arranging the logistics of infidelity, as well as for the mildly illegal ones of income-tax evasion and speeding. Every participant in the underground economy is a future customer of privacy products, legal or not.

A subtler and more worrisome harm to the country caused by a lack of privacy is the formation of a risk-adverse business culture. America's proudest sons and daughters are its businesspeople. The country admires financial success and reveres those who have achieved it because one of our tenets is that those on the road to wealth bring others along for the ride. Some of America's most celebrated business tycoons were viewed as contrarians prior to their success. These are exactly the kind of people who will get flagged for scrutiny prior to becoming successful because entrepreneurs act differently than everyone else. The qualities of intellectual curiosity that made Thomas Edison, Andrew Carnegie, and Bill Gates wealthy might put them on a watch list today.

There's an old Chinese proverb, "The nail sticking up gets pounded down first." Heavily monitored societies make a virtue out of fitting in. Those who look and act "normal" will breeze through checkpoints faster, avoid getting picked on by peers, and in general have an easier, more hassle-free life than those who do not appear "normal." When conformists are confronted by danger, their instinct is to freeze, not to attack. This is a lousy strategy in most business sectors, where the top perch is taken and held by predators. Encouraging conformism as a method for not attracting unwanted government attention is tantamount to breeding out business innovation skills when and where they are needed the most.

As the United States loses its economic king-of-the-hill status, the obstacles to doing business here will grow for many countries. The current Safe Harbor agreement with the European Union regarding privacy is barely sufficient to bridge the legal differences and does nothing for the cultural ones. If U.S. views continue to diverge from those of the Europeans and others, U.S. companies will increasingly run into difficulties doing business with them. Some may embargo U.S. digital goods outright as a protest, just as the United States has used human rights violations as a reason for ending military and trade agreements. Many will have the sneaking belief that the United States is putting encryption back doors in commercial software or in the firmware components of hardware. This is a justifiable concern; the Clinton administration proposed something similar with the Clipper Chip. Some people may even wonder whether U.S. products contain government-sanctioned Trojan horses or remote listening devices, possibly under the guise of copy protection or Digital Rights Management. These fears of cryptographic infection will induce many people outside the United States to buy equivalent products elsewhere that aren't as likely to be tainted. In fact, it wouldn't surprise me in the slightest if the government had already induced several major software vendors and Internet companies to build back doors into their products, allowing at-will access by government agents. U.S. products and services will become less competitive in global marketplaces as the suspicion of U.S. intelligence involvement in commercial industries makes these goods less palatable to many people in the world.

The New Reality of Privacy

Governments need to collect information for security purposes, and they need to retain some of it for a long enough period of time to spot trends. If marketing companies stop keeping information, they lose their reason for existing. They will keep as much as they are legally allowed to and maybe just a little bit more. Some knowledge—about real estate transactions, the actions of a public company and its officers, political contributions—is good for public-policy reasons. Exposing this information is good for the community. People who choose to be leaders in these areas should accept the fact that their lives are going to be a little more open than those of their neighbors.

Collecting Data Doesn't Violate Privacy, Usage Does

As we have seen many times in this book, it's not about the data; it's about what's done with data. If it were possible to safeguard information and ensure that it was used only for its stated purpose and for no other, then most people's objections to data collection would, I suspect, go away. Medical information that stayed in the doctor's office and was used only to treat the patient, not given to the managed-health-care provider to deny coverage. School psychological records that were used only by a counselor to help a child, and not later given to military recruiters to coerce enlistment. Travel information used for booking tickets, not for harassing the traveler.

Data should never be used for anything but its stated purpose. And all information collected by anyone should have a pull date for purging. Both these principles should be legally required. Receipt of a person's personal information is a trust and should be treated as such. The reason medical and legal professions are highly regarded is because we hold them to ethical standards. These principles involve the sanctity of personal information, as in the private, privileged nature of the relationship between a doctor and his patient or a lawyer and her client. How can we expect every middle manager in Homeland Security or every junior database administrator at a direct-marketing firm to uphold the same lofty ethical principles as highly paid doctors and lawyers regulated by their own professions and held accountable for ethical breaches? Proper handling of information and an adherence to the commandments specified in Chapter One will help to build an ethical culture in which our personal information is treated with the professionalism and respect that we deserve by the people we entrust it to.

Profiling Rules Must Be Made Public

The infosphere is too rich and complex to traverse linearly. The amount of digital information out there appears to be doubling every three years.[2] Most textual information now starts out digitally, and increasingly image, sound, and video information is digital too. Intelligent automated software provides the only reasonable way to find complex information in huge databases in a timely manner. Governments will have to use these expert systems, and industry will certainly want to follow suit.

Yet profiling software is responsible for some of the worst privacy abuses. Government no-fly lists and credit-scoring systems are both profilers that can unjustly cause problems for people. It's frustrating for those affected because they don't know why they are being singled out. Even though the process used to put them in a certain category is often held secret, the outcome generally is not. Labels get around quickly.

The only solution to the problem is complete transparency into the programming used for all heuristic systems that affect the lives of citizens or consumers. It's a principle of our legal system that the accused has the right to confront the accuser, and in the future a computer will increasingly be the one pointing the digital finger. It's important to recognize that with the rules built into profiling systems such as FICO, scores are made by humans and enforced by machines, not the other way around. We have a right to know when we're being labeled and a need to know why. Many of us are getting tired of running into bureaucratic obstacles when dealing with the government or big business and getting the big machine run-around, in which the computer is blamed for whatever awful obstacles we've just encountered. A requirement that companies that operate profiling systems publicly expose their rules transfers the blame for ignorant policy away from the machines and back where it belongs, onto the rule makers.

Databases Holding Personal Information Need Oversight

Along with the requirement for transparency of programming is a need for a clear review and appeal system for all databases containing personal information, public and private. With all best intentions, government policy often goes astray in the implementation, usually undermined by the actions of an individual. Sometimes it's the powerful who go astray, as the McCarthyites did; sometimes it's the low-level civil servant who makes a mistake and covers up, who abuses the system for personal reasons, or who sees a golden opportunity to cash in after a lifetime of government work.

On the private side, Americans need an improved process for challenging commercial data that's collected, like credit entries. The current policy is that the credit bureaus "investigate" by asking the company that reported the contested listing to validate the accuracy of the information. These self-regulated systems start with the disingenuous premise that any company is more honest than any citizen. White-collar prisons are full of exceptions.

In both sectors, there needs to be a third, objective party who can rule on incorrect, inappropriate, or illegal data entries. An ombudsman system could be created with the authority to question and correct information in any government or commercial database and levy fines for unresponsiveness.

The single best thing that Congress can do to help protect privacy is to enact legislation charging a regulatory agency with responsibility for guarding the privacy of citizens. Tough legislation, similar to Sarbanes-Oxley, could be enacted that would hold directors of corporations personally responsible for data breaches resulting in exposure of private information. Big enough fines would get shareholders' and thus the corporate boards' attentions. Most companies should improve their computer security anyway, and if tough laws help get their attention, fine. Although technology moves too fast for narrow legislation, organizations that take advantage of rapid technological change can be punished.

The public sector should also be held accountable, both the institutions and the individuals within them. The shameful condition of the U.S. government's computer security needs to be addressed. The first line of defense is better protection of computers everywhere, which is mostly a matter of spending more money. The second is new, tougher legislation that levies personal fines on government workers who leak information. The third is complete and full disclosure of the workings of all profiling systems. Last, the loophole that allows mingling of government and commercial databases needs to be closed. No branch of the government should be allowed to purchase personal information from a private company if the agency wouldn't be legally allowed to collect the information on its own.

No personal data should be allowed to linger in databases forever, either in the public or private sectors. Any data center maintaining other peoples' personal information should be forced to adhere to government-mandated data-erasure policies. Fines should be levied for noncompliance

Transparency and accountability of information and process are the policies that work best in a democratic society.

Rattle the Cage

A panopticon is a kind of prison designed by the English philosopher Jeremy Bentham. His notion was to put prisoners in cells, separated by soundproof walls, centered around an observation tower and backlit in such a way that convicts could be observed both from the outside and from the center without knowing whether they were being watched by unseen guards. Bentham's idea was to create a "sentiment of invisible omniscience"; he figured that inmates would be docile if they knew that they were always under surveillance. The term is also a good description or analogy for our emerging fishbowl society, where the doings of its citizens are visible because of information technology. The collective computer industry is the panopticon.

Technology is a double-edged blade with no hilt, cutting no matter how you hold it. The same solid-state cameras that make modern astronomy possible are used for unapproved surveillance. The databases containing the human genome that will someday help cure many human illnesses will probably also be used to deny employment to those with potential medical problems. The networking equipment that makes all the great things on the Internet possible makes universal surveillance feasible.

Technology has created much of America's opportunity; its potential to damage privacy may eventually cause the opposite effect—driving out people who are uncomfortable living in a panopticon. The United States has always been the kind of magnet that attracts the best. Each wave of immigration has provided scientists, entertainers, and businesspeople who set the standards for their professions. They come and they stay here because of the financial rewards and the freedom, which allow them to live their lives the way they want.

But magnets can repel as well as attract. The United States has never experienced wholesale emigration, but it is one of the few countries that hasn't. Most nations hit bleak stretches in their history where life isn't good and the future looks worse. Then the smart, the lucky, and the ambitious leave. The United States has opened its doors to many riding these immigration waves and has benefited greatly. A combination of long-term economic doldrums combined with a paranoid and privacy-invasive culture could make it tough to retain free thinkers and pioneers.

As citizens get used to the idea of living in a panopticon, those who stay will adjust their behavior to avoid the hassles that come from being under suspicion. The resulting culture of conformity will be ill-positioned to compete in emerging global marketplaces. Business leaders will not rise to the top in this new world unless they have demonstrated the ability to avoid risk, a detrimental skill when managing a company with international competition in a fast-moving market.

The solution to the problem of preserving cultural privacy is moderation. The guiding principle is to affect the smallest number of citizens by minimally encroaching on their privacy for the least possible time that is necessary to get the job done for the greater good. Failing institutional moderation, it's every man or woman for his- or herself.

When all else fails, citizens must take their privacy into their own hands. Ultimately we cannot rely on the government or the good graces of retailers or the sensitivities of our neighbors. Be a curmudgeon. If you feel as though you are living in a cage, rattle the bars once in a while. Turn the tables and watch the watchers for a change. If nothing else works, act like a monkey and throw things. If each of us refuses to meekly provide our SSN, our phone number, our mother's maiden name, and any other information that is not absolutely critically required for a service, then together we will have done our part to stop the invasion.

It takes only a single person to persuade a business to be more privacy-sensitive. Any constituent can get the ear of elected representatives. Groups of people can band together to start pushing back on the data encroachment. Our privacy is becoming lost, but we don't have to let go gracefully. By clinging on, kicking and screaming, we can delay the inevitable, trusting the strength of our community to fill in the gaps with the strongest bonds of all: cultural principles that can preserve our dignity, if not our privacy, far better than a stack of unusable legislation and worthless privacy policies.

Fight back or your privacy will be lost for good.

Recommended Reading

Alderman, E., and C. Kennedy. *In Our Defense: The Bill of Rights in Action*. New York: Perennial Press, 1991.

Brin, D. *The Transparent Society: Will Technology Force Us to Choose Between Privacy and Freedom?* New York: Perseus, 1998.

Cate, F. *Privacy in the Information Age*. Washington, D.C.: Brookings Institution, 1997.

Cole, D., and J. Dempsey. *Terrorism and the Constitution: Sacrificing Civil Liberties in the Name of National Security*. New York: New Press, 2002.

Keefe, P. *Chatter: Dispatches from the Secret World of Global Eavesdropping*. New York: Random House, 2005.

Kelly, K. *Out of Control*. Reading, Mass.: Addison-Wesley, 1994.

Negroponte, N. *Being Digital*. New York: Knopf, 1995.

O'Harrow, R. *No Place to Hide: Behind the Scenes of Our Emerging Surveillance Society*. New York: Free Press, 2005.

Orwell, G. *1984*. Harmondsworth, U.K.: Penguin Books, 2003. (Originally published 1949.)

Rheingold, H. *Smart Mobs: The Next Social Revolution*. New York: Perseus, 2002.

Rosen, J. *The Unwanted Gaze: The Destruction of Privacy in America*. New York: Vintage Books, 2000.

Rothstein, M. (ed.). *Genetic Secrets: Protecting Privacy and Confidentiality in the Genetic Era*. New Haven, Conn.: Yale University Press, 1997.

Solove, D., and M. Rotenberg. *Information Privacy Law*. Gaithersburg, Md.: Aspen, 2003.

Sullivan, B. *Your Evil Twin: Behind the Identity Theft Epidemic*. New York: Wiley, 2004.

Whitaker, R. *The End of Privacy: How Total Surveillance Is Becoming a Reality*. New York: New Press, 1999.

Notes

Preface

1. Judy Garland. 16 March 1967. Interview on NBC TV. Wikiquote.

Introduction

1. <http://www.cia.gov/cia/notices.html#priv> (21 June 2006).
2. G. E. Moore, "Cramming More Components onto Integrated Circuits," *Electronics Magazine*, April 1965, 38(8), 114–117.

Chapter One

1. D. Shipman, *Brando (The Movie Makers)* (New York: MacMillan, 1974).
2. Oxford University Press, "Privacy." *The Oxford English Dictionary* (2nd ed.) (New York: Oxford University Press, 1989).
3. Houghton-Mifflin, "Privacy." *The American Heritage Dictionary of the English Language* (4th ed.) (Boston: Houghton Mifflin, 2000).
4. Merriam-Webster, "Privacy." *Merriam-Webster's Collegiate Dictionary* (11th ed.) (Springfield, MA: Merriam-Webster, 2003).
5. "Nicole Kidman Bugged in Australia," *CBS News*, 25 January 2005, <http://www.cbsnews.com/stories/2005/01/25/entertainment/main669062.shtml> (30 June 2006).

6. Vicky Ward, "The Beautiful and the Damned," *Vanity Fair*, December 2005, 544, 310–317, 352–355, <http://www.vanityfair.com/commentary/content/articles/051212roco01> (30 June 2006).

7. John D. Woodward, "Super Bowl Surveillance: Facing Up to Biometrics," *RAND Issue Paper 209*, 2001, <http://www.rand.org/pubs/issue_papers/2005/IP209.pdf> (30 June 2006).

8. Jane Black, "One in the Eye for Big Brother," *Business Week Online*, 15 August 2002, <http://www.businessweek.com/bwdaily/dnflash/aug2002/nf20020815_7186.htm> (30 June 2006).

9. Sam Tranum, "Proposed Surveillance System Runs Automated Background Checks as Vehicles Enter Town," *South Florida Sun-Sentinel*, 15 April 2004.

10. President's Commission on the United States Postal Service, "Embracing the Future: Making the Tough Choices to Preserve Universal Mail Service." Washington, DC: U.S. Government Printing Office, July 2003.

11. Beth Givens, "RFID Implementation in Libraries: Some Recommendations for Best Practices." Presentation, ALA Intellectual Freedom Committee, American Library Association, ALA Mid-Winter, San Diego, CA, 10 January 2004, <http://www.privacyrights.org/ar/RFID-ALA.htm> (30 June 2006).

12. "Super-Radar, Done Dirt Cheap," *Business Week Online*, 20 October 2003, <http://www.businessweek.com/magazine/content/03_42/b3854113.htm> (30 June 2006).

13. Michael J. Sniffen, "Pentagon Plan Seeks to Track, Record Every Vehicle Within a City," *USA Today*, 1 July 2003, <http://www.usatoday.com/tech/news/techinnovations/2003-07-01-urband-tracking_x.htm> (2 July 2006).

14. GeoSpatial Technologies, Inc., Press Release, August 2002, "Palm Beach School District Protects Students and Bus Drivers with Technology," <http://www.geospatialtech.com/news/press/article/02/prod_08.asp> (30 June 2006).

15. K. C. Jones, "'No GPS In The Cars,' Cabbies Say," *InformationWeek*, 10 October 2005, <http://www.informationweek.com/news/showArticle.jhtml?articleID=171203931> (30 June 2005).

16. Don Oldenburg, "The Snoop in Your Coupe," *Washington Post*, 9 September 2003, Section A, p. A01.

17. Julia Scheeres, "When Cash is Only Skin Deep," *Wired News*, 25 November 2003, <http://www.wired.com/news/technology/0,1282,61357,00.html> (3 July 2006); Applied Digital, <http://www.adsx.com/index.html> (3 July 2006).

18. Privacy International, "PI Submission to Citizenship Committee of Canadian Parliament," 4 October 2003, <http://www.privacyinternational.org/issues/idcard/pi-can-submission-10-03.htm> (30 June 2006).

19. U.S. Government Accountability Office, "Health Information Technology: HHS Is Taking Steps to Develop a National Strategy," Pub. no. GAO-05-628. Washington, DC: U.S. Government Printing Office, May 2005, <http://www.gao.gov/new.items/d05628.pdf> (3 July 2006).

20. Andrew Batson, "China Begins Effort to Replace Citizen IDs With Digital Cards," *Wall Street Journal*, 12 August 2003, <http://www.otiglobal.com/objects/WSJ%2008112003.pdf> (30 June 2006).

21. <http://travel.state.gov/passport/eppt/eppt_2788.html> (21 June 2006).

22. A. Beck, "Data Brokers and Buyers Anger Congress," *Reuters*, 26 June 2006, <http://www.eweek.com/article2/0,1759,1981909,00.asp?kc=EWRSS03129TX1K0000614> (8 August 2006).

23. Craig Bicknell, "Double Click's Single Focus: You," *Wired News*, 14 June 1999, <http://www.wired.com/news/business/0,1367,20205,00.html> (8 August 2006).

24. Robert O'Harrow Jr., "Web Ad Firm to Limit Use of Profiles," *Washington Post*, 27 August 2002, p. E01, <http://www.washingtonpost.com/ac2/wp-dyn/A64716–2002Aug26?language=printer> (21 June 2006).

25. <http://www.websidestory.com/products/web-analytics/datainsights/spotlight/06-28-2005.html>.

26. *Gonzales v. Google, Inc.*, No. 5:06-mc-80006-JW (ND Cal. 17 March, 2006), <http://www.google.com/press/images/ruling_20060317.pdf> (2 July 2006).

27. Ron Leuty, "Banks Come Under Fire for Selling Customer Info," *Sacramento Business Journal,* 12 November 1999, <http://www.bizjournals.com/sacramento/stories/1999/11/15/focus6.html> (21 June 2006).

28. *FTC v. GeoCities,* California Superior Court, Docket no. C-3850, 12 February 1999.

29. Kim Zetter, "California Woman Sues ChoicePoint," *Wired News,* 26 February 2005, <http://www.wired.com/news/privacy/0,1848,66710,00.html> (21 June 2006).

30. Maria Godoy, "Angry 'Brides' Storm Macy's," *Tech Live,* 13 June 2001, <http://www.g4tv.com/> (8 August 2006).

31. *Hatch v. U.S. Bank National Association ND,* No. 99-872 adm/ajb, (D. Minn. filed 9 June 1999), <http://www.ag.state.mn.us/consumer/privacy/pr/pr_usbank_06091999.html> (2 July 2006).

32. Ariana Eunjung Cha, "In Retail, Profiling for Profit," *Washington Post,* 17 August 2005, p. A01, <http://www.washingtonpost.com/wp-dyn/content/article/2005/08/16/AR2005081601906.html> (21 June 2006).

33. "How Do Businesses Use Customer Information? Is the Customer's Privacy Protected?" Hearing, Subcommittee on Commerce, Trade, and Consumer Protection of the Committee on Energy and Commerce, House of Representatives, One Hundred Seventh Congress, first session, Washington, 26 July 2001, <http://energycommerce.house.gov/107/hearings/07262001Hearing336/Zuccarini546.htm> (2 July 2006).

34. Malgorzata Wozniacka and Snigdha Sen, "Credit Scores: What You Should Know About Your Own," *Secret History of the Credit Card,* 23 November 2004, <http://www.pbs.org/wgbh/pages/frontline/shows/credit/more/scores.html> (21 June 2006).

35. "Consumers Now Can Know What Loan Rate Offers to Expect Based on Their FICO Credit Score at MyFICO.com," *myFICO.com,* 6 March 2002, <http://www.myfico.com/PressRoom/PressReleases/2002_03_06.aspx> (2 July 2006).

36. Malgorzata Wozniacka and Snigdha Sen, "Credit Scores: What You Should Know About Your Own," *Secret History of the Credit Card,*

23 November 2004, <http://www.pbs.org/wgbh/pages/frontline/shows/credit/more/scores.html> (21 June 2006).

37. Kristy Welsh, "Notes from the Credit Scoring Conference," *Credit-InfoCenter.com*, 22 July 1999, <http://www.creditinfocenter.com/FeaturedArticles/creditscoringconference.shtml> (21 June 2006).

38. U.S. Public Interest Research Group (PIRG), "Mistakes Do Happen: A Look at Errors in Consumer Credit Reports," June 2004, <http://uspirg.org/uspirg.asp?id2=13649&id3=USPIRG&> (21 June 2006).

39. Wozniacka and Sen, "Credit Scores."

40. Internal Revenue Service, "Reveal System," <http://www.irs.gov/privacy/article/0,,id=137941,00.html> (21 June 2006).

41. Paul Rosenzweig and Michael Scardaville, "The Need to Protect Civil Liberties While Combating Terrorism: Legal Principles and the Total Information Awareness Program," *The Heritage Foundation*, 6 February 2003, <http://www.heritage.org/Research/HomelandDefense/lm6.cfm> (2 July 2006).

42. Farhad Manjoo, "Total Information Awareness: Down, But Not Out," *Salon.com*, 29 January 2003, <http://dir.salon.com/story/tech/feature/2003/01/29/tia_privacy/index.html> (3 July 2006); Ryan Singel, "Total Info System Totally Touchy," *Wired News*, 2 December 2002, <http://www.wired.com/news/politics/0,1283,56620,00.html> (3 July 2006); Gina Marie Stevens, "Privacy: Total Information Awareness Programs and Related Information Access, Collection, and Protection Laws," Report for Congress, Congressional Research Service, 21 March 2003, <http://www.fas.org/irp/crs/RL31730.pdf> (3 July 2006).

43. U.S. Government Accountability Office, "Aviation Security: Computer-assisted Passenger Prescreening System Faces Significant Implementation Challenges," Pub. no. GAO-04-385. (Washington, DC: U.S. Government Printing Office, February 2004), <http://www.gao.gov/new.items/d04385.pdf> (3 July 2006).

44. Bob Sullivan, "ID Theft Again Tops List of FTC Complaints," *MSNBC.com*, 25 January 2005, <http://www.msnbc.msn.com/id/11010464/> (2 July 2006); Beth Givens et al., "Privacy Groups Urge Federal Reserve Board to Protect Consumers from Identity

Theft and Stolen Convenience Checks," *Privacy Rights Clearinghouse*, 28 March 2005, <http://www.privacyrights.org/ar/FRB-IDTheft.htm> (2 July 2006).

45. Matthew Broersma, "Forbes Rich List Fall Prey to High-Tech Fraudster," *ZDNet UK*, 20 March 2001, <http://news.zdnet.co.uk/business/0,39020645,2085145,00.htm> (21 June 2006).

46. "FBI Busts Identity Theft Ring," *BBC News*, 26 November 2002, <http://news.bbc.co.uk/1/hi/business/2513015.stm> (21 June 2006).

47. Wilson P. Dizard, "FBI Analyst Faces Trial for Surfing Law Enforcement Systems," *Government Computer News*, 17 March 2004, <http://www.gcn.com/vol1_no1/daily-updates/25279–1.html> (21 June 2006).

48. Bob Sullivan, "Identity Theft Tops Consumer Woes . . . Again," *MSNBC.com*, 23 January 2004, <http://msnbc.msn.com/id/4029541/> (21 June 2006).

49. Identity Theft Resource Center, "Facts & Statistics," <http://www.idtheftcenter.org/facts.shtml> (21 June 2006).

50. Ira Sager and Ben Elgin, "The Underground Web," *Business Week Online*, 2 September 2002, pp. 67–70, <http://www.businessweek.com/magazine/content/02_35/b3797001.htm> (21 June 2006).

51. Federal Trade Commission, "Identity Theft Survey Report," September 2003, <http://www.ftc.gov/os/2003/09/synovatereport.pdf> (21 June 2006).

52. David Bloys, "The Role U.S. Counties May Be Playing in International Deed Fraud," *News for Public Officials*, 16 February 2006, <http://www.davickservices.com/Link%20Between%20Deed%20Fraud%20and%20Counties.htm> (3 July 2006).

53. Dan Feldstein, "Identity Thieves Stealing Attention; Horror Stories Help Crime Gain Notoriety," *Houston Chronicle*, 27 June 2004, p. 16A.

54. Ibid.

55. Bob Keefe, "Identity Scheme a Riddle," *Atlanta Journal-Constitution*, 27 February 2005, <http://www.ajc.com/hp/content/auto/epaper/editions/today/news_2412e869e1fb614b00d9.html> (21 June 2006).

56. Tom Zeller Jr., "Identity Crises," *New York Times*, 1 October 2005, p. B1.

57. Beth Givens et al., "Nowhere to Turn: Victims Speak Out on Identity Theft, A Survey of Identity Theft Victims and Recommendations for Reform," Privacy Rights Clearinghouse, May 2000, <http://www.privacyrights.org/ar/idtheft2000.htm> (8 August 2006).

58. Robert O'Harrow Jr., "Identity Crisis," *Washington Post*, 10 August 2003, p. W14, <http://www.washingtonpost.com/ac2/wp-dyn?page name=article&contentId=A25358–2003Aug6&notFound=true> (21 June 2006).

59. Sullivan, "Identity Theft Tops Consumer Woes."

60. Laura Bruce, "John Harrison: The Face of Identity Theft," *Bankrate.com*, 18 August 2004, <http://www.bankrate.com/brm/news/advice/IDTheft/ID-home.asp> (21 June 2006).

61. John Markoff and Laura M. Holson, "An Oscar Surprise: Vulnerable Phones," *The New York Times*, 2 March 2005, <http://www.nytimes.com/2005/03/02/movies/oscars/02leak.html?ei=5088&en=ad4f3884 fa663340&ex=1267419600&adxnnl=1&partner=rssnyt&adxnnlx= 1151847514-psZv3LDevl6kaWWX2nfKJw> (2 July 2006).

62. John Hering, "Bluetooth Attack!," *G4tv.com*, 16 September 2004, <http://www.g4tv.com/screensavers/features/48021/Bluetooth_ Attack.html> (2 July 2006); "Long Distance Snarf," *Trifinite.org*, <http://trifinite.org/trifinite_stuff_lds.html> (2 July 2006).

63. Staci D. Kramer, "Paris Hilton: Hacked or Not?" *Wired News*, 23 February 2005, <http://www.wired.com/news/privacy/ 0,1848,66681,00.html> (2 July 2006).

64. Kelley Beaucar Vlahos, "Online Rants Not Always Free Speech," *Fox News*, 20 March 2002, <http://www.foxnews.com/story/ 0,2933,48291,00.html> (21 June 2006).

65. Krysten Crawford, "Have a Blog, Lose Your Job?" *CNNMoney.com*, 15 February 2005, <http://money.cnn.com/2005/02/14/news/ economy/blogging/> (21 June 2006).

66. Jo Twist, "US Blogger Fired by Her Airline," *BBC News*, 3 November 2004, <http://news.bbc.co.uk/1/hi/technology/3974081.stm> (21 June 2006).

67. Rob Capriccioso, "Dental Pain at Marquette," *Inside Higher Ed,* 6 December 2005, <http://www.insidehighered.com/news/2005/12/06/marquette> (21 June 2006).

68. Lee Rainie, "The State of Blogging," Pew Internet & American Life Project, 2 January 2005, <http://www.pewinternet.org/pdfs/PIP_blogging_data.pdf> (21 June 2006).

69. Olga Kharif, "In the Internet's High-Speed Lane," *Business Week Online,* 5 April 2005, <http://www.businessweek.com/technology/content/apr2005/tc2005045_7077_tc206.htm?c=bwtechapr15&n=link8&t=email> (2 July 2006).

70. Servicemembers Legal Defense Network, "McVeigh v. Cohen," 15 January 1998, <http://www.sldn.org/templates/law/record.html?section=95&record=295> (21 June 2006).

71. Janet Kornblum, "Navy Barred from Ousting Sailor," 29 January 1998, <http://news.com.com/2100–1023–207617.html?legacy=cnet> (21 June 2006).

72. Awareness Center, "Rabbi Israel Kestenbaum," <http://theawarenesscenter.org/kestenbaum.html> (21 June 2006).

73. "Man Pleads Guilty in Web Sex Sting," *High Tech NewsBits,* 29 November 1999, <http://www.newsbits.net/1999/19991129.htm> (21 June 2006).

74. Lisa Bowman, "Naughton: Child Porn Unsolicited," *ZDNet News,* 28 November 1999, <http://news.zdnet.com/2100–9595_22–516898.html> (21 June 2006).

75. Jamie Stockwell, "Online Child-Sex Sting Results in Nine Arrests," *Washington Post,* 2 April 2005, p. B05, <http://www.washingtonpost.com/wp-dyn/articles/A19962–2005Apr1.html> (21 June 2006).

76. *Wyman v. James,* 400 U.S. 309 (1971).

77. Electronic Privacy Information Center, "Social Security Numbers," <http://www.epic.org/privacy/ssn/> (21 June 2006).

78. Electronic Privacy Information Center, "Poverty and Privacy," <http://www.epic.org/privacy/poverty/> (21 June 2006).

79. American Civil Liberties Union, "ACLU of R.I. Sues Police over Illegal Strip-Search," press release, 15 May 2002, <http://www.aclu.org//crimjustice/searchseizure/10146prs20020515.html> (21 June 2006).

80. *Spider-Man 2*, directed by Sam Raimi, 127 min., Sony Pictures, 2004.

Chapter Two

1. Robert Frost, "Mending Wall," 1919, <http://www.bartleby.com/104/64.html> (14 July 2006).

2. David Streitfeld, "On the Web, Price Tags Blur: What You Pay Could Depend on Who You Are," *Washington Post*, 27 September 2000, p. A0, <http://www.washingtonpost.com/ac2/wp-dyn/A15159-2000Sep25?language=printer> (1 July 2006).

3. "Ohio Grocer 'Segments' Shoppers with Personalized Prices," Consumers Against Supermarket Privacy Invasion and Numbering (CASPIAN), <http://www.nocards.org/news/archive1.shtml#dlane> (1 July 2006).

4. The Return Exchange, <http://returnexchange.com/> (21 June 2006).

5. "Psychographic," *Wikipedia*, <http://en.wikipedia.org/wiki/Psychographics> (21 June 2006).

6. Claudette Riley, "Schools Put Limits on Camera Use," *Tennessean*, 2 July 2003, <http://www.electronicprivacyinstitute.org/Schools.htm> (21 June 2006).

7. "New York City: A Surveillance Camera Town," NYC Surveillance Camera Project Information, <http://www.mediaeater.com/cameras/overview.html> (1 July 2006).

8. "Surveillance Cameras Keep Watch on Manhattan," *Associated Press*, 19 August 2002, <http://www.enquirer.com/editions/2002/08/19/fin_surveillance_cameras.html> (1 July 2006).

9. "Spotlight on Surveillance," Electronic Privacy Information Center, May 2005, <http://www.epic.org/privacy/surveillance/spotlight/0505/> (1 July 2006).

10. Craig Haney, "The Psychological Impact of Incarceration: Implications for Post-Prison Adjustment," (paper prepared for the "From Prison to Home" National Policy Conference, U.S. Department of Health and Human Services, Urban Institute), 30–31 January 2002, <http://aspe.hhs.gov/HSP/prison2home02/Haney.htm> (1 July 2006).

Chapter Three

1. John Ashcroft, May 2002 interview with Larry King on CNN, *CNN.com*, <http://archives.cnn.com/2002/US/05/31/ashcroft.fbi/index.html> (8 August 2006).

2. G. E. Moore, "Cramming More Components onto Integrated Circuits," *Electronics Magazine*, April 1965, 38(8), 114–117: "The complexity for minimum component costs has increased at a rate of roughly a factor of two per year. . . . Certainly over the short term this rate can be expected to continue, if not to increase. Over the longer term, the rate of increase is a bit more uncertain, although there is no reason to believe it will not remain nearly constant for at least 10 years. That means by 1975, the number of components per integrated circuit for minimum cost will be 65,000. I believe that such a large circuit can be built on a single wafer."

3. CNN, 5 March 1999, <http://www.cnn.com/TECH/computing/9903/05/pentagon.hackers/> (8 August 2006).

Chapter Four

1. Earl Warren, *Lopez v. United States*, 373 U.S. 427 (1963).

2. "Cash Card Taps Virtual Game Funds," *BBC News*, 2 May 2006, <http://news.bbc.co.uk/2/hi/technology/4953620.stm> (21 June 2006).

3. Julian Dibbell, "A Rape in Cyberspace," *Village Voice*, 21 December 1993, pp. 36–42, <http://www.villagevoice.com/specials/0543, 50thdibbell,69273,31.html> (21 June 2006).

4. *Ashcroft v. Free Speech Coalition*, 535 U.S. 234 (2002).

5. "A White Wash at Vanity Fair?" *Radar Magazine*, 14 October 2005, <http://www.radaronline.com/fresh-intelligence/2005/10/14/index.php> (21 June 2006).

6. "Requests for Comment/United States Congress," *Wikipedia*, <http://en.wikipedia.org/wiki/Wikipedia:Requests_for_comment/United_States_Congress> (21 June 2006).

7. Jennifer Lee, "Trying to Elude the Google Grasp," *New York Times*, 25 July 2002, p. G1, <http://tech2.nytimes.com/mem/technology/techreview.html?res=9B05EFDE1338F936A15754C0A9649C8B63> (21 June 2006).

8. John Seigenthaler, "A False Wikipedia 'Biography,'" *USA Today*, 29 November 2005, <http://www.usatoday.com/news/opinion/editorials/2005–11–29-wikipedia-edit_x.htm> (21 June 2006).

9. Shawn P. McCarthy, "INTERNAUT: I Came, I Saw, I Wiki'd," *Government Computer News*, 9 January 2006, <http://www.gcn.com/25_01/content_management/37886–1.html> (21 June 2006).

10. Martha Irvine, "'Star Wars Kid': Internet Star Born Out of Private Moment on Videotape," *SFGate.com*, 21 August 2003, <http://www.sfgate.com/cgi-bin/article.cgi?f=/news/archive/2003/08/21/national1341EDT0610.DTL> (21 June 2006).

11. CBS News, *JetBlue In Privacy Faux Pas*, 20 Sep 2003, <http://www.cbsnews.com/stories/2003/09/20/attack/main574336.shtml> (8 August 2006).

12. Ann Davis, "Far Afield: FBI's Post-Sept. 11 'Watch List' Mutates, Acquires Life of its Own—Bureau Gave it to Companies," *Wall Street Journal*, 19 November 2002, p. A1.

13. "Anthrax 'Person of Interest' Sues Ashcroft, FBI," *CNN.com*, 27 August 2003, <http://www.cnn.com/2003/LAW/08/26/lawsuit.hatfill/> (21 June 2006).

14. David Mery, "Suspicious Behaviour on the Tube," *Guardian*, 22 September 2005, col. 5, <http://www.guardian.co.uk/attackon london/story/0,,1575532,00.html> (21 June 2006).

15. Carl Bernstein and Bob Woodward, *All the President's Men*. New York: Touchstone, 1974, 126.

16. Barbara Warnick, "Parody with a Purpose: Online Political Parody in the 2000 Presidential Campaign," in *Critical Literacy in a Digital Era: Rhetoric, Technology, and the Public Interest* (Hillside, N.J.: Erlbaum, 2002), <http://faculty.washington.edu/barbwarn/com300site/Parody20001.htm> (21 June 2006).

17. Center for the Digital Future, "2005 Digital Future Report," <http://www.digitalcenter.org/pdf/Center-for-the-Digital-Future-2005-Highlights.pdf> (21 June 2006).

Chapter Five

1. Louis Brandeis, *Olmstead v. United States* (1928).

2. "Civil Law," *Wikipedia*, <http://en.wikipedia.org/wiki/Civil_law_(private_law)> (21 June 2006).

3. Samuel D. Warren and Louis Brandeis, "The Right to Privacy," *Harvard Law Review*, 1890, 4, 193–220.

4. Ibid.

5. Prosser stated that a tort is "a term applied to a miscellaneous and more or less unconnected group of civil wrongs other than breach of contract for which a court of law will afford a remedy in the form of an action for damages." William L. Prosser, "Privacy," *California Law Review*, 48, 338–423, 1960.

6. *Roberson v. Rochester Folding Box Co.*, 171 NY 538 (1902).

7. *Pavesich v. New England Life Ins. Co.*, 122 Ga. 190, 50 SE 68 (1905).

8. *Eick v. Perk Dog Food Co.*, 347 Ill. App. 293 (1952).

9. *Carson v. Here's Johnny Portable Toilets, Inc.*, 698 F.2d 831 (6th Cir. 1983).

10. *Midler v. Ford Motor Co.*, 849 F.2d 460 (9th Cir. 1988).

11. *White v. Samsung Electronics America, Inc.*, 971 F. 2d 1395 (9th Cir. 1992).

12. "Rap Group Settles Rosa Parks Lawsuit," *New York Times*, 15 April 2005, <http://www.nytimes.com/2005/04/15/business/media/15settle.html?ex=1271217600&en=97910f02fe14130c&ei=

5088&partner=rssnyt&emc=rss> (1 July 2006); David Shepardson and Joe Menard, "Parks Settles OutKast Lawsuit," *Detroit News*, 15 April 2005, <http://www.detnews.com/2005/metro/0504/15/D01-151386.htm> (1 July 2006).

13. Joseph B. Frazier, "Unflattering Hot Sauce Label Has Skater Tonya Harding All Fired Up," *Associated Press*, 31 October 2002, <http://cnews.canoe.ca/CNEWS/WeirdNews/2002/10/31/3067.html> (1 July 2006).

14. *Hoffman v. Capital Cities/ABC, Inc.*, 33 F. Supp.2d 867 (CDCal 1999).

15. *Zacchini v. Scripps-Howard Broadcasting Co.*, 433 U.S. 562 (1977).

16. *Bartnicki v. Vopper*, 532 U.S. 514 (2001).

17. *Davis v. Temple*, 284 Ill. App. 3d 983 (1996). *Melvin v. Reid*, 112 Cal. App. 285, 297 (1931).

18. *Trammell v. Citizens News Co.*, 285 Ky. 529, 148 S.W.2d 708 (1941).

19. *Shulman v. Group W Productions*, 18 Cal. 4th 200 (1998).

20. *Galella v. Onassis*, 487 F.2d 896 (2d Cir. 1973).

21. *Dietemann v. Time Inc.*, 449 F.2d 245 (9th Cir. 1971).

22. Ken Paulson, "Stolen Conversations and Freedom of the Press," First Amendment Center, 27 May 2001, <http://www.firstamendmentcenter.org/commentary.aspx?id=2313> (21 June 2006).

23. *Wilson v. Layne*, 526 U.S. 603 (1999); *Hanlon v. Berger*, 526 U.S. 808 (1999).

24. *Remsburg v. Docusearch, Inc.*, 149 NH 148 (2002).

25. *Lake v. Wal-Mart Stores, Inc.*, 582 N.W.2d 231 (1998).

26. *Green v. CBS Inc.*, 286 F.3d 281 (5th Cir. 2002).

27. *Sipple v. Chronicle Publishing Co.*, 154 Cal. App. 3d 1040 (1984).

28. *Cox Broadcasting Corporation v. Cohn*, 420 U.S. 469 (1975).

29. *Smith v. Daily Mail Publishing Co.*, 443 U.S. 97 (1979).

30. *Garner v. Triangle Publications, Inc.*, 97 F.Supp. 546 (S.D.N.Y. 1951).

31. *Daily-Times Democrat v. Graham*, 162 So.2d 474 (Ala. 1964).

32 *Barber v. Time, Inc.*, 159 S.W.2d 291 (1942).

33. *Braun v. Flynt,* 726 F.2d 245 (5th Cir. 1984).

34. *Cantrell v. Forest City Publishing Co.,* 419 U.S. 245 (1974).

35. Joe Eszterhas, "Legacy of the Silver Bridge," *Plain Dealer Sunday Magazine,* 4 August 1968, p. 32, col. 1.

36. *Cantrell v. Forest City Publishing Co.*

37. *Griswold v. Connecticut,* 381 U.S. 479 (1965).

38. Ibid.

39. "Bush: New Agency to Secure 'American Homeland,'" *CNN.com,* 6 June 2002, <http://archives.cnn.com/2002/ALLPOLITICS/ 06/06/bush.speech.transcript/> (21 June 2006).

40. Dan Christensen, "Major Information Brokers Face Class Action for Invasion of Privacy," *Daily Business Review,* 24 June 2003, <http:// www.law.com/jsp/article.jsp?id=1056139884864> (21 June 2006).

41. Office of Technology Assessment, U.S. Congress, *Holding the Edge: Maintaining the Defense Technology Base,* OTA-ISC-420 (Washington, D.C.: U.S. Government Printing Office, April 1989).

42. Eric Lichtblau and John Markoff, "Accenture Is Awarded U.S. Contract for Borders," *New York Times,* 2 June 2004, <http:// www.nytimes.com/2004/06/02/technology/02secure.html?ex=14015 95200&en=5363a75d995c3e0f&ei=5007&partner=USERLAND> (1 July 2006).

43. Susannah Patton, "Privacy Is Your Business," *CIO Magazine,* 1 June 2004, <http://www.cio.com/archive/060104/privacy.html> (21 June 2006).

44. *FTC v.Toysmart.com,* LLC, no. 00-11341-RGS (D. Mass. 2000).

45. Jennifer Disabatino, "Web Site Restricted from Selling Customer Data to Third Parties," *Computerworld,* August 2001, p. 10.

46. Brian Krebs, "EPIC: eTour.com Data Sales Violate Privacy Policy," *Newsbytes,* 31 May 2001, <http://www.govtech.net/news/news. php?id=4898> (21 June 2006).

47. Ray Schultz, "Sears Sued over Alleged Data Sharing," *Direct,* 1 November 2001, <http://directmag.com/news/marketing_sears_ sued_alleged/> (21 June 2006).

48. Thomas Claburn, "Albertsons Sued over Customer-Data Privacy," *InformationWeek*, 15 September 2004, <http://informationweek. bizintelligencepipeline.com/47208562> (21 June 2006).

49. Health Privacy Project, "Health Privacy Stories," December 2005, <http://www.healthprivacy.org/usr_doc/Privacy_stories.pdf> (21 June 2006).

50. Susannah Patton, "Privacy Is Your Business."

51. Martin H. Bosworth, "TSA's Privacy Law Violations May Lead to More Abuses," *ConsumerAffairs.com*, 28 July 2005, <http:// www.consumeraffairs.com/news04/2005/tsa_privacy.html> (21 June 2006).

52. Robert Lemos, "Bank of America Loses a Million Customer Records," *CNET News.com*, 25 February 2005, <http://news.com.com/ Bank+of+America+loses+a+million+customer+records/2100-1029_3-5590989.html?tag=nl> (10 July 2006); Saul Hansell, "Bank Loses Tapes of Records of 1.2 Million With Visa Cards," *The New York Times*, 26 February 2005, <http://www.umsl.edu/ ~sauter/spam/26data.html> (10 July 2006).

53. "Info on 3.9M Citigroup Customers Lost," *CNNMoney.com*, 6 June 2005, <http://money.cnn.com/2005/06/06/news/fortune500/ security_citigroup/> (1 July 2006).

54. Brian Krebs, "States Keep Watchful Eye on Personal-Data Firms," *Washington Post*, 1 June 2005, <http://www.washingtonpost.com/ wp-dyn/content/article/2005/06/01/AR2005060100359_pf.html> (21 June 2006).

55. Paul R. Brewer and Emily Marquardt, "Mock News and Democracy: Analyzing *The Daily Show*," 18 May 2006, <http://www.uwm.edu/ ~prbrewer/mocknews.pdf> (1 July 2006); Dannagal Goldthwaite Young, "*Daily Show* Viewers Knowledgeable About Presidential Campaign," National Annenberg Election Survey, Annenberg Public Policy Center, Philadelphia, Penn., 2004, <http://www. annenbergpublicpolicycenter.org/naes/2004_03_late-night-knowledge-2_9-21_pr.pdf> (1 July 2006).

Chapter Six

1. Cartoon by Peter Steiner, *New Yorker*, 5 July 1993, p. 61.

2. Amy Bruckman, "Kibo Is God," *Wired*, 1.04, Sept/Oct 1993, <http://www.wired.com/wired/archive/1.04/eword.html?pg=8> (3 July 2006).

3. Troy Wolverton, "Fraud Lingers Despite eBay Efforts," *CNET.com*, 28 June 2002, <http://news.com.com/Fraud+lingers+despite+eBay+efforts/2100–1017_3–940427.html?tag=nl> (21 June 2006).

4. "eBay Account Theft," <http://www.linksgolfcommunity.com/phpBB2/viewtopic.php?p=10765&> (21 June 2006).

5. Troy Wolverton, "Hackers Find New Way to Bilk eBay Users," *CNET.com*, 25 March 2002, <http://news.com.com/2100–1017–868278.html> (21 June 2006).

6. "eBay ID Account for Sale with Excellent Rating," 20 March 2004, <http://groups.google.com/group/alt.marketing.online.ebay/browse_thread/thread/684b4d0ce7c2c0ba/773c2bb9fd7bc97e?lnk=st&q=usernames+valuable+sold+ebay&rnum=4&hl=en> (21 June 2006).

7. Websense Security Labs, "Security Trends Report," 2005, <http://www.websensesecuritylabs.com/docs/WebsenseSecurityLabs20051H_Report.pdf> (21 June 2006).

8. Trent Youl, "Phishing Scams: Understanding the Latest Trends," FraudWatch International, June 2004, <http://www.fraudwatchinternational.com/internet/phishing/report.pdf> (21 June 2006).

9. Ibid.

10. Ashley Lo, "Phishing from a Global Perspective," <http://www.hkcert.org/ppt/event111/phishing3_edvance.pdf> (21 June 2006).

11. Paul F. Roberts, "IBM Reports Phishing Surge," *eWeek.com*, 30 June 2005, <http://www.eweek.com/article2/0,1759,1833528,00.asp> (21 June 2006).

12. "Security Statistics," <http://www.aladdin.com/home/csrt/statistics/statistics_2005.asp> (21 June 2006).

13. Paul F. Roberts, "IBM Reports Phishing Surge," *eWeek.com*, 30 June 2005, <http://www.eweek.com/article2/0,1759,1833528,00.asp> (21 June 2006).

14. Andrea L. Foster, "ID Theft Turns Students into Privacy Activists," *The Chronicle of Higher Education*, Information Technology Section, p. A27, 2 August 2002, <http://chronicle.com/free/v48/i47/47a02701.htm> (3 July 2006).

15. Matthew Heimer and Stephanie Williams, "Identity Crisis," *SmartMoney Magazine*, 17 December 2002, <http://www.smartmoney.com/mag/index.cfm?story=jan03-identity> (21 June 2006).

16. Ibid.

Chapter Seven

1. William F. Claire. "Thinking of Anais Nin," *The Nation*, 29 March 1971.

2. Geoffrey A. Moore, *Crossing the Chasm* (New York: HarperCollins, 2002), p. 49.

3. Mildred DePallo, "AARP National Survey on Consumer Preparedness and E-Commerce: A Survey of Computer Users Age 45 and Older," American Association of Retired Persons (AARP), March 2000, <http://assets.aarp.org/rgcenter/consume/ecommerce.pdf> (3 July 2006); P. Kumaraguru and L. Faith Cranor, "Privacy Indexes: A Survey of Westin's Studies," ISRI Technical Report, CMU-ISRI-05-138, 2005, <http://reports-archive.adm.cs.cmu.edu/anon/isri2005/CMU-ISRI-05-138.pdf> (3 July 2006).

4. Susannah Fox, "Older Americans and the Internet," Pew Internet & American Life Project, 25 March 2004, <http://www.pewinternet.org/pdfs/PIP_Seniors_Online_2004.pdf> (21 June 2006).

5. David Brin, "Three Cheers for the Surveillance Society!," *Salon.com*, 3 August 2004, <http://archive.salon.com/tech/feature/2004/08/04/mortal_gods/index (8 August 2006).

6. Amanda Lenhart and Mary Madden, "Teens and Technology: Youth Are Leading the Transition to a Fully Wired and Mobile Nation," Pew Internet & American Life Project, 27 July 2005, <http://www. pewinternet.org/pdfs/PIP_Teens_Tech_July2005web.pdf> (21 June 2006).

7. Ibid.

Chapter Eight

1. Douglas, W. *Osborne v. United States*, 385 U.S. 341 (1966).

2. "The Faked World Trade Center Tourist Photo," BluEarthArts, <http://www.blueartharts.com/uhoh.htm> (4 July 2006).

3. K. Silber, "Spy Satellites: Still a Few Steps Ahead," Space.com, <http://www.space.com/news/gov_imagery_990921.html> (September 1999).

4. Privacy International, "Video Surveillance," <http://www.privacy. org/pi/issues/cctv/> (26 June 2006).

5. Leslie Cauley, "NSA Has Massive Database of Americans' Phone Calls," *USA Today*, 11 May 2006, <http://www.usatoday.com/ news/washington/2006-05-10-nsa_x.htm> (1 July 2006).

6. "Two Groups Sue Over NSA Wiretap Program," *CNN.com*, 18 January 2006, <http://edition.cnn.com/2006/LAW/01/17/aclu.nsa/> (4 July 2006).

7. Kim Zetter, "Is the NSA Spying on U.S. Internet Traffic?" *Salon.com*, 21 June 2006, <http://www.salon.com/news/feature/2006/06/21/ att_nsa/> (4 July 2006).

8. Eric Lichtblau and James Risen, "Bank Data Is Sifted by U.S. in Secret to Block Terror," *New York Times*, 23 June 2006, <http:// www.nytimes.com/2006/06/23/washington/23intel.html?ex=130871 5200&en=4b46b4fd8685c26b&ei=5090&partner=rssuserland& emc=rss> (4 July 2006).

9. "Carnivore FOIA Documents," Electronic Privacy Information Center, < http://www.epic.org/privacy/carnivore/foia_documents. html> (4 July 2006).

10. Karen Miller, "NASA Researchers Are Developing an Exquisitely Sensitive Artificial Nose for Space Exploration," National Aeronautics and Space Administration, 6 October 2004, <http://science. nasa.gov/headlines/y2004/06oct_enose.htm> (26 June 2006).

Chapter Nine

1. Anton Chekhov, *The Lady with the Dog*. (Originally published 1899).

2. Bob Sullivan, "E-ZPASS, Now With a Higher Price," *The Red Tapes*, 24 February 2004, <http://redtape.msnbc.com/2006/02/ ezpass_now_with.html> (5 July 2006); "Driving in the USA and Canada—Types of Roads," <http://freespace.virgin.net/john. cletheroe/usa_can/driving/roads.htm#tolls> (5 July 2006); Charlie Schmidt, "The Road Ahead," *Technology Review*, July/August 2001, <http://www.schmidtwriting.com/articles/clients/tr/road.pdf> (5 July 2006).

3. Elisa Batista, "What Your Clothes Say About You," *Wired News*, 12 March 2003, <http://www.wired.com/news/technology/wireless/ 0,58006-0.html> (4 July 2006); Elisa Batista, "Step Back for Wireless ID Tech?" *Wired News*, 8 April 2003, <http://www.wired.com/ news/wireless/0,1382,58385,00.html> (4 July 2006).

4. Katherine Albrecht and Liz McIntyre, *Spychips: How Major Corporations and Government Plan to Track Your Every Move with RFID*. (Nashville, Tenn.: Nelson, 2005).

5. Rick Merritt, "Cellphone Could Crack RFID Tags, Says Cryptographer," *EE Times*, 14 February 2006, <http://www.eetimes.com/ news/latest/showArticle.jhtml;jsessionid=TZK24VTGJG4PIQS NDBESKHA?articleID=180201688> (26 June 2006).

6. Antony Savvas, "IBM RFID System Addresses Privacy Concerns," *ComputerWeekly.com*, 4 May 2006, <http://www.computerweekly. com/Articles/2006/05/04/215764/IBM+RFID+system+addresses+ privacy+concerns.htm> (4 July 2006).

7. Larry Mcshane, "GPS Technology Creeps into the Workplace," *MSNBC.com*, 19 November 2005, <http://www.msnbc.msn.com/id/ 10089674/> (4 July 2006).

8. Adam Geller, "Bosses Keep Sharp Eye on Mobile Workers Via GPS," *USA Today*, 3 January 2003, <http://www.usatoday.com/tech/news/2005-01-03-gps-supervision_x.htm> (4 July 2006).

9. Lini S. Kadaba, "Parents Now Can Be Supersnoopers," *South Bend Tribune*, 31 January 2006, <http://www.southbendtribune.com/apps/pbcs.dll/article?AID=/20060131/Lives06/601310464/-1/Lives/CAT=Lives06> (4 July 2006).

Chapter Ten

1. Richard Perle, *An End to Evil* (New York: Random House, 2003), p. 71.

2. Robert O'Harrow, Jr., "In Age of Security, Firm Mines Wealth of Personal Data," *Washington Post*, 20 January 2005, p. A01, <http://www.washingtonpost.com/wp-dyn/articles/A22269–2005Jan19.html> (26 June 2006).

3. Ibid.

4. Rick Whiting, "Data Demands Respect," *InformationWeek*, 25 October 2004, <http://www.informationweek.com/story/showArticle.jhtml?articleID=51000186> (26 June 2006).

5. Acxiom Corporation, press release, 12 August 2002, "Acxiom Expands Its Customer Solutions by Offering Employment and Security Screening Services," <http://www.acxiom.com.au/default.aspx?ID=1996&DisplayID=87> (8 July 2006); Acxiom Corporation Proxy Statement, Report of the Audit Committee, <http://sec.edgar-online.com/2004/06/25/0000733269-04-000015/Section13.asp> (9 July 2006).

6. Acxiom Corporation, press release, 7 January 2005, "Acxiom Acquires SmartDM," <http://www.acxiom.com/default.aspx?ID=2735&DisplayID=18> (8 July 2006).

7. Richard H. Levey, "Acxiom Acquires MarketsOnDemand," *Direct.com*, <http://www.directmag.com/news/marketing_acxiom_acquires_marketsondemand/index.html> (8 July 2006).

8. Rick Whiting, "Data Demands Respect," *InformationWeek*, 25 October 2004, <http://www.informationweek.com/story/showArticle.jhtml?articleID=51000186> (26 June 2006).

9. Andrew J. McClurg, "A Thousand Words Are Worth a Picture: A Privacy Tort Response to Consumer Data Profiling," *Northwestern University Law Review*, 2003, 98, 63–144.

10. Broadsystem, "Postcode Traits," November 2004, <http://www. broadsystem.com/articles/articles_postcodeanalysis.htm> (26 June 2006).

11. Prime Performance Modeling, Experian, <http://www.experian.com/ prime_performance_modeling/index.html> (9 July 2006).

12. Andrew J. McClurg, "A Thousand Words Are Worth a Picture: A Privacy Tort Response to Consumer Data Profiling," *Northwestern University Law Review*, 2003, 98, 63–144.

13. Federal Trade Commission, "ChoicePoint Settles Data Security Breach Charges," 26 January 2006, <http://www.ftc.gov/opa/ 2006/01/choicepoint.htm> (26 June 2006).

14. Eben Moglen, "Against Honor and Liberty of the Press," speech at the University of Montevideo, Uruguay, 3 May 2001, <http:// moglen.law.columbia.edu/publications/montevideo.pdf> (26 June 2006).

15. EmailLabs, press release, 21 March 2005, "Mom-Focused Marketing Firm Delivers Complex Email Campaigns," <http://www.emaillabs. com/articles/news/marketing_firm_delivers_complex_email_ campaigns.html> (26 June 2006).

16. Electronic Privacy Information Center, "The Children's Online Privacy Protection Act (COPPA)," <http://www.epic.org/privacy/ kids/> (26 June 2006).

17. J. J. McNeal, *Children as Consumers: Insights and Implications* (Lexington, MA: Lexington Books, 1987); Susan Linn, *Consuming Kids: The Hostile Takeover of Childhood* (New York: The New Press, 2004); Dale Kunkel et al., "Psychological Issues in the Increasing Commercialization of Childhood: Report of the APA Task Force on Advertising and Children." (Washington: American Psychological Association, 20 February 2004), <http://www.apa.org/releases/ childrenads.pdf> (8 July 2006).

18. Naomi Klein, *No Logo* (New York: Picador, 2002).

19. Karen Gottlieb, "Using Court Record Information for Marketing in the United States: It's Public Information, What's the Problem?" Privacy Rights Clearinghouse, <http://www.privacyrights.org/ar/courtmarketing.htm> (8 July 2006).

20. *Dennis v. Metromail,* Texas Dist. Ct., No-9604451 (1996); Dante Chinni, "Unlawful Entry," *Mother Jones,* 13 January 1998, <http://www.motherjones.com/news/feature/1998/01/privacy_sidebar.html> (8 July 2006).

21. Adam Liptak, "Free Prozac in the Junk Mail Draws a Lawsuit," *New York Times,* 6 July 2002, <http://query.nytimes.com/gst/fullpage.html?sec=health&res=9C07E2DE1E31F935A35754C0A9649C8B63> (26 June 2006).

22. Amy Goldstein, "HHS Proposes New Standards, Will Protect Medical Privacy," *The Washington Post,* 12 September 1997, p. 3, <http://www-tech.mit.edu/V117/N41/shalala.41w.html> (8 July 2006).

23. Erik Baard, "Buying Trouble: Your Grocery List Could Spark a Terror Probe," *Village Voice,* 24 July 2002, <http://villagevoice.com/news/0230,baard,36760,1.html> (26 June 2006).

24. Ibid.

25. "Customer Loyalty Cards: Price vs. Privacy," *Fayetteville Observer,* 17 April 2002.

26. Kim Nash, "Casinos Hit Jackpot with Customer Data," *CNN.com,* 3 July 2001, <http://archives.cnn.com/2001/TECH/industry/07/03/casinos.crm.idg/> (26 June 2006).

27. Neil Swidey, "Spambusters," *Boston Globe,* 5 October 2003, <http://www.boston.com/news/globe/magazine/articles/2003/10/05/spambusters/> (8 July 2006).

28. Quentin Hardy, "Intertaining Yourself," *Forbes,* 28 November 2005, <http://www.forbes.com/home/free_forbes/2005/1128/180.html> (8 July 2006).

29. Thomas Claburn, "Yahoo's Challenge," *InformationWeek,* 20 February 2006, <http://www.informationweek.com/news/showArticle.jhtml?articleID=180204048> (8 July 2006).

30. Elinor Mills, "MSN Takes on Google AdWords," *CNET News.com*, 26 September 2005, <http://news.com.com/Microsoft+plans+to+ sell+search+ads+of+its+own/2100-1011_3-5881650.html> (8 July 2006).

31. Leslie Walker, "Gmail Leads Way in Making Ads Relevant," *Washington Post*, 13 May 2004, p. E01, <http://www.washington post.com/wp-dyn/articles/A20596-2004May12.html> (8 July 2006).

32. David H. Freedman, "The Future of Advertising Is Here," *Inc. Magazine*, August 2005, <http://www.inc.com/magazine/20050801/ future-of-advertising.html> (26 June 2006).

33. Ibid.

34. Erik Baard, "Smile, You're on In-Store Camera," *Wired News*, 8 August 2002, <http://www.wired.com/news/privacy/0,1848, 54078,00.html> (26 June 2006).

35. Freedman, "The Future of Advertising Is Here."

36. Outdoor Advertising Association of America, Inc., "History of Outdoor Advertising," <http://www.oaaa.org/outdoor/sales/history.asp> (26 June 2006).

37. Emily Turrettini, "Ford Fiesta Ad Campaign Combines Interactive Billboards with SMS," *Textually.org*, 22 July 2004, <http:// www.textually.org/textually/archives/2004/07/004640.htm> (8 July 2006).

38. Mae Anderson, "Yahoo! Billboard Goes Live in Times Square," *Adweek.com*, 24 March 2004, <http://www.adweek.com/aw/ creative/article_display.jsp?vnu_content_id=1000471117> (8 July 2006).

39. Accenture, press release, 2 May 2006, "New Accenture Technology Lands at O'Hare International Airport," <http://www.accenture. com/xd/xd.asp?it=enweb&xd=_dyn%5Cdynamicpressrelease_996. xml> (8 July 2006).

40. Brian Osborne, "New Coca-Cola Sign Responds to Environment," *Geek.com*, 2 October 2003, <http://www.geek.com/news/geeknews/ 2003Oct/gee20031002022026.htm> (8 July 2006).

41. Carol Power, "Billboards Tune in to Show You What You Want," *The Irish Times*, 7 February 2003, <http://www.mobiltrak.com/news/index.cfm?loc=materials/irishtimes_020703.cfm> (8 July 2006).

42. Bob Brewin, "Radio 'Sniffers' Likened to Fed E-Surveillance," *Computerworld*, 31 May 2000, <http://transcripts.cnn.com/2000/TECH/computing/05/31/radio.sniffers.idg/index.html> (26 June 2006).

43. Bruce Schneier, "Real Story of the Rogue Rootkit," *Wired News*, 17 November 2005, <http://www.wired.com/news/privacy/0,1848,69601,00.html> (8 July 2006); Paul F. Roberts, "Sony BMG at Work on Yet Another Patch," *eWeek.com*, 8 December 2005, <http://www.eweek.com/article2/0,1895,1899364,00.asp> (8 July 2006).

44. Ryan Naraine, "Symantec Caught in Norton 'Rootkit' Flap," *eWeek.com*, 11 January 2006, <http://www.eweek.com/article2/0,1895,1910077,00.asp> (8 July 2006).

45. Gregg Keizer, "Rootkit-Armed Worm Attacking AIM," *Information-Week*, 28 October 2005, <http://www.informationweek.com/story/showArticle.jhtml?articleID=172901455> (26 June 2006).

Chapter Eleven

1. Greta Garbo, referring to her role in the film, *Grand Hotel* (1932), <http://en.wikipedia.org/wiki/Greta_Garbo> (8 August 2006).

2. Declan Mccullagh and Elinor Mills, "Feds Take Porn Fight to Google," *CNET News.com*, 19 January 2006, <http://news.com.com/Feds+take+porn+fight+to+Google/2100-1030_3-6028701.html> (9 July 2006).

3. Jefferson was vice president at the time, even though he represented an opposing party, because of a bug in the freshly inked Constitution.

4. The Civil War caused over a million casualties on both sides; almost of all of these young men were of family-starting age.

5. *Schenck v. United States*, 249 U.S. 47 (1919).

6. The committee was formally known as the U.S. Senate Select Committee to Study Governmental Operations with Respect to Intelligence Activities and was chaired by Senator Frank Church.

7. Sara Kehaulani Goo, "Fliers to Be Rated for Risk Level," *Washington Post*, 9 September 2003, p. A01, <http://www.washingtonpost.com/wp-dyn/articles/A45434-2003Sep8.html> (9 July 2006).

8. Position Paper on "No-Fly" Lists, British Columbia Civil Liberties Association, 16 September 2005, <http://www.bccla.org/positions/antiterror/05nofly.htm> (9 July 2006).

9. Dave Lindorff, "Grounded," *Salon Magazine*, 15 November 2002, <http://www.salon.com/news/feature/2002/11/15/no_fly/index.html> (26 June 2006).

10. American Civil Liberties Union, "TSA and FBI Ordered to Pay $200,000 to Settle "No Fly" Lawsuit," press release, 24 January 2006, <http://www.aclu.org/safefree/general/23926prs20060124.html> (26 June 2006).

11. Quoted in Frederick Sweet, "Blacklist Grounds American Passengers," *Intervention Magazine*, 29 December 2002, <http://www.interventionmag.com/cms/modules.php?op=modload&name=News&file=article&sid=278> (26 June 2006).

12. Anne Broache, "Tens of Thousands Mistakenly Matched to Terrorist Watch Lists," *CNET News.com*, 6 December 2006, <http://news.com.com/Tens+of+thousands+mistakenly+placed+on+terrorist+watch+lists/2100-7348_3-5984673.html> (8 July 2006).

13. Sara Kehaulani Goo, "Terror No-fly List Singled Out Kennedy, Senator Was Stopped 5 Times at Airports," *Washington Post*, 20 August 2004, <http://www.sfgate.com/cgi-bin/article.cgi?file=/c/a/2004/08/20/MNGQ28BM1O1.DTL> (9 July 2006).

14. Tom Ramstack and Patrick Badgely, "Name Won't Fly if You Are David Nelson," *The Washington Times*, 17 June 2003, <http://washingtontimes.com/business/20030616-104109-4241r.htm> (9 July 2006).

15. Lindorff, "Grounded."

16. Sweet, "Blacklist Grounds American Passengers."

17. American Civil Liberties Union, "ACLU 'No-Fly' Lawsuit," 6 April 2004, <http://www.aclu.org/safefree/resources/17469res20040406.html> (26 June 2006).

18. Sweet, "Blacklist Grounds American Passengers."

19. Alan Gathright, "No-Fly List Ensnares Innocent Travelers," *San Francisco Chronicle*, 8 June 2003, <http://sfgate.com/cgi-bin/article.cgi?f=/c/a/2003/06/08/MN253740.DTL> (26 June 2006).

20. "No-Fly List Becoming Political Liability," *Rocky Mountain News*, 19 August 2005, <http://www.rockymountainnews.com/drmn/opinion/article/0,1299,DRMN_38_4013121,00.html> (26 June 2006).

21. "GAO: TSA Data Collection Violated Privacy Act," *MSNBC.com*, 22 July 2005, <http://www.msnbc.msn.com/id/8672258/> (26 June 2006).

22. "Bookstores Buck Patriot Act," *CBS News*, 21 February 2003, <http://www.cbsnews.com/stories/2003/02/21/national/main541464.shtml> (26 June 2006).

23. Ibid.

24. Campaign for Reader Privacy, "What We Know About Bookstore and Library Searches Since 9/11," <http://www.readerprivacy.org/info.jsp?id=4> (26 June 2006).

25. Eric Lichtblau, "Libraries Say Yes, Officials Do Quiz Them About Users," *New York Times*, 20 June 2005, p. A11, col. 5, <http://www.globalpolicy.org/empire/terrorwar/liberties/2005/0620library.htm> (26 June 2006).

26. Barton Gellman, "The FBI's Secret Scrutiny," *Washington Post*, 6 November 2005, p. A01, <http://www.washingtonpost.com/wp-dyn/content/article/2005/11/05/AR2005110501366_pf.html> (9 July 2006).

27. Noah Leavitt, "John Ashcroft's Subpoena Blitz," *FindLaw*, 18 February 2004, <http://writ.news.findlaw.com/commentary/20040218_leavitt.html> (26 June 2006).

28. Ibid.

29. Ibid.

30. Eric Lichtblau, "U.S. Uses Terror Law to Pursue Crimes from Drugs to Swindling," *New York Times*, 28 September 2003, <http://www.nytimes.com/2003/09/28/politics/28LEGA.html?ex=1380081600&en=039dd7c0d0c084da&ei=5007&partner=USERLAND> (26 June 2006).

31. J. M. Kalil and Steve Tetreault, "Patriot Act: Law's Use Causing Concerns," *Review-Journal*, 5 November 2003, <http://www.reviewjournal.com/lvrj_home/2003/Nov-05-Wed-2003/news/22521283.html> (9 July 2006).

32. Larry Abramson, "The Patriot Act: Alleged Abuses of the Law," *NPR*, 20 July 2005, <http://www.npr.org/templates/story/story.php?storyId=4756403> (26 June 2006).

33. Ibid.

34. "Summit Accused of Using Patriot Act to Purge Homeless Man from Train Station," 30 June 2005, <http://www.news12.com/NJ/topstories/article?id=144957> (26 June 2006).

35. "Unconscionable USA PATRIOT Act Abuse," 3 August 2004, <http://home.earthlink.net/~exodus22/essays/patriotact02.htm> (26 June 2006).

36. Abramson, "The Patriot Act."

37. Valencia Mohammed, "Black Panthers Are Considered Terrorists Under the Patriot Act," *Afro American Newspapers*, 28 December 2005.

38. Jason Ryan, "FBI Problems Led to Wrongful Terror Arrest," *ABC News*, 6 January 2006, <http://abcnews.go.com/WNT/story?id=1479790&WNTad=true> (26 June 2006).

39. Philip Shehon, "Report on USA Patriot Act Alleges Civil Rights Violations," *New York Times*, 21 July 2003.

40. Dan Eggen, "Anti-Terror Power Used Broadly," *Washington Post*, 21 May 2003, p. A12, <http://www.washingtonpost.com/ac2/wp-dyn/A17171-2003May20?language=printer> (9 July 2006).

41. Ibid.

42. "Boy Investigated by FBI for Researching School Paper on Chesa-peake Bay Bridge," *Baltimore Sun*, 21 October 2003, <http://www.prisonplanet.com/211003boyinvestigated.html> (26 June 2006).

43. Tom Regan, "Artist Falls Afoul of Patriot Act," *Christian Science Monitor*, 7 June 2004, <http://www.csmonitor.com/2004/0607/dailyUpdate.html> (26 June 2006); Critical Art Ensemble Defense Fund, <http://www.caedefensefund.org/faq.html> (26 June 2006).

44. Leslie Cauley, "Bush Lied Repeatedly About Scope of NSA Spying on Americans," *USA Today*, 11 May 2006, <http://www.unknownnews.org/0605190511NSAspying.html> (9 July 2006).

45. Charlie Savage, "Specialists Doubt Legality of Wiretaps," *The Boston Globe*, 2 February 2006, <http://www.boston.com/news/nation/articles/2006/02/02/specialists_doubt_legality_of_wiretaps/> (9 July 2006); Beth Nolan et al., "On NSA Spying: A Letter to Congress," *New York Review of Books*, 53(2), 9 February 2006, <http://www.nybooks.com/articles/18650> (9 July 2006).

46. Carol D. Leonnig and Dafna Linzer, "Judges on Surveillance Court to Be Briefed on Spy Program," *Washington Post*, 22 December 2005, p. A01, <http://www.washingtonpost.com/wp-dyn/content/article/2005/12/21/AR2005122102326.html> (9 July 2006).

47. The United States spends about $3 billion per year on satellites alone, according to James Bamford in a May 1, 2002, online inter-view with the *Washington Post*.

48. After the U.S. embassies in Kenya and Tanzania were attacked with truck bombs, the United States retaliated by firing seventy-nine $1 million Tomahawk cruise missiles at a Bin Laden training camp in Afghanistan and at a pharmaceutical plant in the Sudan.

49. The actual cost was between $33 and $36 billion according to a report published by the Federal Reserve Bank of New York: Jason Bram, James Orr, and Carol Rapaport, "Measuring the Effects of the September 11 Attack on New York City," *Federal Reserve Bank of New York Economic Policy Review*, November 2002, 8(2). This range includes lifetime-earnings loss for the victims, property damage, and cleanup costs.

50. The indirect expense was over $150 billion on top of the actual costs. This number reflects the budgetary difference between projected spending for the military and antiterror efforts and what was actually spent. The proposed 2003 budget, not passed as of this writing, adds a yearly increase of nearly $20 billion.

51. Traffic, or network, analysis is an intelligence technique for extracting information about relationships in a community without necessarily understanding the contents of the messages themselves. Participants are drawn in a diagram showing who initiated a call and when. By looking at the diagram, trained analysts can determine the organizational hierarchy. By comparing the amount of traffic with some norm, they can get an indication of upcoming activity along with its severity. One of the most powerful capabilities of such analyses is that the shape of a network will always look the same, even if the encryption or password scheme changes.

Chapter Twelve

1. *Plan 9 from Outer Space*, Ed Wood, 79 min., 1959.

2. David Brin, *The Transparent Society* (New York: Perseus Books, 1999).

3. Seth Ackerman, "Hit the Rewind: Bork's Video Subpoena Was a Story Too Good to Check," *FAIR.org*, April 1999, <http://www.fair.org/index.php?page=1456> (8 July 2006).

4. Theo Francis, "Trial Will Test Privacy Rules for Health Files," *Wall Street Journal*, 10 December 2003, pp. B1, B10.

5. Beth Givens, "Medical Records Privacy: Fears and Expectations of Patients," speech given at the Toward an Electronic Patient Record Conference, Sheraton Harbor Hotel, San Diego, Calif., 15 May 1996, <http://www.privacyrights.org/ar/speech2.htm> (26 June 2006).

6. Tom Regan, "ACLU Accuses FBI of 'Spying' on Activists," *The Christian Science Monitor*, 19 May 2005, <http://www.csmonitor.com/2005/0519/dailyUpdate.html> (8 July 2006).

7. Terry M. Neal, "Satirical Web Site Poses Political Test," *Washington Post*, 29 November 1999, p. A02, <http://www.washingtonpost.com/wp-srv/WPcap/1999-11/29/002r-112999-idx.html> (8 August 2006).

8. *O'Grady v. Superior Court* (Apple Computer, Inc.) (2006), Cal.App.4th. [No. H028579. 6th Dist. May 26, 2006.]; "Apple v. Does," Electronic Frontier Foundation (EFF), <http://www.eff.org/Censorship/Apple_v_Does/> (8 July 2006).

9. John Schwartz and Robert O'Harrow Jr., "Databases Start to Fuel Consumer Ire," *Washington Post*, 10 March 1998, p. A1, <http://www.washingtonpost.com/wp-srv/frompost/march98/privacy10.htm> (26 June 2006).

10. Quoted in Toby Lester, "The Reinvention of Privacy," *Atlantic Monthly*, March 2001, pp. 27–39 <http://www.theatlantic.com/doc/prem/200103/lester> (26 June 2006).

11. Boing Boing, "Arkansas Salon Requires Thumbprint to Get a Tan," 27 April 2005, <http://www.boingboing.net/2005/04/27/arkansas_salon_requi.html> (26 June 2006); "Would You Submit Biometric Data to Join a Gym?" *Slashdot*, 29 April 2005, <http://ask.slashdot.org/article.pl?sid=05/04/28/1925226> (26 June 2006).

12. Mike Stollenwerk, "'Show Me Your Papers!' Demands the New Yorker Ramada Hotel," Privacy Rights Clearinghouse, 14 April 2003, <http://www.privacyrights.org/ar/NYRamada.htm> (26 June 2006).

13. Ibid.

14. Dennis Roddy, "Grounded: Millionaire John Gilmore Stays Close to Home While Making a Point About Privacy," *Pittsburgh Post-Gazette*, 27 February 2005, <http://www.postgazette.com/pg/05058/462446.stm> (26 June 2006).

15. Forrester Research, "The Privacy Best Practice," <http://www.forrester.com> (26 June 2006); Pew Internet & American Life Project, "Trust and Privacy Online: Why Americans Want to Rewrite the Rules," press release, 21 August 2000, <http://www.pewinternet.org/PPF/r/6/press_release.asp> (26 June 2006); Harris Interactive, "Privacy On and Off the Internet: What Consumers

Want," 7 February 2002, <http://www.aicpa.org/download/webtrust/priv_rpt_21mar02.pdf> (26 June 2006).

16. Schwartz and O'Harrow, "Databases Start to Fuel Consumer Ire."

17. Ibid.

18. Association of American Physicians and Surgeons, Inc., "New Poll: Doctors Lie to Protect Patient Privacy," 31 July 2001, <http://www.aapsonline.org/press/nrnewpoll.htm> (26 June 2006).

19. Ibid.

20. Privacy Rights Clearinghouse, "School Posting Photos of Students Online," February 2005, <http://www.privacyrights.org/Media/scoop.htm> (26 June 2006).

21. Aimee Molloy, "No Child Left Unrecruited," *Salon Magazine,* 21 March 2005, <http://www.salon.com/news/feature/2005/03/21/schools_recruiters/index_np.html> (26 June 2006).

22. <http://epistolary.org/rob/bonuscard/> (18 July 2006).

23. <http://www.wired.com/news/business/0,1367,59589,00.html> (18 July 2006); <http://www.usatoday.com/tech/columnist/cceli017.htm> (18 July 2006).

Chapter Thirteen

1. Ayn Rand, *The Fountainhead* (New York: New American Library, 1952), p. 683.

2. Peter Lyman and Hal R. Varian, "How Much Information?" 2003, <http://www.sims.berkeley.edu/how-much-info-2003> (26 June 2006).

Index

The Author

David Holtzman has done many things and worn many hats. In many ways his life experience has made him especially qualified to truly understand both the implications and effects of technology on our culture and society.

During the Dot Com Boom of the late 1990s, Holtzman ran one of the most critical networks in the world—the domain name system. As Chief Technology Officer of Network Solutions and the manager of the Internet's master root server, Holtzman oversaw the growth of the commercial Internet from five hundred thousand to over twenty million domain names.

Early in his technology career Holtzman was a cryptographic analyst, Russian linguist, and submariner with the U.S. Naval Security Group. He worked at the Defense Special Missile and Astronautics Center as an intelligence analyst, focusing chiefly on the Soviet Manned Space program. As chief scientist at IBM's Internet Information Technology group, Holtzman managed the development of IBM's information product and service offering to encrypt and sell digitized content across the Internet, which was called *cryptolopes*. He served as a senior analyst for Booz | Allen | Hamilton for several years, where he ran technology-driven restructuring initiatives for Wall Street firms and large financial institutions. He also designed and built a networked, heterogeneous database and text retrieval system called *Minerva*, which was used by NATO and several trade associations before being sold to IBM in 1994.

Holtzman has designed and built numerous information-based software systems and is the author of several major patents. Mr. Holtzman was CEO and chairman of Opion, a venture-backed start-up company he founded in 2000. While there, he developed and patented innovative marketing intelligence technology. He has consulted on marketing strategy for several large corporations, including Amazon.com. He has been a security consultant for several organizations, private and public, including Wesley Clark's 2004 presidential campaign. He has been an advisor to over a dozen high-tech companies throughout North America. He has taught business courses as an adjunct associate MBA professor at American University in Washington, D.C., and entrepreneurship via a cutting edge "Lecture On Demand" technique for the University of Pittsburgh using distance learning software and podcasts.

In addition to writing and consulting, Holtzman is currently the president of GlobalPOV, a firm he founded to explore significant technology issues and their affects on society. He has been interviewed by major news media including the *New York Times*, CNN, and USA Today. Holtzman wrote a monthly ethics and privacy column called "Flashpoint" for *CSO* [Chief Security Officer] *Magazine*, and his essays have been published in *BusinessWeek*, *Wired Magazine*, *CNET*, and *ZDNet*. Holtzman publishes daily on topics such as privacy, intellectual property, business, and pop culture on his blog, www.globalpov.com.

Holtzman has a B.S. in Computer Science from the University of Maryland and a B.A. in Philosophy from the University of Pittsburgh. He is the father of five children, whom he raised as a single parent. He likes to sail, watch Shakespearean plays, and cook.